Bc
MENL(

D0436585

THE END OF THE REPUBLICAN ERA

THE JULIAN J. ROTHBAUM DISTINGUISHED LECTURE SERIES

THE END OF
THE REPUBLICAN
ERA

BY

THEODORE J. LOWI

UNIVERSITY OF OKLAHOMA PRESS : NORMAN AND LONDON

To the memory of
Annick Percheron

Also by Theodore J. Lowi

At the Pleasure of the Mayor: Patronage and Power in New York City, 1898–1958 (New York, 1964)

(ed.) *Legislative Politics, U.S.A.* (Boston, 1962, 1965, 1974)

(with Robert F. Kennedy) *The Pursuit of Justice* (New York, 1964)

(ed.) *Private Life and Public Order* (New York, 1967)

The End of Liberalism: The Second Republic of the United States (New York, 1969, 1979)

The Politics of Disorder (New York, 1971, 1974)

(et al.) *Poliscide: Scientists, the Giant Accelerator and the Metropolis* (New York, 1975, 1990)

American Government: Incomplete Conquest (New York, 1976, 1977, 1981)

(et al.) *Nationalizing Government: Public Policies in America* (Beverly Hills, 1978)

The Personal President: Power Invested, Promise Unfulfilled (Ithaca, 1985)

(with Benjamin Ginsberg) *American Government: Freedom & Power* (New York, 1990, 1994)

(with Benjamin Ginsberg) *Democrats Return to Power: Politics and Policy in the Clinton Era* (New York, 1994)

Book and series design by Bill Cason.

Library of Congress Cataloging-in-Publication Data

Lowi, Theodore J.
    The end of the republican era / by Theodore J. Lowi.
        p.   cm. —(The Julian J. Rothbaum distinguished lecture series ; v. 5)
    Includes index.
    ISBN 0–8061–2701–5 (alk. paper)
        1. Political science—United States—History.   2. Republicanism—United States—History.   3. Liberalism—United States—History.   4. Conservatism—United States—History.   5. United States—Politics and government.   6. Ideology—United States—History.   I. Title.   II. Series.
JA84.U5L69   1995
320.973—dc20   94-31038
                                                                              CIP

The End of the Republican Era is Volume 5 in the Julian J. Rothbaum Distinguished Lecture Series.

The paper in this book meets the guidelines for permanence and durability of the Committee on Production Guidelines for Book Longevity of the Council on Library Resources, Inc. ∞

1 2 3 4 5 6 7 8 9 10

CONTENTS

v

TABLES

FIGURES

FOREWORD

AMONG THE MANY GOOD THINGS that have happened to me in my life, there is none in which I take more pride than the establishment of the Carl Albert Congressional Research and Studies Center at the University of Oklahoma, and none in which I take more satisfaction than the Center's presentation of the Julian J. Rothbaum Distinguished Lecture Series. The series is a perpetually endowed program of the University of Oklahoma, created in honor of Julian J. Rothbaum by his wife, Irene, and son, Joel Jankowsky.

Julian J. Rothbaum, my close friend since our childhood days in southeastern Oklahoma, has long been a leader in Oklahoma civic affairs. He has served as a Regent of the

University of Oklahoma for two terms and as a State Regent
for Higher Education. In 1974 he was awarded the University's
highest honor, the Distinguished Service Citation, and in 1986
he was inducted into the Oklahoma Hall of Fame.

The Rothbaum Lecture Series is devoted to the themes of
representative government, democracy and education, and
citizen participation in public affairs, values to which Julian J.
Rothbaum has been committed throughout his life. His life-
long dedication to the University of Oklahoma, the state, and
his country is a tribute to the ideals to which the Rothbaum
Lecture Series is dedicated. The books in the series make an
enduring contribution to an understanding of American democracy.

CARL B. ALBERT

Forty-sixth Speaker
of the
United States House of Representatives

PREFACE

WHEN *The End of the Republican Era* was nothing but a plan for three lectures at the University of Oklahoma in 1991, it was greeted as a bold prediction in the face of President Bush's historically high performance ratings. I did win a few dinner bets on the 1992 election, but prediction was the least of my concerns in 1991. I did not expect the Republican era to end with the mere defeat of a Republican president any more than I expected it to be perpetuated by his reelection. Partisanship does not define eras; ideology does. Just as Richard Nixon was the last New Deal president, it is very likely that Bill Clinton will be the last Republican-era president. Partisanship does not have much to do with it. And prediction is merely a device to round out the analysis and to dramatize the relationship between end as objective and end as decline and fall.

This is in many ways a revisit to my 1969 book. *The End of Liberalism* was a deliberately ambiguous title intended to convey the two objectives of that book. The first objective was to assess the actual character of liberalism as the ideology of the New Deal era. The second objective was to expose its weaknesses in order to hasten its end, either through replacement or fundamental reform. It was replaced, and the time has now come for the end of its replacement. *The End of the Republican Era* will be an outcome of the same causal connection between its objectives and its collapse—its ends and its end. But because it follows the end of the New Deal era and inherited all the institutional baggage of what had become the Second Republic of the United States, there is a lot more at stake. I fear we could be confronting not only the end of the twenty-year Republican era but also the end of the two-hundred-year *republican* era. Thus, the title is playing with not one but two deliberate ambiguities. The book is inevitably about ambiguities because it is about belief systems or ideologies that have been hegemonic in America at one time or another, and it is only when a belief system is in power that its fundamental contradictions are fully exposed.

"_____ is a great system. Too bad it's never been tried." Anyone can play this game and win, by filling in the blank with one's favorite belief: Christianity, capitalism, democracy; conservatism, liberalism, socialism. Most believers have said this in frustration, not realizing how lucky they are that circumstance intervened to save them from the fulfillment of their wish. Marx put it very well in his observation that "capitalist production begets, with the inexorability of a law of nature, its own negation." But Marx was much too modest. He should have universalized his proposition, because all systems, including his own, are similarly flawed.

In that spirit I have identified four systems or bodies of political belief that have a popular base broad enough in American society to be occasionally hegemonic and occupy a place in American history long enough to qualify as a tradition. Louis Hartz wrote a volume about the two traditions of liberalism, which he duly entitled, *The Liberal Tradition in America*. No one wrote the equivalent volume on the two traditions of conservatism. And it is quite possible no one could, because there has been a gigantic rhetorical mix-up that has effectively blocked good analysis as well as constructive discourse. Proving once again that truth is stranger than fiction, the first liberal tradition (Old Liberalism) came to be called conservatism, though no two bodies of belief could be further apart than Old Liberalism and conservatism. Meanwhile, the second liberal tradition (New Liberalism) came to be defined as the Left (socialism), despite the fact that the Left and the New Liberalism were separated by the great gulf of their contrasting attitudes toward capitalism, which both traditions of liberalism embrace just as strongly as the most orthodox tradition of socialism rejects. Capitalism is, in fact, the economic expression of liberalism. Meanwhile, and equally strange, few Americans appreciate the fact that *genuine* conservatives are the Americans most ill at ease with capitalism. That is why, as we shall see, they have put so much effort into trying to work out a politically viable concordance with capitalism.

My book does not provide the complete and comprehensive account of the four traditions that comprise the politics of ideology or belief back of *public policy* in the United States. My goal is the more modest one of making such an account possible. I hope also to set the tone for that more comprehensive synthesis by telling the four stories as tragedies. When in power, the end of the two liberalisms and the two conservatisms is the same. Power corrupts, but it tends to corrupt intellect earlier than character, and in predictable ways. Any belief system, when it becomes a theory of government, will self-destruct, *unless its adherents recognize the limits of its applicability*. True believers, whether they are educated or not, seem to have learned little from the 2,500-plus years of experience with tragedy, or, as William Fleming puts it in his seminal *Arts & Ideas,* with "tragic necessity [wherein] the hero's downfall comes because he carried the seeds of his own destruction within his breast."[1] Heroes are the ultimate example of true believers—persons who so believe in their own virtue that they cannot imagine, or indeed reject, the very idea that there could be or should be a limit to its pursuit. How could there be a limit? Can there ever be "too much of a good thing" when the good thing is goodness itself?

This, finally, is why the political theorist tries to make a distinction between private life and public life, between civil society and the polity. The good in one may not carry over as

[1]William Fleming, *Arts & Ideas* (New York: HR & W, 1991), 30.

an equal amount of good in the other. What is true for a part is not necessarily true for the whole. In the economy, it may be prudent for each farmer to produce as much as possible yet imprudent for farmers as a whole to do so. In the society, it is never good to kill; in the polity the same argument hardly applies. Most Americans, regardless of ideology, insist upon the distinction between private and public, but mainly in order selfishly to define the sphere or realm of their personal activity as immune from public interference. But they are less likely to carry this distinction to an equal but opposite expression of it, applying it to that sphere or realm in which private tastes and values ought not to intrude upon public discourse or policy decision. When truly believing Christians speak of a Christian nation, they fail to recognize how perilously close they come to crossing the line from private (and civic) observance to public (and coercive) intrusion. When they seek to christianize politics, they have indeed crossed the line; and afterwards, retreat back across the line is difficult if not impossible.

Professor Stephen Carter confesses that he does not understand why "one good way to end a conversation . . . is to tell a group of well-educated professionals that you hold a political position . . . because it is required by your understanding of God's will." In fact, his entire best-selling book, *The Culture of Disbelief*, is a lament that religious beliefs can no longer "serve as the basis of policy," indeed, that religious beliefs "cannot even be debated in the forum of public dialogue on which a liberal politics crucially depends."[2] My answer throughout these pages is that true believers systematically misrepresent or misunderstand the requisites of politics. Note, for example, the subtitle of Stephen Carter's book, *How American Law and Politics Trivialize Religious Devotion*. The very purpose of politics is precisely to trivialize all manner of beliefs drawn from private life and to render them into a discourse about consequences that can moderate and balance

---

[2]Stephen Carter, *The Culture of Disbelief* (New York: Basic Books, 1993), 22 and 30.

the coercive forms by which public decisions are ultimately expressed. That is to say, when beliefs are pursued without full appreciation of their consequences, Act I of the tragedy of the true believer has begun. Permit me to draw inspiration from one of the modern masters of the private realm, T. S. Eliot. Having made observations that might give the impression he had a theory of the overall disintegration of the intellect in modern Europe, Eliot quickly adds: "I would remind you that I am here concerned primarily with poetry, not with modern Europe and its progress or decline; but that if and when I speak of 'disintegration,' 'decay,' or 'decline,' I am unconcerned with the emotional or moral co-efficient of these terms. [That] is an occupation for prophets and makers of almanacks of whom I am not one."[3]

Separation of private from public, of which separation of church and state is one small part, is the necessity driving this book. It is a necessity because so much more is at stake when the end in question is not only the Republican era but also the republican era. Although an end is generally followed by a new beginning, the start-up of another *republican* era may not be so certain, at whatever cost. The signs are all around us. Dare I cite the two most ominous, signs so commonplace that they are accepted as signs of health: the drainage of power from elected officials to the executive bureaucracy, and the drainage of power away from elections toward what my colleagues Benjamin Ginsberg and Martin Shefter refer to as "politics by other means."

I begin this book and I also conclude it with an appeal inspired by Dante, to be engraved in large letters over the portals of politics: "Abandon God, all ye who enter here." Whenever the true believers of all faiths can take that as good advice, the light will again shine more brightly on this, the greatest of all republics—if we can keep it.

[3]Christopher Lehmann-Haupt, review of *The Varieties of Metaphysical Poetry: The Clark Lectures at Trinity College, Cambridge, 1926, and the Turnbull Lectures at the Johns Hopkins University, 1933*, by T. S. Eliot, "Books of The Times," *The New York Times*, May 23, 1994.

ACKNOWLEDGMENTS

MY ACKNOWLEDGMENTS AND THANKS are accompanied by a warning that my colleagues will detect in these pages a far greater influence than they could possibly have anticipated. This is a responsibility each of them will have to bear even though it is not one for which their consent was or for that matter could have been sought.

First of all, I am indebted to the Julian J. Rothbaum family, the Honorable Carl Albert and Carl Albert Center, and the University of Oklahoma community for making this book *necessary*—a Yogi Berra faux pas that was never more appropriate. The original three lectures comprising the Rothbaum Lecture Series grew into a serious book because University of Oklahoma faculty and students took what I said so seriously that I had to make good on the many implicit promises embodied in the tantalizing overstatements understood best as visiting lecturer's license. Those who played a special role during my visit and afterwards were Ronald Peters, Director of the Carl Albert Center, Danney Goble, Allen Hertzke, Larry Hill, and LaDonna Sullivan as well as Julian and Irene Rothbaum, their son Joel Jankowski, and Carl and Mary Albert, all of whom attended the lectures and participated in the discussions along with the other students. My thanks also to Kimberly Wiar and George Bauer and other staff at the University of Oklahoma Press.

Although the Oklahoma invitation produced the book, I had been working on aspects of it for two or three years. Godfrey Hodgson gave me the opportunity to try out the scheme of classifying ideologies in a chapter for a book under his thoughtful editorship, "Before Conservatism and Beyond: American Ideology and Politics in the 1990's."[1] Part of a year's leave in France, thanks to the support of Cornell University and the hospitality of the Fondation Nationale des Sciences Politiques, was devoted to preparation of that chapter and profited immensely from my French associates at the Observatoire Interrégional du Politique (OIP) and the Fondation, most particularly Marie-France Toinet and the late Annick Percheron. A special expression of gratitude is due to Serge Hurtig and the late Georges Lavau, who worked tirelessly to translate the aforementioned article for publication in *Revue Française de Science Politique*. It was Georges Lavau's last project before his death.[2]

A series of lectures and seminars in Italy also helped provide a larger perspective on the range of ideology in Western democracies. My host, guide, and indispensable colleague and formidable critic in all matters was Professor Mauro Calise. I profited from a similar tour in Australia, beginning with the distinguished Wolfsohn Lecture at Melbourne University and continuing at the Universities of Deakin and Sydney as well as Australian National University in Canberra. Aynsley Kellow, then of Deakin now of Griffith in Brisbane, has been, before and since my visit, one of my most valued colleagues.

Opportunities to teach the materials were not lacking in the United States. Most important of these, as always, were in my own classes at Cornell, with my own students, graduate and

[1]Theodore J. Lowi, "Before Conservatism and Beyond: American Ideology and Politics in the 1990's," in Godfrey Hodgson, ed., *Handbooks to the Modern World: The United States, Volume 2* (New York and Oxford: Facts on File, 1992), 619–43.

[2]Georges Lavau, trans., "Avant le Conservatisme et Au-Dela les Ideologies et la vie Politique Americaines dans les Années 1900," *Revue Française de Science Politique* 40, no. 5 (1990): 669–98.

undergraduate. Several of my faculty colleagues made worthwhile contributions to the ideas as well, most particularly Benjamin Ginsburg (now of Johns Hopkins), Elizabeth Sanders, Joel Silbey, and Martin Shefter. I am especially indebted to Professor Timothy Byrnes of Colgate and Professor Allen Hertzke of the University of Oklahoma, who read the entire manuscript, and Professor Thomas Dumm of Amherst and Professor Michael Minkenberg of Gottingen, who read significant portions of it. All of them flattered me with the diligence and care of their reading and criticism; they strengthened my arguments even when they disagreed with me.

Finally, there is my family nucleus. That includes Rose Zakour and her successor Jackie Discenza, each of whom began as secretaries and quickly became my managers and then my friends. And it includes my wife Angele, my son Jason, my daughter Anna, and her husband Dan Ferguson. Their debunking style helped maintain my sense of reality and their constant support and affection maintained my sense of purpose.

THEODORE J. LOWI

East Hill, Ithaca

THE END OF THE REPUBLICAN ERA

CHAPTER 1

THE CONSTITUTION
AND THE PUBLIC PHILOSOPHY

Thus, in the beginning,
everything was America.
JOHN LOCKE, 1689

TO JOHN LOCKE, mankind began in "the state of nature," a place of "peace, goodwill, mutual assistance and preservation," where all individuals were guided by their own conception of moral good and all earned their rights by their own labor. The state of nature was a useful fiction, a logical starting point for a distinctly modern view of the individual as the point and purpose of society and of government.

If to Locke in 1689 everything began with America, in the America of 1789 everything began with John Locke. Americans had marched out of the state of nature to the cadence of the social contract, just as John Locke had laid it all out.[1]

Actually, Americans had discovered the social contract forty-eight years before Locke. In 1620, while still aboard ship, heads of household formed their government and signed what became known as the Mayflower Compact.

> We . . . do by these presents solemnly and mutually in the presence of God and one of another, covenant and combine ourselves together into a civil body politic . . . ; and by virtue hereof to enact, constitute, and frame such just and equal laws,

[1]For another indication of the experience of early American settlements with the practice of creating government by contract, see Kenneth A. Lockridge, *A New England Town: The First Hundred Years* (New York: W. W. Norton, 1970). Lockridge provides an account of the founding of the town of Dedham, Massachusetts, in 1836 with a social contract called the Dedham Covenant (4–7).

ordinances, acts, constitutions and offices, from time to time, as shall be thought most meet and convenient for the general good of the colony, under which we promise all due submission and obedience.

The Mayflower Compact was not brought to light until 1802, by the future president, John Quincy Adams, who hailed it as "the first example in modern times of the social compact or system of government instituted by voluntary agreement."[2] But it demonstrates that Americans were more than ready for Locke's theory, and the framers of the Constitution were very much aware of Locke. Their Constitution made the United States the first and probably the only polity to be formed self-consciously according to Locke's blueprint.

If man in the state of nature be so free, . . . if he be absolute Lord of his own person and possessions, equal to the greatest, and subject to nobody, why will he part with his freedom . . . ? To which, it is obvious to answer, that though in the state of nature he hath such a right, yet the enjoyment of it is very uncertain. . . . This makes him willing to quit this condition, which, however free, is full of fears and continual dangers; and it is not without reason that he seeks out and is willing to join in society with others . . . for the mutual preservation of their lives, liberties, and estates.[3]

Not by divinity, not by a conquest, and not by a tradition or evolution; the American state was founded by contract.

John Locke's views can be traced back half a century to Thomas Hobbes and a century and a half before that to Niccolò Machiavelli; both contributed to this distinctly modern conception of human nature or psychology as one of individual self-preservation and acquisitiveness, and both were beginning to recognize state authority as justifiable only to the extent that it enabled individuals to satisfy their own individual wants. But they were distant sources of the Ameri-

[2]Quotes and references from Kate Caffrey, *The Mayflower* (New York: Stein and Day, 1974), 114–15 and 340–41.
[3]From John Locke, *Second Treatise of Civil Government and a Letter Concerning Toleration*, pars. 123 and 131.

can founding, while Locke was the proximate source. As the historian Bernard Bailyn put it,

> Referred to on all sides, by writers of all political viewpoints in the colonies, the major figures of the European Enlightenment and many of the lesser, contributed substantially to the thought of the Americans; but except for Locke's, their influence . . . was neither clearly dominant nor wholly determinative.[4]

Real interests were at stake in the founding. But contract theory was not merely a cover for them, because opposing interests—for example, commercial versus plantation—as well as opposing principles—anti-Federalists versus Federalists— would not have been able to sustain such a conspiracy. The framers were the power elite in America, and the power elite made the Constitution. Basing the new polity on contract was a calculated risk. The Constitution was a contract between elites and the people. Essentially, the elites agreed to put limits on their power in return for consent on the part of the people to permit government to take place. On this basis, a genuine national government could be formed with sovereignty over thirteen jealous former colonies who would submit to being states in a single national system in exchange for giving that national government only limited powers. Moreover, these powers were not given over to a European type of national state but were highly specific powers delegated to the elected legislature, the Congress of the United States, in Article I, Section 8.

The consequences were immediate and durable. Table 1.1 is an indispensable picture of American government in actual operation for virtually its first century and a half. This is a picture of the real government but also the government designed by the Constitution. In the history of government, there has never been a closer concordance between the formal and the real. And even today, few elements of American

[4]Bernard Bailyn, *The Ideological Origins of the American Revolution* (New York: Harvard University Press, 1967), 30.

Table 1.1

The Federal System: Specialization of Functions Among the Three Levels of Government, the Traditional System, ca. 1800–1933

National Government Policies (Domestic)	State Government Policies	Local Government Policies
Internal improvements	Property laws (incl. slavery)	Adaptation of state laws to local conditions ("variances")
Subsidies (mainly to shipping)	Estate and inheritance laws	Public works
Tariffs	Commerce laws (ownership and exchange)	Contracts for public works
Public lands disposal	Banking and credit laws	Licensing of public accommodations
Patents	Labor and union laws	Assessable improvements
Currency	Insurance laws	Basic public services
	Family laws	
	Morals laws	
	Public health and Quarantine laws	
	Education laws	
	General penal laws	
	Public works laws (incl. eminent domain)	
	Construction codes	
	Land use laws	
	Water and mineral resources laws	
	Judiciary and criminal procedure laws	
	Electoral laws (incl. political parties)	
	Local government laws	
	Civil service laws	
	Occupations and professions laws	
	Etc.	

government or politics can be understood except within the context of table 1.1.[5]

Column 1 is an accurate, if not exhaustive, list of the types of domestic policies that the national government in Congress produced day by day, decade after decade. Americans called it limited government, and Europeans called it a weak state. The national government was indeed limited and weak compared to Europe. But that only masks the two important facts about our system that can be appreciated after a moment's study of the items in column 1. First, the items of policy reveal a national government whose purpose was one of promoting commerce. If there was a vision shared by the leaders and elites of the national government throughout the nineteenth century and a goodly part of the twentieth century, that vision was not one of morality but one of utility. Europeans have quite properly called us a commercial republic, because the policies listed in column 1 existed literally for the purpose of promoting commerce. This was intended. And it was laid out in an explicit plan by Alexander Hamilton in his famous *Report on Manufactures* (1791), written as secretary of the treasury on order from the First Congress.

Further study of column 1 reveals still another common trait, a trait conspicuous by its absence: direct coercion. There is none of what later came to be called regulation, or intervention in the economy. Cash subsidies, land grants, and licenses and contracts were specific privileges distributed by the national government to encourage individuals to do more of what they were already doing or to undertake things that they would not otherwise have done. Patents, copyrights, and so on, existed to facilitate action, not to restrict it. A government engaging virtually exclusively in such promotional, nonregulatory policies can most accurately be referred to as a patronage state.

[5]See, for example, Theodore J. Lowi, *American Government: Incomplete Conquest* (New York: Holt, Rinehart and Winston, 1976), 130; Lowi, *The Personal President: Power Invested, Promise Unfulfilled* (Ithaca: Cornell University Press, 1985), 24; and Lowi and Benjamin Ginsberg, *American Government: Freedom and Power* (New York: W. W. Norton, 1994), 62.

Patronage has to be properly understood. The concept arises out of the medieval practice of the patron who aids individual clients. That is what feudalism was all about. Patronage. The term has been bastardized in modern usage, suggesting that it has to do only with the handing out of jobs and that there is something basically corrupt about it. But the fact is that patronage is a fundamental way in which people can deal with resources. Some wealthy families are patrons of the arts or the university. In the same manner, all governments some of the time and some governments all of the time use their public policy powers for patronage. The end (or objective) of this, the First Republic of the United States, was to promote commerce by using the resources available to the national government—money, privilege, access—on an individualized and personalized basis to encourage individuals, firms, and corporations, to help individuals who sought the help, whether to occupy and own a parcel of farmland or to build a railroad. Patronage.

This is the secret of the longevity of the national government operating under the original Constitution. It lasted beyond and despite the Civil War. Once Reconstruction was over, the national government went back to the same system of patronage as pictured in column 1 of table 1.1, engaging in virtually no regulation of individual conduct, engaging in no redistribution of wealth, just husbanding commerce in a variety of ways. Exceptions such as the Interstate Commerce Act and the Sherman Antitrust Act are so weak and infrequent that they confirm the overwhelming pattern of patronage policies in a commercial republic.

However, it was a patronage state without a monarchy, a bureaucracy, or an army. It was a patronage state with a Bill of Rights for individuals and a bill of particulars against autonomous bureaucratized governmental institutions. It was an instrumental state, short on coercions and obligations, long on freedoms, opportunities, and incentives.

In sum, it was a liberal state. It was a state under a Constitution that did its best to avoid taking positions on substantive morality. In fact, an exhaustive examination by one of the most distinguished constitutional scholars, Lawrence Tribe, turned up exactly two substantive positions in the Constitution—religious freedom and private property.[6] And even these are not expressed as substantive moral obligations. That is to say, no individual is obliged to attend a church, to express a religious idea, or to observe a religious ceremony; and no individual is obliged to own property or to make contracts with regard to it. The Constitution embraces religion and property by providing that the national government may take no actions depriving persons of their enjoyment of religion or of their acquisition and exchange of property. Thus, even as to moral substance, the Constitution is virtually procedural in its recognition. And with these as with virtually everything else, the Constitution is permissive, supportive, utilitarian. Everything is interests and opportunities; virtually any objective can be included as one of the "blessings of liberty." Conservatives today decry the decline of America toward "moral equivalence" and "moral relativism." What decline? That is precisely what the original Constitution embraced. Quintessential liberalism.

In this sense America actually began with the Constitution. The Constitution set the terms of political discourse. The preeminent national public philosophy had to be one that was fully consonant with this Constitution. That is where, or how, John Locke came in.

Numerous belief systems competed for preeminence.[7] But as one belief was wont to assert, many are called but few are chosen. The choice was determined largely by the Constitution. It occupied the conceptual space, it distributed the

[6]Lawrence Tribe, *Constitutional Choices* (Cambridge: Harvard University Press, 1985), 11. He also includes antislavery, but that is a position taken only after the Civil War. Before that, slavery was subsumed under private property. So that leaves us with only two substantive positions.

[7]Outstanding inventories and evaluations will be found in Bailyn, *Ideological Origins*; Isaac Kramnick, *Republicanism and Bourgeois Radicalism* (Ithaca: Cornell University Press, 1990); and Gordon S. Wood, *The Creation of the American Republic, 1776–1787* (New York: W. W. Norton, 1969 and 1972).

governmental powers, it created the architecture of government; and these shapes and forms, and the political dynamics following therefrom, have determined which ideologies would become the primary sources of political discourse. The Constitution shaped power, and power shaped ideology.

Louis Hartz, in trying to account for "the liberal tradition in America," drew on Richard Hildreth's 1850s observation that America was producing "one code, moral standard, by which the actions of all are to be judged." Hartz then extended this observation with the following interpretation:

> Hildreth knew that America was a marvelous mixture of many peoples and many religions, but he also knew that it was characterized by something more marvelous even than that: The power of the liberal norm to penetrate them all.[8]

This power of the liberal norm was enough to "[kill] the socialist dream here at its very bourgeois roots."[9] But Hartz then made a fatal error by extending his analysis to the conclusion that the power of the liberal norm also prevented the development of a "conservative tradition."[10] We shall soon see quite clearly that there is a conservative tradition, as old and as strong as the liberal tradition. The Constitution did in fact provide a home for Edmund Burke, the Bible, civic religion, communitarian republicanism, and whatever. But the relationship between the Constitution and their American ideology can be understood only by first defining liberalism and conservatism within the context of that constitutional structure.

I will begin with a definition of liberalism that may make political theorists and intellectual historians cringe, because I am going to do it briefly and I am going to do it by listing what

[8]Louis Hartz, *The Liberal Tradition in America* (New York: Harcourt, Brace, Jovanovich, 1955), 56.

[9]Ibid., 78. For a complementary interpretation, see Theodore J. Lowi, "Why No Socialism in America: A Federalist Perspective," in Robert T. Golembiewski and Aaron Wildavsky, eds., *The Costs of Federalism* (New Brunswick, N.J.: Transaction Books, 1984).

[10]Hartz, *Liberal Tradition*, 57.

appear to be its main characteristics.[11] These are displayed on the middle column of table 1.2. I will call this an operational definition not because it meets the requirements of an operational definition in hard science but because it meets the need for dealing with "beliefs in operation." It is an effort to bring theory into practice or to engage in practical reason with theoretical constructs.

First, the single defining attribute of liberalism is individualism. Liberalism embraces the individual as the purpose of society and the state. Liberalism defines the individual *in opposition to the collectivity*. This may also be the single most inspirational aspect of liberalism to people throughout the world whose countries are casting off the various forms of moral absolutism that had suppressed them for most of this century.

The second attribute flows inexorably from the first. The individual is defined in terms of wants and the striving for their satisfaction. This restates and reinforces individualism as the primacy of the self, to which society itself must be subordinated: "Each person possesses an inviolability founded on justice that even the welfare of society as a whole cannot override."[12] Liberalism as a public philosophy is anti-Christian, or extra-Christian, because it encourages individuals to pursue their wants without shame. Wants do not have to be defined as needs, nor do they have to be subordinated to any larger moral code. In brief, liberalism envisions a society built on greed, which Americans call "the pursuit of happiness." This also defines capitalism; capitalism is nothing more than the economic manifestation of liberalism.

Critics of liberalism who try to make a concordance between capitalism and Christian theology insist that there is a

[11]I am not in such bad company. Russell Kirk will be seen later trying to do the same for conservatism.

[12]John Rawls, quoted in Michael J. Sandel, *Liberalism and the Limits of Justice* (Cambridge: Cambridge University Press, 1982), 16. Although Sandel's book is a critique of liberalism, it provides a treatment that is fairly consistent with the definitional efforts I am making here.

Table 1.2
Ideologies — Some Definitions

Left	Liberal	Right
1. Society must be made moral for the individual	1. Individual above all	1. Individual subordinate to moral code
2. Needs define rights; society obliged to meet them	2. Individual defined by wants; society built on greed, the pursuit of happiness	2. Need over greed
3. Morality guides discourse, drawn from concept of a just society	3. Against morality in public discourse	3. Morality guides discourse, drawn from tradition or sacred texts
4. Collectivity over contract, after society reconstituted	4. Linkage to collectivity through contract	4. Community over contract
5. Government justification: move society toward equality of condition	5. Government justification: intervene only against conduct deemed harmful *in its consequences*	5. Government justification: intervention into conduct deemed good or evil *in itself*

"moral and cultural dimension of capitalism" and claim that they can find it even in Adam Smith and such other pure liberals as Milton Friedman.[13] They speak of selfish interest "properly understood," which becomes their linkage to an argument against selfish interest itself. The critics have every right to insist that people espouse principles of honesty, goodwill, and philanthropy as ends in themselves. But that is not liberalism, and it is not the liberal foundation of capitalism. Nor is it a view espoused consistently by Adam Smith: "The natural effort of every individual to better his own condition . . . is so powerful a principle, that it is alone, and without any assistance, . . . capable of carrying on the society to wealth and prosperity."[14] The greed or avarice basis of liberalism and of capitalism is purely individualist. The only limit to the pursuit of individual satisfaction is the harm that such pursuit might do to another individual. This is the dividing line between productive, socially positive greed and the destructive forms of greed we call fraud, theft, exploitation, corruption. But the limit as well as the principle of greed is instrumental. Respect for one's own individualism takes its very meaning from respect for the same quality in others. What the liberal economist George Stigler said of economists can be generalized to the whole liberal public philosophy: "Economists . . . believe that economic transactions are usually conducted on a high level of candor and responsibility, because it is in the interest of the parties to behave honorably in repetitive transactions. Hence honesty pays."[15] This will be confronted more fully in chapter 5.

As already anticipated, the third characteristic of liberalism is its steadfast opposition to the involvement of morality in public discourse. To Locke, and to virtually all who espouse

[13]Michael Novak, *The Catholic Ethic and the Spirit of Capitalism* (New York: Free Press, 1993), 8.

[14]Quoted with approval in libertarian George Stigler's *The Economist as Preacher and Other Essays* (Chicago: University of Chicago Press, 1982), 7.

[15]Ibid., 24. This comment was the introductory passage of a section in his book entitled "What is Ethics?"

liberalism, every individual has a moral code; that is what distinguishes human beings from the simpler forms of animal life. However, although certain that every individual possesses a moral code and a conscience by which to determine moral obligations, liberalism is equally doubtful that one can ever know the absolutely true and only moral code. And since we cannot know which morality is exclusively the best, it is desirable to try to keep morality out of public life. According to George Sabine, "Locke, whose personal life was a distillation of the best qualities of puritanism, was able to pass the whole question over except as it affected his argument for toleration. . . . [He] could meet theological dispute with the deadliest weapon, indifference."[16] Alexis de Tocqueville was quick to recognize the same in his famous passage about the separation of church and state in America.

> When a religion founds its empire only upon the desire of immortality that lives in every human heart, it may aspire to universal dominion; but when it connects itself with a government, it must adopt maxims which are applicable only to certain nations. Thus, in forming an alliance with a political power, religion augments its authority over a few and forfeits the hope of reigning over all.[17]

The fourth attribute concerns the linkage between the individual and the collectivity, which, to the largest extent possible, is made by contract. Another formulation of contract is "voluntary association." This, in turn, reinforces the individualistic, essentially private, aspect of morality. To liberals like Locke, morality is less a matter of substance than one of the individual's right to conscience and the freedom to use it. This is self-interest "properly understood," that each person can enter into contracts only if each person has "the moral

---

[16]George Sabine, *A History of Political Theory* (New York: Henry Holt, 1951), 518.

[17]Alexis de Tocqueville, *Democracy in America* (New York: Alfred A. Knopf, Vintage Books, 1945), I: 319–21.

independence to determine the nature and content of ethical obligation."[18]

The fifth attribute is the most complex and problematic because it carries the heaviest burden. The first four attributes point toward one compelling conclusion, that liberalism means anarchy—the absence of rule. Liberal government is an oxymoron. Government is collective; liberalism is individualist. Government is a moral force; liberalism is against morality. Government is by definition a coercive force; liberalism rejects coercion in favor of voluntary association. How, then, can liberalism justify government under any conditions? I can locate only one: liberalism can justify government intervention against *conduct deemed harmful or injurious in its consequences*.

The unanimous opinion in *Brown v. Board of Education of Topeka* (1954) can be taken as the paradigm of the liberal approach to government. Virtually everyone in America except a few rabid racists agreed that racial segregation was morally bad. Yet the Supreme Court of the United States did not invoke moral arguments in its decision to declare legally prescribed racial segregation unconstitutional. The Court examined the original intent of the framers of the Fourteenth Amendment (1868) and declared that their investigation was "at best . . . inconclusive." The Court examined the history of school segregation and its own precedents regarding the doctrine of "separate but equal" articulated in *Plessy v. Ferguson* (1896) and found these inconclusive because the schools were being equalized "with respect to buildings, curricula, qualifications and salaries of teachers, and other 'tangible' factors." After having eliminated those standards, the Court forthrightly concluded,

We must look instead to the effect. . . . Does segregation of children in public schools solely on the basis of race, even

[18]David A. J. Richards, "Constitutional Liberty, Dignity and Reasonable Justification," in Michael J. Meyer and William A. Parent, eds., *The Constitution of Rights: Human Dignity and American Values* (Ithaca: Cornell University Press, 1992), 78.

though the physical facilities and other "tangible" factors may
be equal, deprive the children of the minority group of equal
educational opportunities? We believe that it does. . . . To separate [minority children] from others of similar age and qualifications solely because of their race generates a feeling of
inferiority as to their status in the community that may affect
their hearts and minds in a way unlikely ever to be undone. . . . Whatever may have been the extent of psychological
knowledge at the time of *Plessy v. Ferguson*, this finding is
amply supported by modern authority. . . .

We conclude that in the field of public education the doctrine
of "separate but equal" has no place. Separate educational
facilities are inherently unequal.[19]

This is what gives liberalism such an affinity for science—
and also what makes liberalism so often appear to be wishy-
washy. Liberals felt a deep moral antipathy to segregation; but
liberalism made the antisegregation argument on consequential grounds, avoiding moral imperatives altogether. Such a
formulation disappointed many, especially in the black community, who had become much more radicalized after World
War II. Surely they would have liked to see their moral
antipathy reflected in the Court's reasoning. Nevertheless,
the liberal argument of the Supreme Court treated segregation as a conduct whose consequences justified government
intervention.

In sum, although liberals are not always and forever consistent in their own behavior, the standard liberal approach to
public policy is to identify the conduct, to listen carefully to
arguments regarding the harmful consequences of that conduct, to feel an obligation to consider government intervention with regard to those consequences, and to accept a policy
of intervention if the evidence confirms the theory that there
is a significantly probable causal connection between the
conduct and the consequences. From John Dewey at least
through John Kennedy's 1962 Yale University commencement
address, the liberal faith was that the public could always

---

[19]*Brown v. Board of Education of Topeka*, 347 U.S. 483.

agree on how to solve its problems if it could just do enough good research.

NEW REPUBLIC, NEW LIBERALISM

The five attributes discussed above constituted the operational foundation of what came to be accepted as "the liberal tradition in America." And this tradition extends virtually unchanged in the nation at large through the epoch of the First Republic, which came to an end at some point after 1937.

The "Roosevelt Revolution" is not particularly interesting as a revolution in the size of the national government, although there was significant growth. However, it was a genuine revolution in the functions it was called upon to perform. From a constitutional standpoint, the government created by Roosevelt was a double revolution, because two lines of constitutional decision making were required to validate it: the first was *NLRB v. Jones and Laughlin Steel Corporation*, to establish the constitutionality of national regulatory power and the administrative agency approach to it; the second was *Helvering v. Davis* and *Steward Machine Company v. Davis*, to validate the welfare and fiscal (redistributive) programs of the New Deal.[20]

With such fundamental governmental and constitutional change, ideological change could not be far behind, and that would complete the Roosevelt Revolution. I give 1961 as the date of the Second Republic, because until at least the late 1940s, the general impression conveyed by most mainstream New Dealers was that the new domestic programs were a kind of necessary evil, adopted to meet the emergencies of the Great Depression but not necessarily designed to last beyond it.[21] Until pluralism became the official political theory and until Keynesianism became the official economic ideology (and Richard Nixon could confess, "I am now a Keynesian"),

[20]*NLRB v. Jones and Laughlin Steel Corporation*, 301 U.S. 1 (1937); *Helvering v. Davis*, 301 U.S. 619 (1937); *Steward Machine Company v. Davis*, 301 U.S. 548 (1937).
[21]For example, see Richard Hofstadter, *The American Political Tradition* (New York: Knopf, 1948), 336–42.

there was no new all-encompassing statement of a New Deal public philosophy. But by 1961, a new public philosophy for the Second Republic had emerged.

Yet this new public philosophy was still part of the "liberal tradition." Much as the Republicans in the 1950s tried to stigmatize the New Deal and Harry Truman's Fair Deal as "creeping socialism," most Republican candidates themselves ran as though they were Democrats who could do the same job better and cheaper. *Both* parties were liberal parties.[22]

Table 1.3 will help explain how it was possible to have an ideological sea change without drowning the liberal tradition. Indeed, it may seem strange to classify as an ideological revolution a change that left us with two liberal parties, but that seems to be what happened. Note first that the Liberal column in table 1.3 applies equally to New Liberalism (box 4) as well as to Old Liberalism (box 3). No new defining characteristic needs to be added to the list; this is why it can be said that the New Liberalism has not departed from the liberal tradition. The difference between the two liberalisms is one of degree: At what point can governmental intervention be justified? How injurious does the conduct have to be? What is the probability that the conduct will cause injury? What is the probability that the intervention will cost less than the injury? Simply put, the threshold of governmental intervention is much lower for the New Liberalism than for the Old.

Few foreign observers were misled by the New Deal or New Liberalism. They understood that both of the major American political parties were liberal parties. They also understood clearly that both parties, being liberal, are *right of center* in the European (and world) ideological context—the litmus test being the positive, supportive attitude of both parties toward capitalism. This has not changed with the collapse of the

[22]The "Compact of Fifth Avenue" between presidential candidate Nixon and Nelson Rockefeller, with Nixon capitulating on fourteen of Rockefeller's platform positions, indicated quite explicitly that the GOP was for the moment a *New* Liberal party. See Peter Collier and David Horowitz, *The Rockefellers: An American Dynasty* (New York: Holt, Rinehart and Winston, 1976), 340–43.

Table 1.3
Traditions of American Political Thought

EPOCHS		Positions		
		Left	Liberal	Right

OLD		1. Old Socialism
		Components:
		  Marxist socialism
		  Christian socialism
		Justification for government: achieving equal outcomes, then withering away
		Ideal: a *communal* society of equals
			3. Old Liberalism
			Components:
			  Free market (laissez-faire)
			  Smithian
			  Libertarian
			  Corporate ideology
			Justification for government: intervene only against conduct palpably harmful *in its consequences*.
			Government to support contract.
			Ideal: A society free *for* risk.
				5. Old Conservatism
				Components:
				  Christian Right
				  Traditional Right
				  Movement conservatism
				Justification for government: intervene against conduct deemed good or evil *in itself*. Government to impose morality.
				Ideal: a *good* society

NEW		2. Social Democracy
		Components:
		  Neo-Marxism
		  Statist socialism
		  New Left
		  Public interest Left
		  Civil rights radicalism
		Justification for government: permanent to maintain equal outcomes
		Ideal: a *participatory* society of equals
			4. New Liberalism
			Components:
			  Liberalism
			  Progressivism
			  Statist liberalism
			  Keynesianism
			Justification for government: same as above but with a lower threshold. A *theory* of harm sufficient to justify intervention.
			Ideal: a society free *from* risk
				6. New Conservatism
				Components:
				  Neoconservatism
				  Statist conservatism
				  International conservatism
				Justification for government: same as above, with a mixture of Old Left.
				Ideal: a *strong and virtuous* society

Soviet Union, because only totalitarianism died. Socialism is far from dead, and as long as it lives, even in memory, liberalism is clearly a right-of-center ideology. Making New Liberalism out to be socialism, stigmatizing the "L-word" as an alien, almost treasonable philosophy, is the sheerest piece of irresponsibility on the part of Republican party strategists, and its success was built on the ignorance of all those who followed their lead. Richard Nixon became a New Liberal in order to deal with what was still then a big Democratic voting majority in the country. George Bush was always a fairly orthodox Old Liberal whose problems with a resurgent right wing led him to keep his genuine liberalism in the closet. It is grotesque that such an orthodox liberal as George Bush would permit, indeed celebrate, the stigmatization of his own beliefs and those of his father and of the Bush/Yankee/Connecticut liberal Republican party tradition.

TO THE LEFT AND RIGHT OF LIBERALISM—THE OTHER IDEOLOGIES

Table 1.3 is once again needed in order to put the boundaries around liberalism. Ordinarily Americans tend to use the term "ideology" when they look at the Left (boxes 1 and 2). Correspondingly, the Left tends to apply "ideology" as a term of denunciation against its opposition. In its dictionary meaning, ideology refers to the "science of ideas" or to the scientific study of ideas and to the use of ideas in language. But at the very dawning of its usage, ideology was already being used as a term of abuse. (See chap. 6.)

Eventually, the term was cleansed by social scientists to refer to any system of ideas and values held by members of a particular social class or group, the hypothesis being that all groups, all the way up to the state itself, develop rationalizing and justifying beliefs appropriate to the long-term interests of the group, particularly its leaders. That practice is followed in this book, wherein "ideology" refers to ideas that defend and justify one's present position or that of one's group or class. Arguments referred to as ideology only characterize the justifying intentions of that particular discourse. The term is not intended to suggest that the beliefs held are false.

Locating the Left

Leftist ideology is distinctive in its core belief that capitalism, or a society built on it, is morally suspect and imposed by force for the purpose of exploitation of one class by another. The genuine Left, as identified on table 1.2, is not simply an extreme position on a continuum of ideologies, with liberalism in the middle and the far Right defining the other end. The Left is its own body of ideas; it is a dimension of beliefs quite separate and independent, just as liberalism and the Right are, respectively, separate bodies of belief and justification. (See also chap. 6.) A radical leftist, then, is a person who emphasizes the need to maintain the purity of the socialist position toward capitalism and would tend to view any compromise as immoral. A moderate leftist is far from a liberal. A moderate leftist is a person who believes, along with the radical leftist, that capitalism is problematic and will and should ultimately collapse of its own internal contradictions. The moderateness comes not from being a liberal at all but from the willingness either to take a longer view of the demise of capitalism or to participate in governments dominated by capitalist parties with a view toward influencing them in a leftist direction as much as possible. Called revisionist by the radical Left, these moderate leftists are often more reviled by their own socialist colleagues than by the members of the opposing liberal or conservative parties.

By the same token, there can be radical as well as moderate liberals, although that may at first exposure sound like the kind of oxymoron that brings a smile. But actually radical liberals are easy to identify. They are the virtual anarchists identified earlier, individuals who so believe in the self-perfecting dynamics of competition and the market that they would tend to reject any argument favoring government intervention against a particular conduct even if everybody else agreed it was injurious. To the radical liberal, whom we now tend to call libertarian, even Adam Smith was a compromiser.[23]

Having said this, it is necessary to say immediately that there is virtually no Left in America, or, no "socialist tradition in America." There is, of course, a history of *socialists* in America, and not all of them are Marxist. (See boxes 1 and 2 of table 1.3.) But most observers would agree with the empirical premise underlying the question first posed by Friedrich Engels, "Why is there no socialism in America?" According to Marxist theory there ought to have been a mobilized and class-conscious proletariat in America; in fact, there ought to have been a mobilized working class in America before any other capitalist country. There being none in nineteenth-century America, it would be impossible to say that by the twentieth century there was a "socialist tradition." There are all sorts of theories about why there is no socialism in America,[24] but they all reinforce the empirical proposition that there is no such tradition. That is a fascinating inquiry, but it is an unnecessary one here. The absence of a bona fide socialist tradition in America helps only to justify the lack of attention to ideologies of the Left in this book. It will enter into the analysis only to the extent that the New Left has been an influence on the Democratic party and the Old Left has been an influence of a different sort on the far Right.

The Right will receive only brief treatment in this chapter, not because of its insignificance but because it will become, in

[23]In a conversation with F. A. Hayek, Nobel Prize winner and one of the most notable Old Liberal economists, I had the opportunity to ask him if he had ever met the celebrated libertarian novelist Ayn Rand and what he thought of her and her philosophy. He confessed that they had met just once at a party given for the two of them and that they chatted rather briefly. Then, he said, "she called me a compromiser and walked away." Few would be willing to call Hayek, author of *Road to Serfdom*, a moderate, but it is clear from this story and from any comparison of the writings of the two people that his writing is moderate by the standards of a radical like Rand.

[24]Probably the best review of the various efforts to explain why there is no socialism in America will be found in S. M. Lipset, "Why No Socialism in the U.S.?" in Seweryn Bialer and Sophia Sleyar, eds., *Sources of Contemporary Radicalism* (Boulder: Westview Press, 1977), 3–149, 346–63n.

due course, the primary problem of the book. The purpose of its treatment here is one of definition and of logical placement as the other boundary of liberalism.

Locating the Right

Unlike the Left, the Right is not only a third dimension of public philosophy but also a genuine American tradition. Hartz wrote only half the truth in *The Liberal Tradition in America*. Not a half-truth, but half of the truth. There *is* a conservative tradition in America, alive today and as old and as strong as the liberal tradition. It is labeled "Right" on table 1.2 to make it more inclusive and also to make it more consonant with European understandings. That not only gives it greater stature but also strengthens the contention that, far from being ignored, it should have been Hartz's volume 2. Although such a volume will not be written here, one of the more important goals of this book is to explain why the genuine conservative tradition went unappreciated as a regular intellectual force in American politics.

The first step in that endeavor is to identify and define conservatism (or the Right) as a public philosophy. What will prove to be ironic here is not its absence but the fact that it got lost through a misapplication of terminology. For reasons largely of political strategy, Franklin Roosevelt appropriated liberalism as the New Deal's primary campaign label; and as the popularity of the New Deal grew, liberalism strengthened in its association with it and gained a halo effect. (See also chap. 3.) Liberalism in the New Deal combined the optimistic connotations of progressivism with the energetic associations of "reform" and the egalitarian connotations of populism and nationalism. Meanwhile, being on the losing side and fighting a retreat, the Republicans under Herbert Hoover got saddled with the term "conservatism," which took on the distinctly negative connotation of defense of the status quo and opposition to change. Republicans became "Neanderthal" in their defense of existing institutions and social elites.

What was missed entirely in this characterization was the historic commitment of the Republican party to genuine liberalism. The Republican party was founded as the liberal party, and the era of its dominance after the Civil War has been referred to as "the liberal era" by intellectual historians.[25] There was, in fact, far more genuine conservatism in the Democratic party, pre-1930s, than in the Republican party. What people *saw* in the Republican party was Old Liberalism. After 1932, what they *called* it—conservative—was plainly incorrect, misleading, and fundamentally harmful to political discourse as well as political analysis. But terminological misuse does not explain why real conservativism went unappreciated. On the contrary, it was the lack of appreciation of genuine conservatism in America that made such terminological misapplication possible.

It is time now for a more methodical definition. At the risk of some distortion, I have designed the definition of conservatism (the Right on table 1.2) as a set of characteristics in a point-by-point direct opposition to those characteristics listed for liberalism.[26] This enormously simplifies the presentation, but, to repeat, care should be taken to resist conceiving of *Left, liberal* and *Right* as a single continuum, with liberal being a moderate or compromised version of the other two.

The first characteristic has to do with the place of the individual in conservatism and the general tendency among conservatives to speak of the individual and of interests "properly understood." This means understanding the individual within and subordinating individuals to their social, institutional, and moral matrix. Here, as so often, the Right has more in common with the Left than with liberalism. To

[25]See, for example, Larry I. Peterman and Louis F. Weschler, eds., *American Political Thought* (New York: Meredith Corporation, 1972). Their chapter, "The Liberal Era," includes selections by such radical liberals as William Graham Sumner and such radical liberal views of the good society as the majority opinion in *Lochner v. New York*, 198 U.S. 45 (1905).

[26]Compare to Kirk's list of "six canons of conservative thought," in Russell Kirk, *The Conservative Mind* (Chicago: Henry Regnery, 1953), 7–8. Note also his contrasting list for "radicalism," p. 9.

conservatives, "the vaunted independence [of the individual] is a liberal illusion. It misunderstands the fundamentally 'social' nature of man, the fact that we are conditioned beings 'all the way down.'"[27] The extreme individualism of the French Revolution was one of the primal causes of philosophical conservatism in the first place. Conservative founding fathers such as Edmund Burke and Georg Hegel agreed that the philosophy of the Revolution was false in two respects: it failed "to recognize that the citizen's personality is a social being which requires as a condition of its moral significance a part to be played in the life of civil society and it failed to recognize that the institutions of civil society are organs of the nation, which must be embodied in a public authority consonant in dignity with the nation's moral significance."[28]

Item two follows inexorably from the first. Individual striving for the satisfaction of wants is the evil liberal vision of a society built on greed. It is a vulgar rendition of the pursuit of happiness and must be capped, in conservative thinking, by a more guided definition of wants. One of the primary purposes of religion is to restrict wants—to introduce restraint through shame. That is the difference between wants and needs. Wants are individual goals defined by the individual. Needs are individual goals defined by somebody else, according to some external moral standard.

This immediately drives into item three: morality trumps individual claims and the conservative has confidence that true morality can be known. It can be known by reason applied to appropriate texts and to existing traditions. And once known, morality ought to be imposed—preferably by parents and community, but by law if necessary.

In America, summation of items one, two, and three is essentially Bible plus Burke. The Bible or some other text is first embraced as an act of faith. Once that leap has been made, the text can be carefully studied for moral truth; and,

[27]Sandel, *Liberalism and the Limits of Justice,* 11.
[28]Sabine, *History of Political Thought,* 651.

through reason, moral guidance can be discovered. Following Burke, tradition is also a source of moral truth. Burke's conservatism is not merely a worship of the past for its own sake or of things because they exist. Respect for the past is based on the reasonable assumption that there must be virtue in human arrangements that have existed from beyond memory.

The following are illustrative quotes from the *National Review* and the Heritage Foundation, two enormously influential sources of contemporary conservative thinking.

> Lord Acton got it right: "Freedom is not the power to do what you want, but rather the right to do what you ought." [Republican Congressman Henry Hyde of Illinois, author of the Hyde Amendment, denying the use of Medicaid funds for reimbursing medical expenses attributable to abortion]

> Imaginative conservatives [seek above all] to conserve order: Both order in the soul and order in the state. . . . Libertarianism [Old Liberalism] properly understood, is as alien to real American conservatives as is communism." [Russell Kirk, author of *The Conservative Mind* (1953), a pathbreaking work in the nationalizing of the conservative movement][29]

Conservatives are even more fundamentally at odds with liberals on item four, the matter of contract. Conservatives do not see contract as immoral but as problematic; it is a radically dangerous principle on which to found a society or a polity. Burke probably gave the best statement of opposition to the principle of contract, indeed by ridicule.

> Society is indeed a contract . . . but the state ought not to be considered as nothing better than a partnership agreement in a trade of pepper and coffee, calico and tobacco, or some other such low concern, to be taken up for a little temporary interest, and to be dissolved by the fancy of the parties. . . . It is a partnership . . . not only between those who are living, but

[29]Both quotes from Bradley Miller, "The Right's Nanny Agenda for Running Your Life," *Washington Post*, 1991 June 10–16, pp. 25–26, national weekly edition. Many conservatives have used the aphorism attributed to Acton. But I have tried to track it down, and none of the users could identify the original source. Each relied on some other secondary user. I continue to doubt it came from Acton.

between those who are living, those who are dead, and those who are to be born. Each contract . . . is but a clause in the great primeval contract of eternal society, linking the lower with the higher natures, connecting the visible and invisible world, according to the fixed compact sanctioned by the inviolable oath which holds all physical and all moral natures, each in their appointed place.[30]

The fifth and final item is not so weighty a problem for conservatism as it is for liberalism, because conservatives are basically statists, while liberals are basically anarchists. To conservatives, as observed earlier, moral obligation, once known, should be imposed, *by law* if necessary. Note also in the long passage from Burke that morality, society, and state are all tied together in the conceptualization of the continuity of all contracts. But for our own time a more effective and useful formulation of the statist implications of the moral approach to individual and society can be provided by probably the most outstanding conservative writing today, the columnist George Will.

> In a famous opinion in a famous case (one concerning compulsory flag salutes in schools), Justice Felix Frankfurter wrote: "Law is concerned with external behavior and not with the inner life of man."
> I am not sure what Frankfurter meant. I am sure that what he said cannot be true. The purpose of this book is to say why that proposition is radically wrong.[31]

Even the title of Will's book, *Statecraft as Soulcraft*, is anathema to genuine liberals, Old or New. Liberals have been slow even to accept the notion of a "state" and cannot sit comfortably with the idea of "statecraft." But statecraft as "soulcraft" is beyond liberal conception.

Here, then, with some exaggeration, is "the conservative tradition." Once identified, its size and longevity in America should be obvious and undeniable, deserving its own treat-

[30]Edmund Burke, *Reflections on the Revolution in France* (1790), quoted in Sabine, *History of Political Thought*, 615.
[31]George Will, *Statecraft as Soulcraft* (New York: Simon & Schuster, 1983), 20.

ment as a volume 2 to Hartz's volume 1. But how could such a formidable tradition have gone so long unappreciated, virtually unnoticed, or casually treated in political analysis? How could a whole generation of political historians, political scientists, and journalists have been so confused about liberalism and conservatism that they could have mislabeled Old Liberalism as conservative?

Once again, the Constitution provides the answer. Another look at table 1.1 will reveal that the federal principle in the Constitution did more than merely recognize the states as a second layer of government. It reserved to that layer of government a very specialized set of functions. If the typical policies of a national government made it a "patronage state," the policies of the state governments, as identified in column 2, could characterize each of the states as a "regulatory state." The theory of federalism in the original Constitution—made explicit in the Tenth Amendment of the Bill of Rights (1791)— was that "the powers not delegated to the United States by the Constitution, nor prohibited by it to the States, are reserved to the States respectively, or to the people." These so-called reserved powers have been characterized as "police power"— the power to control the health, safety, and morals of the community. And the standard policy output of the state legislatures and courts ever since was precisely such an exercise, as seen in virtually all of the items in column 2. The modern word for this is *regulation*—from the French *régle* (rule) and *réglementation* (to impose rules upon). Column 2 demonstrates, as did column 1, that things worked out in reality almost precisely as the framers had intended. There are no national property laws; property is the result of all of the state laws of trespass, breach of contract, and so forth. There are no national family laws or morals laws or compulsory education laws or corporate laws—only state provisions.

And for these profoundly important, and generally conservative, state powers, *there was no Bill of Rights:* There was no national constitutional protection of individuals from the arbitrary exercise of police powers by state legislatures, state courts, state administrators, or state police (or their local agents). The Bill of Rights is an individualist document rendering liberal all principalities to which it applies, because it places no higher value on religion over nonreligion or one religion over another, one speech over another, one status over another, one want over another. When the Bill of Rights applies, the public discourse is in fact one of moral equivalence, moral relativism. Consequently, since the Bill of Rights did not apply to the states, a state could be as moral and as absolutist as a majority of its people wished. When the Tenth Amendment provided that "the powers not delegated to the United States . . . are reserved to the States respectively, or to the people," it meant that if a majority of the people decided to require stores to close on Sunday or to require religious instruction in schools, they could delegate this power to the states but could not delegate it to the national government even if an overwhelming national majority wished to do so.

The determinative document for the states was not the Bill of Rights at all but *Barron v. Baltimore* (1833).[32] The issue in *Barron v. Baltimore* was whether Mr. Barron's property was protected from the city of Baltimore's taking, under the Fifth Amendment's provision that no citizen can be "deprived of life, liberty, or property, without due process of law; nor shall private property be taken for public use, without just compensation." Chief Justice John Marshall's answer was a resounding No, unless the State of Maryland had such a provision in its own constitution.

> The Constitution was ordained and established by the people of the United States for themselves, for their own government, and not for the government of the individual states. Each state established a constitution for itself, and, in that constitution, provided such limitations and restrictions on the powers of its particular government as its judgment dictated. . . . [The] Fifth Amendment must be understood as restraining the power of the general government, not as applicable to the states. In their

[32]*Barron v. Baltimore*, 7 Peters 243 (1833).

several constitutions they have imposed such restrictions on their respective governments as their own wisdom suggested; such as they deemed most proper for themselves. It is a subject on which they judge exclusively.

This case merely recognized what the framers had probably intended, which was the power of the states to deal with their citizens as they saw fit. In this sense, if the Bill of Rights was the charter of the status of the individual citizen within the context of national power, *Barron v. Baltimore* was the charter of the status of citizens within the power of the states.

This duality of constitutional federalism produced two separate and specialized structures of government—a patronage government and a regulatory government—and each developed a governmental tradition that would be consonant with a distinctive ideological tradition. The national government became the house of liberalism, and the state governments became the house of conservatism. Granted, state legislatures have veered occasionally Leftward, for example, attempting to declare a moratorium on private debt or attempting to repudiate public debt. But the laws and judicial decisions of state after state, decade after decade, testify to the persistent conservative reality of state governments, the keepers of morality and community.

By the time Louis Hartz was writing his book, there was in fact a new national liberal consensus—New Liberal, but liberal nonetheless. Hartz's book was written in 1954, the year of *Brown I*, and published in 1955, the year of *Brown II*. This was the beginning of the social revolution that would give us the Constitutional Revolution of the 1960s, in which, by a succession of cases, *Barron v. Baltimore* was finally and fully overturned and the Bill of Rights was nationalized and applied to the states.[33] But it would take the entire 1960s for liberalism to

[33]The Supreme Court effectively overruled *Barron* in 1897 when it held that the due process clause of the Fourteenth Amendment did in fact "incorporate" the Fifth Amendment and thus prohibited states from taking property for a public use without just compensation even if that particular state did not have such a provision in its own constitution. *Chicago, Burlington and Quincy Railroad*

succeed in nationalizing the Bill of Rights, and until then, conservatism would remain content within the home of the state governments.

Here we will find the principal reason why conservatism went unappreciated by most political analysts. The Constitution can explain the existence and location of the conservative tradition, its relative obscurity despite its strength, and the preeminence nationally of the liberal tradition and the liberal consensus, extending through the epoch of the New Liberalism. But can it also explain "the end of liberalism," the nationalization of conservatism, and the Europeanization of America? New Liberalism had been extremely popular. It was so popular that Republican candidates ran like Democrats who would simply do the same job more cheaply. New liberalism was so strong that it was able to maintain its grip on its own southern right wing (box 5) in the long-standing New Deal coalition. And New Liberalism was so strong that it continued to grow during the Nixon administration and was still strong enough during the Reagan administration to prevent the New Liberal (New Deal) policy apparatus from being dismantled.[34] Why did it collapse? Why did its end bring on a genuine national conservatism?

Chapter 2 deals with the end of New Liberalism. It revisits my earlier volume and adds the perspective of twenty-five years since its first publication and fifteen years since the writing of the second edition. Chapter 3 deals with the Republican era and the end of *Old* Liberalism. Chapters 4 and 5 concern what the end of liberalism was the beginning of: the

---

v. Chicago, 166 U.S. 226 (1897). However, in a broader sense, *Barron* remained the charter of state government because the Supreme Court did not "incorporate" any of the other provisions of the Bill of Rights into the Fourteenth Amendment until it acted on the First Amendment in 1925. No other provisions of the Bill of Rights were applied through the Fourteenth Amendment to the states until the 1960s. For a thorough and lively treatment of that process, see Henry Abraham, *Freedom and the Court* (New York: Oxford University Press, 1977).

[34]The Civil Aeronautics Board was the only New Liberal program terminated in the name of deregulation, and that action was taken by the Democratic Carter administration.

conservative era. In effect, they deal politically with the origins of modern conservatism and with the nature of its success during the Republican era. The final chapter evaluates the end of conservatism and makes a few speculative gestures toward what that end could be the beginning of.

CHAPTER 2

THE END OF LIBERALISM

> *Hegel says somewhere that all great*
> *events and personalities in world*
> *history reappear in one fashion or*
> *another. He forgot to add: the first*
> *time as tragedy, the second as farce.*
> KARL MARX, 1852

THE DEMOCRATIC PARTY spend sixty years trying to recover from the Civil War. It was the oldest electoral party in the world and one of the few institutions left unbroken by the war. But it was the party of the Old Republic and of the Old South—the party in retreat. Between 1860 and 1900, Democrats won the presidency only twice, with Grover Cleveland in two unconnected terms. And Cleveland belongs to a category of presidents, including James Buchanan and Herbert Hoover, that supports an important generalization formulated by Walter Dean Burnham, "that established 'old politics' leadership in any given period responds to growing political crisis by a rigidity and a rejection of emergent demand which contributes in no small way to the magnitude of the subsequent explosion, and the completeness of their own repudiation."[1] Democrats did little better in the House of Representatives or Senate between 1860 and 1900, winning House majorities eight times, against thirteen for the Republicans, and three times (with one tie), against twelve, in the Senate. The so-called critical election of 1896 actually reinforced Democratic minority status. Woodrow Wilson squeaked through in 1912 with a historically low 42 percent of the popular vote, thanks

[1]Walter Dean Burnham, "American Politics in the 1970s: Beyond Party?" in William N. Chambers and Walter Dean Burnham, *The American Party Systems*, 2d ed. (New York: Oxford University Press, 1975), 346.

to the William Taft/Theodore Roosevelt split of the true majority. And between 1902 and 1930, Democrats won majorities in the House and the Senate three times, to twelve for the Republicans. That last figure indicates that Democrats were in the minority in state elections as well, because, until 1912, most of the states still selected their U.S. senators by state legislative vote rather than by statewide popular vote.

That critical election of 1896 not only reinforced the minority status of the Democratic party. It produced the conditions for political decadence in both parties, because the most dramatic development attributable to the 1896 "system" was the end of the two-party system as we had known it. Up until 1896, most elections were contested by two or more candidates representing two or more different political parties. This was just as true of counties, wards, and assembly districts as it was for statewide elections. After 1896, the Republican party virtually disappeared from the South and the Democratic party shrank to noncompetitive status in most of the northern states and local districts. The myth of a national two-party system was sustained only by the persistence of two-party competition inside the United States Congress and vigorous two-party contests for the presidency. But in both of these contexts—legislative and executive—the United States did not have a genuine two-party system between 1896 and the 1950s; instead, there was a system of two one-party systems whose respective regional strength produced two-party confrontation at the national level. To a large degree, this extreme sectionalization of the two parties was a reaction within each against the populism and progressivism that had begun to sweep throughout the country in the early 1890s.[2] And unquestionably these new interests, which were to become so important to the New Liberalism of FDR, were for their first thirty-plus years suppressed or kept at arm's length at the periphery of politics. They were first and most dramati-

[2]See, for example, the excellent analysis of the 1896 impact and the reaction to populism in E. E. Schattschneider, *The Semisovereign People* (New York: Holt, Rinehart and Winston, 1960), chap. 5.

cally suppressed in state Democratic party organizations. After 1912, they were pushed to the periphery of the GOP, if not outside altogether. But suppression of these new interests was not the only decadent aspect of the post-1896 development. Parties were losing strength in legislatures. Elections were losing their scale and vitality, with dramatic reductions in the number of contested elections as well as in the size of the voter turnout. And the electoral process was in many instances being displaced altogether by intraparty primaries. This turned out to be an especially effective way to disenfranchise black voters.

The 1932 election has been tagged by political scientists as another critical election, producing a historic "electoral realignment" comparable to 1860 and 1896, when shifts in partisan electoral affiliation were massive, meaningful, and as close to permanent as things can be in politics. But an election can be a critical realignment only in retrospect, and in fact nothing of great significance could have been known immediately from the 1932 campaign or election. Franklin Roosevelt had won it more by Republican party failure than by Democratic party success. Any non-Republican candidate could have won, even if running on what New York politicians used to call the Chinese laundry ticket. Roosevelt had given little indication in his campaign that his administration would depart radically from its predecessors or that it would make any special effort to absorb those populist and progressive movements referred to earlier. As one quite friendly biographer put it, some of Roosevelt's ideas were "more orthodox than Hoover himself. . . . And in one of the most sweeping statements of his campaign he berated Hoover for spending and deficits, and he promised—with only the tiniest of escape clauses—to balance the budget."[3] In other words, even as late as 1932, Roosevelt was running as a Republican.

[3]James MacGregor Burns, *Roosevelt: The Lion and the Fox* (New York: Harcourt, 1956), 143.

TOWARD THE NEW AMERICAN STATE—AND
NEW LIBERALISM

Yet the significance of the 1932 election could be seen very soon after it was over. There were, of course, strong elements of pure symbolism and opportunism, quickly improvised shots to meet mass fear and establish as widely as possible the impression that government was responsive to people's needs. There was an immense amount of improvisation in the early New Deal. Agriculture groups virtually wrote their own legislation, which Congress passed and the president signed with a minimum of deliberation. Although labor did not have the power of agriculture, labor legislation did arise out of close consultation with most available labor leaders. Industrial and economic policies were an accumulation of concessions to corporations and corporate trade associations under the banner of the National Recovery Administration (NRA) and other programs covering banking, securities, mining, and transportation. Yet there was also method and vision to the New Deal. The so-called Roosevelt Revolution was a revolution that defied Lenin's rule that you cannot have a real revolution without a revolutionary theory. The New Deal created a new American state out of the cumulative enactments of presidential and interest-group proposals to Congress. From the standpoint of constituencies and budgets, the policies were merely additive. But they also added up. Table 2.1 presents a picture of the architecture of the new American state, or eventually, the Second Republic of the United States. Properly understood, it is also a pictorialization of New Liberalism.

FDR might well have met his 1932 mandate with expansion of traditional federal policies and programs (as shown in column 1 of table 1.1): patronage, the traditional stuff of the First Republic. A number of existing traditional programs were in fact expanded in 1933–34, including rivers and harbors projects, highway construction, agriculture assistance, and other programs that had been called "internal improvements"

Table 2.1
The Political Economy of the New Deal

Program Category	Acronym	Year
1. Traditional State		
Civil Works Administration	CWA	1933
Public Works Administration	PWA	1933
Civilian Conservation Corps	CCC	1933
Works Progress Administration	WPA	1933
Tennessee Valley Authority	TVA	1933
Rural Electrification Administration	REA	1933
Soil Conservation Service	SCS	1935
2. Regulatory State		
Agricultural Adjustment Administration	AAA	1933
National Recovery Administration	NRA	1933
Securities and Exchange Commission	SEC	1933
Public Utility Holding Company Act		1935
National Labor Relations Act and Board	NLRB	1935
Fair Labor Standards Act	FLSA	1938
Civil Aeronautics Act and Board	CAB	1938
3. Redistributive State		
Federal Deposit Insurance Corporation	FDIC	1933
Bank holiday		1933
Home Owners Loan Corporation	HOLC	1933
Devaluation		1934
Federal Housing Administration	FHA	1934
Federal Reserve Reforms	FED	1935
Social Security Act	SSA	1935
Farm Security Administration	FSA	1935
Internal Revenue tax reforms	IRS	1935
4. Organizational State (Constituent Policies)		
Judiciary reform		1937
Executive Office of the President	EOP	1939
Budget Bureau	OMB	1939
White House staff		1930s
Administrative law		1930s
Federal Bureau of Investigation	FBI	1940s
Joint Chiefs of Staff	JCOS	1940s

in the nineteenth century. In fact, from the budgetary stand-point, the three largest new programs enacted during the famous Hundred Days—the Works Progress Administration (WPA), the Public Works Administration (PWA), and the Civil Works Administration (CWA)—accounted for nearly 53 per-cent of the 1934 budget, 46 percent of the 1935 budget, and 41 percent of the 1936 budget. Although proclaimed as recovery and relief programs, they were essentially extensions of the patronage state.

If Roosevelt had done nothing more than expand tradition-al approaches, he might well have brought the United States out of the depression. Given the sorry condition of the coun-try by 1939, he might have done no worse than to stay the course and increase the velocity. But that is not what he did. Although lacking in theoretical finesse and totally committed to the practical question, "Will it work?" Roosevelt's improvi-sation produced a new state as surely as if he had been a philosopher king.

The need for several categories in table 2.1 demonstrates with little explication required that the national government would no longer be merely a patronage state. Here it can be clearly seen that a mere expansion of the size of the national government was the least significant aspect of the 1930s change. The most significant aspect was that for the first time the national government established a direct and coercive rela-tionship between itself and individual citizens. The Roosevelt administration had discovered that the national government, not merely the states, possesses police power. The new regu-latory programs (table 2.1, category 2) are functionally identi-cal to traditional state regulatory programs in the sense that each seeks through law to impose obligations directly on the conduct of citizens, backing those obligations with sanctions.

The second new function added during the 1930s (table 2.1, category 3) is referred to as redistributive policy. These poli-cies are novel in comparison to traditional patronage policies but also in comparison to regulatory policies—state or feder-al. For although coercive and involuntary in relation to citi-

zens, redistributive policies deserve to be separately cate-
gorized because, rather than attempting to impose direct
obligations on individual conduct, they attempt to influence
individuals by manipulating the *environment of conduct*. These
policies seek to create new structures, to influence people by
manipulating the value of property and money, or to categor-
ize people according to some universalized attribute, such as
level of income or age or status of occupation. As referred to
earlier, regulatory and redistributive policies were recognized immediately as two distinctively novel functions, because two separate lines of constitutional litigation were
required to validate them. Regulatory power was validated in
NLRB v. Jones and Laughlin Steel Corporation. Redistributive
power was validated in *Steward Machine Company v. Davis* and
Helvering v. Davis.

Of particular significance for our purposes is that, although
these new policies are clearly and definitively statist, they are
liberal, not Left or socialist. First, they share the same outlook
or temperament as the Supreme Court opinion in *Brown v.
Board* in that they focus on potential injury (and theory about
the causes of injury), and they focus on how to intervene
against the causes of those injuries either to reduce the
frequency of the injuries or to indemnify the victims. Beyond
that, these policies are liberal in that they accept capitalism—
that is, the existing economic system—and they attempt self-
consciously to deal with its imperfections. This is precisely
why European observers accepted the New Deal as liberal
and as right of center, not even social democratic, a successful
attempt to save or salvage (depending on one's assessment of
the consequences of the depression) the capitalist system.

Most Europeans were consequently skeptical of the notion
of a "Roosevelt Revolution," feeling rather that it was only
moderately reformist in saving the existing capitalist system.
But from an American perspective, these policies, taken as a
bundle of innovations, were revolutionary in the degree to
which they altered the constitutional position of the national
government and in the degree to which they produced or

contributed to the change in the relative institutional power and functions of the branches of the national government.[4] Judged by standards drawn from within American historical experience, this was genuinely a new republic. Yet within American as well as world standards, it was a liberal state—a positive, discretionary state but still a liberal state.

It should also be called a "positive state" for the obvious reasons that it committed itself to being affirmative rather than reactive; and it was also expansionist, because growth had become the criterion of responsiveness or accountability within a modern understanding of democracy. As a positive liberal state, the new republic was willing to be responsive to any widely held theory of injury. This is the primary reason why there was tremendous growth in the research apparatus of the executive branch, followed by an almost equivalent or proportionate growth in the research apparatus of Congress. Growth of senior staff in executive agencies—once not only moderate but dominated by lawyers and career personnel who simply knew the procedures and workings of the agencies—came to be matched and sometimes surpassed by the recruitment of economists, engineers, and biomedical technicians who were experts in the subject matter of a particular agency rather than the mere procedures. This expansion of substantive research apparatus went beyond responsiveness toward what came to be called "affirmative action" to take initiatives in order to prevent injuries from taking place or to determine how compensation for past injuries can be worked out. Affirmative action took on a particular meaning in the

[4]For a more elaborate argument on this point, see Lowi, *The Personal President.* The Supreme Court attempted to prevent this transfer of power, holding that Congress was not constitutionally permitted to delegate its broad legislative power to the executive branch without accompanying that delegation with clearer standards as to how to implement the powers so delegated. *Schechter Poultry Corporation v. U.S.,* 295 U.S. 495 (1935); and *Panama Refining Company v. Ryan,* 293 U.S. 388 (1935). However, Congress proceeded essentially to disregard that doctrine. For an effort to convince European colleagues that the evidence supports a "revolution," see also Mario Einaudi, *The Roosevelt Revolution* (New York: Harcourt, 1959).

area of civil rights, but it is a useful generic term for the rise of the positive state.

The new state was from the start also a discretionary state because of the delegation of vast areas of discretion by law from Congress to the president and executive agencies. Amounting to suspension of the rule of law, delegated discretion was justified during the dark days of the depression, when, in desperation, bad policies could be considered superior to no policies at all. This is precisely what the Supreme Court rejected in *Schechter* (1935; see chap. 1, n. 4) with its rule that Congress should accompany every delegation of discretion with standards and guidelines for executive agency decisions. Although this ruling has never been explicitly reversed by the Court, it has been extinguished by disuse.[5] Thus we remain a highly discretionary state even when there is no emergency to deprive Congress of the time for deliberation and the proper drafting to determine what the rules of conduct and the standards of intervention ought to be.

What we can also add is that this positive, discretionary, liberal state was from the beginning a very popular state and, to a large extent, a legitimate one. The proof: none of the legal or administrative apparatus of this state has ever been terminated. In fact, no serious effort has ever been made to terminate any of it. Two Republican administrations during the 1980s tried earnestly for twelve years to change the direction and reduce the vigor of the liberal state, but they made no serious effort to disestablish it or to dismantle any particular

[5]The authors of one important administrative law textbook ask rhetorically at the end of a long discussion of the problem of delegation, "If, as appears, the delegation doctrine has no operative effect . . . why waste [time] discussing this arcane bit of legal history? Our answer is, first, so long as *Panama* and *Schechter* are not overruled, they serve as a warning that there are some limits. . . . More important, although the delegation doctrine may not result in the invalidation of any attempted congressional delegation, the *problem* . . . is real and significant." Walter Gellhorn et al., *Administrative Law: Cases and Comments* (Mineola, N.Y.: Foundation Press, 1979), 68. See also Theodore J. Lowi, *The End of Liberalism: The Second Republic of the United States*, 2d ed. (New York: W. W. Norton, 1979).

part of it. All told, despite the charges of "creeping socialism" made by critics in the 1950s and the stigmatization of liberalism successfully engineered by Republican campaigns of the 1980s, the positive, discretionary, liberal state had proven itself, not necessarily as a success, but as a genuine effort at representative government not incompatible with American capitalism.

Yet although the apparatus of the New Liberal state endured, the New Deal coalition came unstuck and the liberal consensus collapsed, all within the brief span of less than a decade between the last New Liberal presidents—Lyndon Johnson, Richard Nixon, and Jimmy Carter—and the beginning of the Republican era. The Republicans succeeded miraculously well in their not-so-subtle redefinition of liberalism as Left and as Socialism. As President Ronald Reagan himself put it, the Democrats are "so far Left, they've left America." A Republican governor and convention keynoter tied in the international with the domestic aspects of liberalism with his reference to the Democratic party as a party of "pastel patriotism" that tried to "hide its true colors." This went along nicely with the accusation initiated by the Christian conservative Pat Robertson that the American Civil Liberties Union (ACLU) is a subversive organization and that the 1988 presidential candidate Michael Dukakis was "a card-carrying member." So successful were these efforts to associate liberal with far Left, and foreign, that the liberal Democratic candidates quickly began to avoid associating themselves with the term, which contributed further to the discrediting of liberalism. It was in fact the embarrassment of liberals in their liberalism that enabled Reagan to confirm its stigmatization with his reference to the "L-word," as though it were an obscenity.[6] No matter that the majority wing of the Republi-

[6]This enabled the Republicans to run against Richard Nixon as well as against the 1960s Democrats. A number of worthwhile references to this successful Republican campaign will be found in Gerald M. Pomper, ed., *The Election of 1988: Reports and Interpretations* (Chatham, N.J.: Chatham House, 1989); see the contributions by Gerald Pomper, Marjorie R. Hershey, and Wilson Carey McWilliams.

can party was itself liberal. That only suggests how confused and deranged was the political discourse of the 1980s in the dust of the collapse of the liberal consensus. The question is, why?

THE END OF LIBERALISM: A TRAGEDY IN THREE ACTS

This is the continuation, perhaps the conclusion, of a story I began literally thirty years ago. My account of the end of liberalism at that time remains an essential part of the story, because that account was sufficient to anticipate the collapse of the liberal consensus, and it provided at least the beginnings of an explanation. As early as 1964, I could see that liberalism had become its own worst enemy.[7] No external opposition or circumstances were endangering liberalism. Even by 1968, the year I completed *The End of Liberalism*, the Republican party under Nixon won the presidential election with a liberal consensus campaign. With all the friends it had at that time, liberalism did not need enemies.

Stories of internal collapse, of self-defeat, and of heroic death by heroic misjudgment are usually known as tragedies. In characterizing tragedy in classical Greek theater, A. C. Bradley observed that what actually occurs "is not so much the war of good with evil as the war of good with good."[8] I would add only one particular dimension: tragedy arises out of ignorance or disregard of the limits of one's own strengths and virtues.

[7]My first effort to capture and put in print a case study of liberalism gone awry was "How Farmers Get What They Want," *Reporter*, May 1964. The owner and publisher of *Reporter*, Max Ascoli, earned my eternal gratitude by urging me to change the title of that piece from "Big Estates from Little Acres Grow" and also for encouraging me to expand for later publication my all too lengthy critique (at that time) of liberal policy making as a reemerging form of European corporatism. Two years later I wrote what was to become the organizing critique of liberalism: "The Public Philosophy: Interest-Group Liberalism," eventually published in *American Political Science Review* (March 1967).

[8]Quoted in David Ricci, *The Tragedy of Political Science* (New Haven: Yale University Press, 1984), 22. I am grateful to Ricci for his use of this characterization in his treatment of the history of political science as a profession, although I do not agree with his analysis in all its particulars.

In the theatrical spirit, the analysis will be presented in three acts, with a few changes of scene. And each act will be concluded with reflections by the chorus (a single voice).

Act I: How Success Produced Decadence

The *Oxford English Dictionary* (*OED*) defines decadence as "the process of falling away or declining (from a prior state of excellence, vitality, prosperity, etc.); decay; impaired or deteriorated condition." This we can associate with Acton's aphorism, "Power corrupts," because corruption goes beyond the mere breach of public trust, as by the taking or giving of bribes, to include, according to the *OED,* "dissolution of the constitution which makes a thing what it is." Corruption is a particular form of decadence, the derangement of judgment, the wearing away of the capacity to think, the capacity to sustain action consistent with original position.

Scene 1: The Conceptual Overexpansion of Liberalism—Making Frontiers Out of Boundaries: Boundaries are clear and formally recognized lines of division; frontiers are vague and indeterminate separations. In international relations, one generally assumes that diplomatic progress has been made when frontiers between nations have been converted to boundaries. One could possibly consider such a thing progress in domestic law and administration as well, for a boundary indicates recognition of the limits of the reach of the law and the jurisdiction of the agency.

Table 2.2 indicates that the pattern of development has been virtually the reverse of what might have been expected and what ought to be preferred. It seems, at least to me, that as Congress, the agencies, the president, and the regulated groups gained experience with regulation, they would all have been able to define more clearly the laws and rules in each existing regulatory program as well as to improve on the definitions and boundaries in new programs of regulation. There is no learning curve in the history of national lawmaking.

Table 2.2
Rule of Law: From Boundaries to Frontiers*

Scope	Objects	Development Characteristics
1. Monopoly (1887)	Railroads Trusts—oil, sugar, etc.	Concrete Specific Traditional Rule-bound Proscriptive
2. Bad products and goods (1906)	Qualities of things Substandard foods, etc.	*Abstract*** Specific Traditional Rule-bound Proscriptive
3. Unfair competition (1914)	Relationships	Abstract *General* Traditional *Discretionary* Proscriptive
4. Factors (1933)	Goods and services, by sector	Abstract *Universal Nontraditional Prescriptive*
5. Systems (1940s)	The whole economy Total environment of conduct	Abstract Universal *Integrated* Prescriptive

*An abridged and revised version of table 5.1, pp. 98–99, in Lowi, *The End of Liberalism*.
**Italicized to indicate a major innovation.

The first entry in Table 2.2 refers of course to the first two important regulatory laws enacted by Congress—the Interstate Commerce Act and the Sherman Antitrust Act. In each of these, the goal was to fight unfair trade and unfair competition. Although the concepts of unfair trade and restraint of trade may initially seem too abstract to perform as good standards to guide delegations of regulatory power from Congress to the executive branch, the history of competition and the experience of Anglo-American common law in the states in dealing with unfair competition and restraint of trade had "freighted them with meaning," informing the statutory definitions with concrete cases and holdings.[9] The category of unfair competition/restraint of trade was rendered still more concrete by the prevailing understandings of the objects to be regulated. In the Interstate Commerce Act, the objects were quite explicitly the railroads and the problem was primarily rates. Under the Sherman act, the concept of the trust sounds at first more abstract, but everyone knew that this was a concrete reference to *the* trusts, namely, the oil trust, the sugar trust, and so on. Consequently, the characteristics provided in the third column of table 2.2 suggest that these early regulatory laws were relatively concrete, specific as to object and conduct, traditional (having been drawn from English and state common law experience), rule-bound (to the degree that the regulated parties could have a good understanding of their obligations under the laws), and proscriptive (inasmuch as the obligations involved were statements of what *not* to do).

The second stage of development, item 2, indicates a clear step in development, although not a quantum leap. As with item 1, these regulatory efforts arose out of a rich tradition of state control of adulterated substances. In other words, people could come to an agreement as to some goods that were unsafe, even if they disagreed as to whether the probability of injury was sufficient to require prohibition. Moreover, the techniques of regulatory control were fairly standard and familiar, such as a regulatory (virtually prohibitive) tax on

[9]Donald Dewey, *Monopoly in Economics and Law* (Chicago: Rand-McNally, 1959), chaps. 9–11. Although the common law from state to state gave a confused picture, the concepts and understandings regarding the primary category, restraint of trade, were unmistakably clear. The expectation was that the national law would make the application more consistent, but the understanding of the concept was already clear.

certain undesirable goods, inspection and publicity regarding unsafe consumable products, and in some instances (although most of this was to come later), outright, hands-on control of some aspect of the particular product or conduct. The new step in item 2 was that for the first time the scope and jurisdiction of the law were to be defined not by concrete designation of known companies and recognized behaviors but by *abstract categorization*. That is to say, the objects of regulation were not designated but were indicated more abstractly through definition of a quality or characteristic that inheres in all of a designated class of objects. Following that, flexible guidelines could be set down for the administrator's decision on how to designate the actual objects that fell below the cutoff point, as *sub*standard, *im*moral, *un*healthy. Obviously the ability of Congress to provide standards to guide administrative decisions is far more limited in such a situation, because definition by abstraction and categorization involves philosophic questions that transcend practical experience and available technology. At what point of odor or of bacteriological content is meat spoiled or a drug unsafe? At what point does the purpose of a woman's movement across state lines become immoral? This step from concreteness to abstractness in the definition of a regulatory policy may well have been the single most important change in the entire history of public control in the United States. And it may be the most problematic.[10]

The next item in table 2.2 moves the abstraction of item 2 a step further and then adds some novelty of its own. The relative definiteness of the Sherman Antitrust Act was beginning to cause some political trouble to the degree that its intent was to forbid all conspiracies to restrain trade. The courts began to retreat from this by drawing distinctions between reasonable and unreasonable restraints of trade; the category itself became increasingly muddied. In 1914, Con-

[10]A longer treatment of this phenomenon will be found in Lowi, *The End of Liberalism*, 99–101.

gress tried to define what it had in 1890 only needed to designate, virtually by pointing its finger. The Clayton Act of 1914 did manage to list two or three specific evils, but the language of the Clayton Act and of the Federal Trade Act of the same year was on net both abstract and general or open-ended. There was also a large step in the amount of discretion delegated to this new agency, the Federal Trade Commission (FTC). Although a goodly amount of discretion is inevitable in the enforcement of any regulatory law, a large step in degree can amount to a change in principle; and this is precisely what happened in 1914. In referring to "unfair methods of competition . . . and unfair or deceptive acts or practices," the 1914 laws created an abstract category of behavior (commerce or competition), decreed an abstract characteristic that is to be sought in any such behavior (competition), and provided an abstract standard to guide decisions (fairness). This may at first exposure appear similar to the previous abstract category of "bad goods," but in the regulation of goods, the categories (beef, morphine) and the qualities (even the notion of morality applied to transporting women) possessed both a plain meaning and some capacity for measurement. Laws governing competition could have very little of either—especially when the key adjective was *reasonable*. To add to the degree of discretion granted the agency, the 1914 laws also provided that the agency would have power to determine not only when conduct was unfair but also "when it is in the public interest" to take action against the conduct. Thus the conduct could be unfair but untouched, according to whether at a particular point in time it was in the public interest to touch it.[11]

Although innovations in the previous phases of regulatory development were clear enough to be detectable, they did not come into full flower until the 1930s, when the largest number of new regulatory programs was instituted. Item 4 is obvi-

[11]See Douglas Jaenicke, "Herbert Croly, Progressive Ideology and the FTC Act," *Political Science Quarterly* 93, no. 3 (Fall 1978): 471–94.

ously a large step toward far greater abstraction, toward *universality* in the scope and applicability of the regulatory measure. Moreover, as Congress was making the effort to move further and further behind commerce along the causal chain to the factors that comprise commerce or affect the flow of commerce, it was also moving the law toward more and more "nontraditional" applications in the sense that there was less and less established legal meaning through the experiences of state legislatures and state common law. Programs moved away from a relatively restricted realm of conduct deemed threatening to persons or to the flow of commerce toward the sum total of all transactions and toward forms of conduct further and further away from commercial activity. Another innovation noted on the table is "prescriptive," to indicate that many agencies were being given the power to include "thou shalts" as well as "thou shalt nots." Orders to raise prices to make commerce more uniform would be an example of a prescriptive regulation. Laws requiring companies to print securities brochures or to adopt a particular method of accounting for purposes of welfare programs or taxation are prescriptive. Here are the beginnings of efforts to reach entire systems through regulation, and it is very difficult even for physical scientists, much less policy makers, to be able to define the boundaries of a system.

Up to this point, one could say that social and economic necessity explains the spreading of the scope and the softening of the boundaries of public policy. It could be argued that the explosive expansion of the scale of the economy, coupled with the increasingly complex and interdependent economic relationships, rendered federal government intervention more and more difficult even as demand for intervention intensified. The culmination should have come in the 1930s when the collapse of the economy produced an urgency for bold action that justified the vaguest and sloppiest legislative drafting. There was a popular clamor for legislation not merely in the first hundred days but in the first thousand days. An overwhelming majority in Congress was ready to commit legiscide to provide the president with the means to restore faith that America could control its own fate. But if the emergency explained the New Deal's leap into great scope coupled with limitless abstraction, there should have been a change toward better legislation once the emergency was over. But that is not what happened. Public policies after World War II indicate that developments in the positive, liberal state were driven not by social/economic necessity but by ideology.

There had been some systems thinking prior to the 1960s. For example, the Interstate Commerce Commission (ICC) under the Transportation Act of 1920 was expected to take into account the entire rail system as it determined its regulatory provisions. Some thinking of a similar nature was partly the obligation of the Federal Communications Commission (FCC) with regard to the new industry of radio, and similar thinking was to be expected of the Civil Aeronautics Board (CAB) and the Federal Aviation Administration (FAA) in regard to the fledgling industry of commercial airline service. But the sector by sector scale of those earlier efforts gave only the barest intimation of what was to come.

Systems thinking drifted fairly quickly from the academic disciplines in the 1940s into the minds and hearts of public policy makers in the 1960s. From that point on, virtually all new programs defined the jurisdiction of the relevant agency as an entire system. The best example for purposes here is the language setting up the Environmental Protection Agency (EPA), because it is language provided by Republican President Nixon in his message to Congress conveying to them his executive order proposing the creation of the agency. In this message, President Nixon said that the purpose of his reorganization plan was to respond to "environmentally related activities" and to organize them "rationally and systematically." He went on to argue that "we need to know more about the *total environment*" if we are effectively to "insure the protection, development . . . and enhancement of the total environment."[12] EPA was then charged with doing its job by "setting standards consistent with national environmental goals . . . [of] protecting the environment by abating pollution." EPA would "monitor the condition of the environment, . . . establish quantitative environmental baselines, . . . [and] set and enforce standards for air and water quality and for individual pollutants."[13] In other words, EPA's jurisdiction was the whole universe. Since pollution can come from anywhere, we must naturally equip our agency with power to cover anything and everything.

Similar language will be found in most of the regulatory programs established in that epoch. For example, the universe of the Occupational Safety and Health Administration (OSHA) was "working conditions . . . and human resources." The jurisdiction of the Consumer Products Safety Commission (CPSC) was the whole universe of risk from household products and other consumer durables. And in each statute, *an ultimate goal for that system* was ordained by law. The product was to be safe, the conditions sound, the environment clean; and in many cases, the goal was specified with precision, for example, down to so many parts per billion. This was not rule of law. It was not even rule of jurisdiction where the "metes and bounds" of territory were specified. It was rule even beyond dominion, to an open-ended universe in which agencies had to grope for standards that applied to individual conduct yet somehow might be related to the larger system. These points will return soon to the analysis, when the chorus speaks.

Scene 2: The Institutional Overextension of Liberalism—The Binge of 1965–75 Actually there were two binges, one in the welfare state, the other in the regulatory state, roughly in that order,

[12]*President's Message to Congress Transmitting Reorganization Plans to Establish Two Agencies*, 6 Weekly Comp. Pres. Doc. 908 (9 July 1970). Emphasis added.
[13]Quoted from the full text of President Nixon's *Environmental Reorganization Plan of July 9, 1970*, reprinted from Government Printing Office in *Congressional Quarterly Almanac* (1970), 119A–20A.

as they shall be treated here. The welfare binge got off to an inauspicious beginning in 1962, with a policy initiated by the Kennedy administration to provide social services to Aid to Families of Dependent Children (AFDC) in addition to cash benefits. The service programs provided a federal share of 75 percent, with 25 percent provided by the states. This eventually produced a significant increase in the AFDC rolls, but its impact was not noticed during the first four years because the increase in the number of recipients was less than 1 percent a year until the end of the decade. Another precursor of the welfare takeoff was the food stamps program, in effect reborn in 1964. It was to become very significant, but at first no one appreciated that for two reasons. First, the initial appropriation was comparatively small ($250 million); second, it was widely advertised among the more sophisticated observers as less a welfare program and more a program to help in a constructive way to get rid of some farm surpluses.

These programs did not weaken the support that had been building for adding health insurance to the welfare state. Medicare and Medicaid were adopted as new titles amending the Social Security Act, and there was no mistaking their novelty. One of the more interesting features of these new programs is that they covered precisely those people who were not in the workforce: Medicare covered those who had permanently left the workforce by virtue of their age, and Medicaid covered persons, mainly those already eligible for AFDC, who were, by demonstration of need, in a situation of long-term dependency, especially in matters of medical care.

The Vietnam War was a cataclysmic intervention into American political life but merely delayed what appears to have been a genuine consensus in favor of continued expansion of the welfare state. For a new administration under a man dedicated to the virtual destruction of the Democratic party produced a set of welfare programs that would have been the envy of any Democrat. Three of these will be singled out as the most significant contributions to the structure of the welfare state.[14]

The first of these structural expansions was the Supplemental Security Income Program (SSI). The purpose of SSI was to federalize most of the welfare costs for older welfare recipients, so that they would receive their benefits virtually as a matter of right and so that these benefits would not vary in the extreme from one state to another. This led to a very steep increase in the old age assistance rolls. The second structural change was indexing of social security benefits. This meant tying by formula the basic social security benefit payments to the cost of living (the Cost of Living Adjustment, COLA), and it became a major commitment in Richard Nixon's 1968 party platform and a central proposal in his first program presented to Congress in 1969. It was attractive to Nixon and the mainstream of the Republican party because they would share some of the credit for increased generosity in welfare. Indexing was also attractive to the Republicans because it promised to put an end to the tendency of the Democratically controlled Congress to increase benefits during every election year. Hidden from view was the fact that an indexing commitment coming on top of a large benefit increase (the 20 percent referred to earlier), coming then on top of steadily high rates of inflation could produce a runaway increase in benefits. A vicious spiral was possible, inasmuch as substantially increased social security benefits could contribute to inflation, which in turn could contribute to another round of automatic social security benefit increases, and so on. Also suppressed or repressed from discussion in 1972 was the fact that the ratio of wage earners to benefit receivers was dropping from 18:1 toward 8:1 and then 6:1 and then below 5:1.

[14]The others include revenue sharing, consolidation of social services, addition of a family planning program to a Public Health Act, assorted health legislation, and the Comprehensive Employment Training Act (CETA). Nixon also made serious proposals for a Family Assistance Program and national health insurance. Both were turned down by a Democratic Congress.

The debate in 1972 about the revenue base and the general solvency of the welfare system was entirely optimistic. Yet less than one year later, unofficial as well as official reports projected near-run crisis, avoidance of which would require very substantial social security tax rate increases. Quite suddenly, news stories began to spread that bankruptcy was threatening the system.

Martha Derthick, a social security expert, observed in her important 1979 book that "the financial troubles of the system demonstrated the limits of the policy maker's vision. Policy making for social security had always been conducted as if the policy makers could tell what the future held."[15] Bruce Jansson concludes his history of the "reluctant welfare state" with a characterization of 1968–80 as "the paradoxical era." After a closer examination of the logic of liberalism, we will see that it was no paradox at all.[16]

The 1968–74 binge in the new regulatory programs was anticipated by the conceptual expansion of regulation, as dealt with earlier in this chapter. Thus, even as the boundaries and frontier of each regulatory law were being expanded, more and more substantive areas of economic and social life were being covered by new regulatory programs. Table 2.3 is a pictorialization of the regulation binge, and it needs little elaboration, except to explain the role of the Republicans, since the entire regulation binge happened on the Republican watch.

Republicans can respond to charges of collaboration with New Liberalism with two arguments. First, they can insist that their interest in regulation is strictly limited to local law and order—within a "state's rights" tradition—not to the national economy. Second, they can argue that the 1970s regulation binge was imposed on President Nixon by the Democratic Congress.

[15]Martha Derthick, *Policy Making for Social Security* (Washington, D.C.: Brookings Institution, 1979), 382.
[16]Bruce Jansson, *The Reluctant Welfare State* (Belmont, Cal.: Wadsworth, 1988), chap. 10.

Table 2.3
The Regulation Binge of the 1970s

Year Enacted	Statute
1969–70	Child Protection and Toy Safety Act
	Clean Air Amendments
	Egg Products Inspection Act
	Economic Stabilization Act
	Fair Credit Reporting Act
	Mine Safety and Health Act
	National Environmental Policy Act
	Occupational Safety and Health Act
	Poison Prevention Packaging Act
	Securities Investor Protection Act
1971	Economic Stabilization Act Amendments
	Federal Boat Safety Act
	Lead-based Paint Elimination Act
	Wholesome Fish and Fisheries Act
1972	Coastal Zone Management Act
	Consumer Product Safety Act
	Education Amendments Preventing Sex Discrimination
	Equal Employment Opportunity Act
	Federal Election Campaign Act
	Federal Environmental Pesticide Control Act
	Federal Insecticide, Fungicide, and Rodenticide Act
	Federal Water Pollution Control Act Amendments
	Marine Mammal Protection Act
	Marine Protection, Research, and Sanctuaries Act
	Motor Vehicle Information and Cost Savings Act
	Noise Control Act
	Ports and Waterways Safety Act
1973	Agriculture and Consumer Protection Act
	Economic Stabilization Act Amendments
	Emergency Petroleum Allocation Act
	Endangered Species Act
	Flood Disaster Protection Act

Table 2.3 *(continued)*

Year Enacted	Statute
1974	Atomic Energy Act
	Commodity Futures Trading Commission Act
	Consumer Product Warranties Act
	Council on Wage and Price Stability Act
	Employee Retirement Income Security Act
	Federal Energy Administration Act
	Hazardous Materials Transportation Act
	Housing and Community Development Act
	Pension Reform Act
	Privacy Act
	Safe Drinking Water Act
1975	Age Discrimination Act
	Energy Policy and Conservation Act
	Equal Credit Opportunity Act
1976	Consumer Leasing Act
	Medical Device Safety Act
	Toxic Substances Control Act
1977	Clean Air Act
	Clean Water Act
	Federal Mine Safety and Health Act
	Safe Drinking Water Act
	Surface Mining Control and Reclamation Act

Sources: Theodore Lowi, "Europeanization of America? From United States to United State," in Theodore Lowi and Alan Stone, eds., *Nationalizing Government: Public Policies in America* (Beverly Hills: Sage Publications, 1978), 19; as supplemented by Cass Sunstein, *After the Rights Revolution: Reconceiving the Regulatory State* (Cambridge: Harvard University Press, 1990), 26–28. This is a conservative listing, including only those programs that seemed comfortably to fit my definition of regulation: laws imposing control on individual conduct, backed by sanctions. The list obviously could vary in length depending on one's definition.

As to the first, it is true that President Nixon was with the Republican right wing in favor of strong intervention by the states on matters of individual beliefs and values, ranging from anticommunism to safe streets. However, as president,

Nixon could not have gone much further in encouraging state and local regulation than the Democrats had already gone by the end of 1968 during the Johnson administration. It was the Democrats who had formulated and enacted the Safe Streets and Crime Control Act of 1967 and the Crime Control Act of 1968. These programs made millions of federal dollars available to local law enforcement agencies to beef up their police forces, modernize their equipment, and so on. The Democrats instituted most of the conspiracy trials against the leaders of dissenting movements in the 1960s. And the Democrats were responsible for putting thousands of people under illegal surveillance.[17] The Democrats could argue, of course, that their record of collaboration with local regulation during the 1960s was temporary and forced on them by the political radicalism of the period, while Republicans like Richard Nixon actually advocated those kinds of policies because they truly believed in them. But a more consistent line of argument would be that both political parties had become committed to the positive, discretionary, liberal state and that each administration, regardless of party, was drawn into doing whatever seemed necessary to cope with the problems of this kind of state. Federal troops and federal regulators were drawn into local matters as the federal government became more and more involved in local transactions. This is inherent in the notion of establishing a national *presence*. Intervention at all levels is built into the logic of this situation, as President Bill Clinton confirmed with his war-on-crime proposals of 1994.

As for the second Republican argument, it is undeniably true that a strongly Democratic Congress often imposed its will on the Nixon administration. Few of the regulatory laws identified in table 2.3 were explicit parts of President Nixon's program, and the most ambitious enactment—wage and price

[17]For more on the commitment of the Democratic party to state and local as well as national regulatory programs, see Lowi, *The End of Liberalism*, 113–19. Some of this section is drawn from those pages. See also Victor Navasky, *Kennedy Justice* (New York: Atheneum, 1971); and Adam Yarmolinsky, *The Military Establishment* (New York: Harper & Row, 1971).

controls—was passed despite his grumbling that such authority was not needed and that he would not use it if it were
handed over to him. Nevertheless, President Nixon did not
veto any of these laws and his administration did more than
merely accept the domination of the Democrats. There is
ample evidence to support the argument that the continued
expansion of the regulatory authority of the federal government was a direct consequence of the modern liberal state and
that this had come to be accepted almost as much by Republicans as by Democrats.

The most telling evidence of positive Republican collaboration with New Liberalism would probably be the Nixon
administration's involvement in wage and price control (under
the Economic Stabilization Act) and in its creation of the
Environmental Protection Agency. Although President Nixon
did not support the enactment of the Economic Stabilization
Act of 1970, he quickly became convinced that the unholy
matrimony of recession and inflation (stagflation) required
inauguration of a program of economic regulation unpar-
alleled in U.S. peacetime history. Moreover, since the 1970 act
had to be renewed within a year and since Nixon not only
requested congressional extension of the act but also requested extension of its jurisdiction to cover interest rates and
dividends as well as wages and prices, we can say that Nixon
made wage and price control his own program. Beyond that,
Nixon made certain that the programs within the act would be
vigorously pursued by delegating authority to the one U.S.
agency that not only had a great deal of integrity but had the
size and presence in every region and locality in the United
States necessary for vigorous implementation: the Internal
Revenue Service (IRS). And to ensure constant updating of
the ceilings and schedules for price adjustments and increases, Nixon set up the Cost of Living Council, a domestic version of the National Security Council. Several other
important boards and commissions were set up to feed the
Cost of Living Council and to guide the regulatory work of
the IRS.

Although President Nixon cooperated with Congress in the drafting and implementation of such vast regulatory programs as OSHA and CPSC, he actually took the initiative and the leadership in the creation of the EPA with executive orders issued in 1970. Through these orders, Nixon sought to consolidate several major programs in a single agency, the better to ensure that the national government would be "setting standards consistent with national environmental goals." The enormous breadth of this agency has been remarked already. The point here is that a president who would create such an agency to ensure the more efficient and effective implementation of all the preexisting environmental protection legislation is not a president who was drawn kicking and screaming into the positive, discretionary, liberal state.

Here again, these vastly increased regulatory activities, on top of the welfare state expansions, were taking place within both parties in the face of the tremendous widening of the "confidence gap," the bipartisan disillusionment with Keynesianism, the mystery of stagflation, and the growing awareness of at least the possibility of the insolvency of entitlement programs. In sum, the welfare and regulatory binges were taking place despite the imminent collapse of the liberal consensus.

Chorus—Explaining Away the Paradox   The plight of the liberal, positive state since the 1970s presents no paradox that a proper understanding of liberalism and public policy cannot dispel. 1.) The Constitutional Revolution of 1937 eliminated the external, constitutional basis for saying No. Everything became good to do. 2.) The logic of liberalism itself eliminated the internal, political basis for saying No. Everything became logically imperative to do. 3.) Systems thinking, particularly through the concept of insurance, eliminated the technical basis for saying No. Everything with theoretical support became scientifically compelling to do. This three-cornered approach to explaining the success-to-decadence story is by no means exhaustive. In fact, additional reinforcing arguments will be presented at the end of Act II.

The Constitutional Revolution. Although the contemporary liberal state was validated by a series of Supreme Court decisions in the late 1930s, there had always been two dimensions of constitutional government, and only the first was settled at that time. The first dimension concerned the actual substantive scope or reach of governmental power. The second concerned the form by which governmental power could be exercised, whatever its scope. The Court in 1937 conclusively settled the first by establishing the principle that in a democracy there can be no effective substantive limit to the scope of governmental power. With that principle accepted, however, the second dimension became all the more important. The second, concerning forms, included majority rule, proper procedure in elections and in legislatures, and due process in judicial conduct. But it went beyond these to what is rather vaguely referred to as "rule of law."

Although rule of law means a lot of things to a lot of people, there is a minimum position with which few could disagree. This is that no government official should exercise coercive power over any person except according to standards, guidelines, and a substantive jurisdiction laid down in advance by a constitutionally authorized body and that, while some discretion must be given to the enforcer, it cannot include the decision to determine what the law is and whether the law should be enforced. In other words, the rule of law says to rulers, "You must tell us what you are going to do to us before you do it to us."[18]

---

[18] A more extensive argument will be found in chapter 6. One defining passage will suffice here: "The desideratum of clarity represents one of the most essential ingredients of legality. . . . Today there is a strong tendency to identify law, not with rules of conduct, but with a hierarchy of power or command. This view — which confuses fidelity to law with deference for established authority — leads easily to the conclusion that while judges, policemen, . . . [etc.] can infringe legality, legislatures cannot, except as they may trespass against explicit constitutional restrictions on their power. Yet it is obvious that obscure and incoherent legislation can make legality unattainable by anyone, or at least unattainable without an unauthorized revision which itself impairs legality." Ron L. Fuller, *The Morality of Law* (New Haven: Yale University Press, 1964; rev. ed., 1969), 63.

Rather than confront this second dimension of constitutional government, liberal jurisprudence defined it away. This was done largely by importing traditional European administrative state theory and mixing it with recent American political theory. The administrative theory is largely this, that experts know best and will exercise their judgment neutrally within the limits set by elected officials. The political theory is pluralism, based on a bastardization of the belief of Adam Smith and James Madison that competition among adversary interests is both a necessary and a sufficient solution to representative government. That is to say, when you have process you do not need form. This was the source of the discretionary aspect of the positive, discretionary, liberal state.

Laws without substance, delegating raw discretion to administrative agencies, were understandable, perhaps justifiable during the period of emergency in the 1930s. But when this practice persisted after thirty years of modern government, into the 1960s and beyond, when government was strong and emergencies were not present and when older statutes were never amended in light of programmatic experience, it was clear that liberals believed in formless democracy as a virtue in itself and that, consequently, liberalism was undoing itself. It did not need enemies.

The Logic of Liberalism. To understand the self-destructive tendency built into the logic of liberalism, it is necessary to return briefly to the definition of liberalism provided in chapter 1, specifically, item 5: Government intervention is justified when directed against conduct deemed *harmful in its consequences.* For most Americans, including this author, this is the most virtuous aspect of liberalism. It appeals to reason. It demands research before action. Debate can focus clearly on the issues, and the winner is likely to be the side with the best argument and evidence. However, *under some circumstances,* any conduct can be harmful in its consequences. For example, making steel or farming tobacco is morally neutral activity. And for generations, people engaged in such industries without government interference. But a theory about the relationship between the product and health or safety can justify significant government intervention. That is all well and good, *unless any theory of harm that embodies any argument as to cause and effect becomes a claim to government action.*

When the Court swept away substantive constitutional barriers to government action and when Congress was freed from having to formulate a clear rule of conduct that would address the injury, it became extremely difficult for liberal government to turn its back on any strong cause-and-effect argument. If the proposed action promised to reduce, even minutely, the overall level of risk in society, it was not only difficult to say No but there was also something of an imperative to say Yes. Like prohibition under Hoover, each program became a kind of "noble experiment." Beyond that, liberalism became driven by its own rhetoric as well as its own logic and began to match the breadth of delegated power with the eloquence of the goals it set in the statute. The language was often virtually biblical. Here is a moderately exaggerated mock statute:

> Whereas the air is dirty [defined in parts per billion], and whereas dirty air is harmful to health [defined by biomedical theory estimating increased lung cancers], now therefore let there come to pass clean air [defined precisely in parts per billion with a precise date provided]. In pursuance of this goal, the agency is authorized to make whatever rules and standards it deems necessary, using the best available technology, to give us clean air by [the date provided].

More will be said of the implications of such statutory formulation below. Here it is sufficient to observe that this kind of high-flown rhetoric creates mass expectations that later define the program as a failure even if it had made a measurable improvement in air quality. More relevant to the larger point being made here, such bold efforts to cleanse the air became a center of gravity for other demands that might also clean the air or for still other demands that might in other respects reduce the sum total of risk to the society. So much did each effort generate additional efforts that the objective (or end) of liberalism was ultimately defined as the achievement of a "risk-free society." A ridiculously extreme formulation, it is both cause and reflection of the virtually totalitarian tendency of a liberalism that recognizes no substantive or formal constitutional limitations but takes both its obligations and its limits from the claims about injury made by competing interest groups.

As a liberal myself, I do not utilize totalitarianism for the purpose of impugning liberalism or shocking people away from its basically virtuous tenets. The main argument here is that liberalism came to a point where it considered itself *responsible* for every injury, every harm, and every potential cause thereof. Although the U.S. national government has taken on only a small proportion of so large a universe of obligations, a liberalism that recognizes no constitutional limits had no way to distinguish ethically between or establish priorities among competing theories of cause and effect. This is a burden that no public philosophy can long bear.

Systems and Insurance. The third factor is the insurance perspective of the American welfare state.[19] Whatever its virtues may be for social security—and those are ample—the insurance perspective writ large helps explain the collapse of liberalism.

The totalistic, societywide scope of liberalism rendered virtually impossible the task of locating individual blame and fault in each instance of injury. *New Liberalism can be said to have arisen literally out of the decline of the ability to find individual blame and fault in the allocation of responsibility for injury.*[20] The modern outlook is to recognize statistically a certain incidence of injury and to accept this as systemic. This means laying the blame on the system, even though individual

[19]See, in particular, J. Douglas Brown, *An American Philosophy of Social Security* (Princeton: Princeton University Press, 1972).

[20]An effort to trace out a history of this development will be found in Theodore J. Lowi, "The Welfare State: Ethical Foundations and the Constitutional Remedies," *Political Science Quarterly* 101, no. 2 (1986): 197–220.

negligence can be located in many such injuries. The ultimate expression of this point of view is called insurance. And the limiting case is no-fault insurance, in which victims are indemnified regardless of fault. Though much of this indemnification is provided by private liability insurance companies and is paid for by individual subscribers, the ethical situation is the same whether public or private. This is the very essence of the American welfare state—the public assumption of some of the responsibility for indemnifying and supporting persons rendered dependent for whatever reason. President Reagan called it the safety net. It can also be called the "socialization of risk." This is not intended to invoke the notion of socialism. Its purpose is only to indicate the public assumption of part of what had developed as collective private responsibility and to demonstrate the connection of the liberal state to the long line of ethical development of private, liberal, capitalist society—the costing and spreading of risk, or risk management.

Although the insurance perspective worked well for social security (despite the fact that it was never actuarially sound), it proved counterproductive to the extent that it had an influence on the perspectives of the regulatory state. Insurance works best, in fact, it works *only*, within the largest possible definition of the universe of conduct. This is necessary if statistics are to produce dependable probabilities of injury (risk) and if there are to be enough paying customers to cover indemnities. Within that context, an insurer, including a government insurer, develops a very special point of view: *insurance may be the only enterprise in which the patron is more concerned than the client for the welfare of the client*. This is not for reasons of altruism but arises out of a keen concern for keeping costs under control. Consequently, as government expanded welfare policies for indemnifying victims, concern for the absolute level of injury and for the cost of injuries spread at the same rate, if not faster.

This culminated in the 1970 Occupational Safety and Health Act, whose scope could hardly be broader: "Each employer shall furnish to each of his employees employment and a place of employment which are free from recognized hazards that are causing or are likely to cause death or serious physical harm to employees." Moreover, this protection was intended to cover employees against substances and experiences (including noises) whose harmful effects might come only from slow accumulation, not only during their careers but long after severance or retirement. The OSHA statute is only one example of many modern regulatory statutes that are as broad as they are because they had to be *coextensive with the welfare state itself.* This is precisely why the term "social regulation" is an appropriate one.

Once again it must be said that the reason for the point of view or ethic of the new social regulation was not sentimentality but cost control, and its scope had to be defined then by the welfare state's acceptance of injury as a system to be dealt with systemically. But if the insurance perspective of the largest possible statistical universe was good for the welfare state, the opposite—the smallest possible behavioral universe—is required for rational regulation. At the level of a system, patterns of behavior and causal relationships can be dealt with in the aggregate and by probability. But, even though a regulatory rule is stated in general terms, regulation requires identifying a specific cause for a specific effect, and this is extremely difficult even in the most advanced sciences. Defining the jurisdiction of a regulatory agency as a system and obliging the agency to formulate rules and standards for all the possible causes of categorically identified effects produced an explosion of demands for rules—as manifested by the explosion of the number of pages in the *Federal Register* during the 1970s.[21] More will be said of this later; it is

[21]In 1936, the *Federal Register* had a total of 2,400 pages. By 1960, it was up to 14,000; ten years later, in 1970, it contained 20,000 pages. By 1976, it contained 60,000 pages and was growing by at least 5,000 pages a year. Not all of the material in the *Federal Register* consists of rules proposed and enforced by regulatory agencies, but a substantial portion of its growth came from such activity. It might be added here just as a matter of interest that most of Ronald

sufficient here simply to emphasize that the growth of regulatory activity was driven by the logic of liberalism as much as—nay, more than—the complexities of modern industrial society.

Act II: How Success Produced Fragmentation

Scene 1: A Brief History of Social Policy   It is worth repeating here that the regulatory programs of the New Deal were quite popular after World War II and were widely accepted even among business people. Robert E. Lane's study of business attitudes revealed two very significant things: first, the number of unfavorable references to federal regulatory programs dropped precipitously; and second, the substance of those criticisms changed drastically, from broad ideological objections to narrower, instrumental questions concerning how to deal with the agencies.[22]

Moreover, the Roosevelt Revolution was far from over. It was kept alive and extended by the postwar Truman administration and by the Roosevelt/Truman Court even after it came to be led by the Eisenhower-appointed Earl Warren. Table 2.4 gives a thumbnail sketch of the additions and extensions of the New Deal after 1948. One quickly gets the sense that these were all quite different from the policies of the New Deal.

Another impression drawn from a quick review of the table is that much of the policy of this epoch was court driven. But that only proved what most realistic people already knew, that the courts are and always have been instruments of the state and not merely umpires in private disputes. What could not have been anticipated even by the most sophisticated observers was that the federal courts would become leaders and not just legitimizers in the second half of the Roosevelt Revolution, the social revolution.

Reagan's success at "deregulation" came not from the termination of any regulatory agencies (which he did not succeed in doing) but from the reduction by about half of the number of rules and regulations being promulgated.

[22]Robert E. Lane, *The Regulation of Businessmen* (New Haven: Yale University Press, 1953), 38.

Table 2.4
Post–New Deal Policies:
The New Social Regulation and Social Policy

Policies	Institutional Initiative
Higher education	Congress
Desegregation	Court, Congress, executive order
Welfare, from cash to services	Congress, Executive
Elementary and secondary education	Congress
Criminal justice	Court
Equal pay for women	Congress
Reapportionment	Court
Privacy	Court
Voting rights	Congress
Age and disability rights	Court, Congress
Church-state relations	Court
Women's rights	Congress, Court

"Social regulation" was introduced earlier to distinguish the broader regulatory programs of the sixties from the 1930s regulation. "Social policy" is a label developed in the 1960s that is a kind of code for all sorts of policies whose intent was to improve the life chances of people of lower income and status who were not so well represented by organized groups. In other words, "social policy" was code for policies generated by the politics of class and race, later to be joined by gender, while the New Deal majority was governed by organized economic interests playing the coalitional political game. Although these so-called social policies were a logical extension of the 1930s and utilized techniques of government and constitutional principles already well accepted, they were beginning to cut heavily into the bonds between the southern and northern wings of the Democratic party, whose tacit covenant had been "Be as [New] liberal as you want, so long as you stay away from race and class." The curtain closes on scene 1.

Scene 2: Social Policies Become Wedge Issues "Wedge issue"
refers to an issue that alienates a segment of a party or
coalition no matter what position the leadership takes. Wedge
issues began to afflict the Democratic party from virtually the
moment it returned to the White House in 1961. Civil rights
split South from North. Federal aid to education—especially
after the 1964 civil rights law incorporated federal aid as a
sanction against segregation—further separated North from
South but added to this the beginnings of a wedge along class
lines. This wedge cut deeper with the new welfare policies,
which provided strong incentives for more indigent people to
join the AFDC rolls. Increases in social security benefits
created a wedge along lines of age; welfare services divided
welfare beneficiaries against each other. The racial implications of AFDC, along with civil rights, eventually created a
larger wedge in the relations between working-class whites
and the entire black community. One did not need public
opinion polls to anticipate the fault lines of an endangered
New Deal coalition.

These wedges cut still more deeply in the 1970s as the
national government and then the national economy ended
their growth mode. As long as there was an expectation of
government expansion, party leaders could buy off some of
the pressure of a disaffected component of their coalition.
Without the prospect of expansion, issues would look more
and more like zero-sum games. Politics on the way down is
obviously a lot more intense and conflictive than politics on
the way up. This would eventually afflict the Republican
coalition as well, but not until Democratic fragmentation had
completed itself and contributed in its fullest measure to
Republican rejuvenation.

Wedges cut still more deeply into the New Deal/Democratic
coalition because of radical influences from the Left of the
party. Table 2.5 is a replication of the two boxes depicting the
Left in table 1.3. During the depths of the depression, there
had been a left wing within the Democratic party comprised
basically of Old Left ideology. But it remained extremely

Table 2.5
Elements of the American Left

Old Left	1. Old Socialism
	    Components:
	       Marxist socialism
	       Christian socialism
	    Justification for government:
	       achieving equal outcomes, then withering
	       away
	    Ideal: a *communal* society of equals

New Left	2. Social Democracy
	    Components:
	       Neo-Marxism
	       Statist socialism
	       New Left
	       Public interest Left
	       Civil rights radicalism
	    Justification for government:
	       permanent, to maintain equal outcomes
	    Ideal: a *participatory* society of equals

small, first, because the Marxist element would remain tiny as long as its ties to the USSR and especially to Soviet foreign policy remained strong and, second, because what little there was of an Old Left either lost itself in tiny single-issue "third parties" or remained even more obscure by rejecting the political system altogether. However, out of the 1950s and 1960s the New Left emerged (box 2). There was very little genuine Marxism in the New Left, even among the radical activists of the student antiwar movement. More participants in a rebellion than a revolutionary group, the student activists were using extreme and often illegal methods to shock the establishment into redeeming itself, to conduct itself more consistently with its own ideals. This was also true of the civil rights movement. Given the profound grudge all people of color deserved to have against the "white power structure," it is nothing less than a miracle that the leadership of the civil rights movement and other racially composed organizations carried so little genuinely revolutionary feeling or thought in their rhetorical knapsacks.

What, then, was radical in the influence of the Left on the Democratic party? Their radicalism was not simply that they occupied the left side of an imaginary ideological continuum. *It was the morality they brought to political discourse that made them radical*. (This is equally true of the Right. It bears repeating here that radicalism has nothing to do with the direction of one's position but how deeply it orients itself toward the roots and foundations of the system it addresses.) Thus, the Left, in particular the New Left, brought morality to the Democratic program. The New Left changed almost nothing substantively about the liberal program of the Democrats of the 1960s.[23] Yet the radicals of the Left added to the liberal program precisely what the liberal Supreme Court had deliberately and successfully avoided in *Brown v. Board*—a morally absolute position against racial segregation and a morally absolute position against the inequitable distribution of wealth. The soft pragmatism of liberalism—indeed, the steadfast commitment of liberalism to keep morality out of public discourse even if it required toleration of much inequality—looked as weak and immoral to the Left as it did to the Right. Repeating an earlier characterization, the Left and Right, in their radicalization, have a lot more in common with each other than either has with liberalism, Old or New.

However, the more important point here is that the radical influence on the Democratic party from the Left—even though it was never that strong—deepened the cut of the wedges into the liberal consensus and the New Deal coalition until the coalition finally broke apart and the liberal consensus collapsed. The so-called McGovern takeover in 1972 was not an important factor in this collapse. Quite the contrary: George

[23]Many of the Old Left were deeply antagonistic to the welfare state because of their justifiable feeling that it was helping to salvage capitalism. But they had virtually no influence in this regard, and none of this entered into the thinking of the New Left.

McGovern's nomination was possible only because the Democratic coalition had already broken and the "end of liberalism" was already at hand.

Chorus: Reflections on Goals and Rights Fragmentation was inevitable. The New Deal coalition had been in power too long to avoid decadence. And its demise was far from dishonorable. It had possessed enough vision and enough high motive to be proud even in failure. Only a politician so narrow as to measure success exclusively in terms of reelection could be embarrassed by the demise of a consensus that had brought about and had sustained for a generation the Roosevelt Revolution. However, the fragmentation is important here because of what it reveals about the decadent phase of liberalism, what that did to liberalism itself, how it contributed to the coalition that would take its place, and what all this did to its own prospects of regeneration. This will be explored through two lines of analysis: (1) how goals generate rights, and (2) the internal logic of rights.

How Goals Generate Rights. Delegation of fairly broad discretionary power from Congress to administrative agencies is of course unavoidable. But there has to be a reason why the discretion that is delegated is so much broader after more than fifty years of experience as a modern state. One possible answer is that life today is so much more complex and time is so much more pressing that Congress can no longer make law as well as state legislators of 1840 or 1880. Since this issue will come up again in chapter 6, suffice it to say here that the complexity defense is phony. The 1840s was the dawn of the industrial revolution. In the 1880s, capitalism was still poorly understood and germ theory was still in its infancy. And state legislators had no professional staff. No, the greatness of the legislature is to be measured by how it deals with its ignorance, not by the superiority of its knowledge.

Another possible explanation for the emptiness of modern legislation is "the electoral connection." In other words, legislators must design the language as well as the substance of legislation to evade responsibility. But there always has been an electoral connection and yet the legislation is worse. We already have confronted an example of the biblical language that modern legislators often resort to. But beyond that, note how legislators increasingly dress up their statutes with fancy names embodying wished-for results. Here are a few examples: Clean Air Act, Environmental Protection Act, Air Quality Act, Fair Credit Act, National Defense Education Act, Medicare, Medicaid, Consumer Product Safety Act, Safe Drinking Water Act, Comprehensive Environmental Response, Compensation, and Liability Act, and so on, and so on. No, the electoral connection is realistic but most inadequate as an explanation because it is not unique to our epoch.

A far better explanation can be found inside liberalism, in the derangement of liberal thought produced by its commitment to the most modern of analytic methods—professional knowledge and systems thinking. Systems thinking and systems analysis arose out of the academic sciences and entered into the thinking of public policy makers first through its applicability to the insurance base of the welfare state. Thanks especially to Keynes and the application of systems thinking and probability mathematics to economics, systems thinking spread quickly from insurance to every field and every dimension of public policy. As this new science spread, so did professionally trained specialists increase in the agencies and congressional committee staffs. To cope with the elaborate research and technical analysis necessary to think and analyze in systems terms, even the interest-group staffs had to expand in this direction, and the weight of this kind of responsibility led to the drastic expansion after World War II not only of the policy analysis staffs in the executive branch and not only to an explosive expansion of the same types on the personal and committee staffs in the House and Senate but also in research agencies (literally, think tanks) created by Congress to serve it independently of the executive branch. The Legislative Reference Service in the Library of Congress was expanded and renamed the Congressional Research Service. That being insufficient, Congress then also created the Office of Technology Assessment, which is much more literally a think tank. And this does not count the very large policy research component in the General Accounting Office, another servant of Congress. The Congressional Budget Office, albeit smaller, is still another source of technical staff trained in systems thinking and economic analysis.

When these specialists in the agencies and congressional committee staffs and government think tanks bring to Congress a proposal for legislation, it is usually in the form of lawlike findings (in the *scientific,* not the legal sense), based on professional knowledge derived formally from established scientific methodology and confirmed both by statistics and by causal theories and models with good academic standing. Members of the relevant congressional committee recognize the described pattern as unanswerable and undebatable (for example, the relation between a toxic substance and cancer or between drugs and crime). Although some members of Congress will oppose a bill on principle or on grounds that the findings are inadequate, all the members will tend to recognize that no amount of added knowledge can deny the findings as such. Scientific systems analysis has set the terms of discourse. Therefore, if legislation is to be adopted on a given subject, Congress will not reject the systems approach and resort to a more amateur, piecemeal approach to legislation on specific aspects of the problem but will instead enact the system-level pattern as law (in the *legal* sense). In other words, *Congress accepts the causal pattern as determined by the systems analysis and ordains it as the goal of the statute.* It is from this that we tend to get the inflated, biblical language in modern public policy, for example, "Whereas we have dirty air, and whereas every particle of dirty air adds to the number of cancers in the population, now therefore let there come to pass rules and regulations. . . ."

This is a new kind of law in the American experience. And it calls for the distinction made most clearly by David Schoenbrod between "rules statutes" and "goals statutes." A rules statute identifies a particular conduct and either restricts or encourages it; in contrast, a goals statute ordains the outcome and delegates to the agency the power to make all the rules pertinent to the conduct.[24]

I take Schoenbrod's distinction a step further: *Rules statutes convey obligations; goals statutes convey rights.* It is my contention that when Congress enacts a statute ordaining a desired outcome—clean air, safe consumer products, or safe working conditions—it is conveying a right to that outcome, whether that was intended by Congress or not. And even though the responsible agency will later make rules restricting or encouraging the relevant conduct, the goal in a goals statute remains as a criterion by which agency action is judged; moreover, the statutory goal can become a *cause of action* in the courts against the agency. Since no agency rule can obtain more than a fraction of a legislated goal, especially given the grandiose rhetoric of modern statutes, each rule, or the whole bundle of rules, adopted by an agency can be seen as an inadequate remedy for the legislated right to the clean air or the safe working conditions. Consequently, the lack of full attainment of the benefit defined in the legislated goal amounts to the denial of the right to that goal. The right conveyed by a legislated goal is, of course, not a right in the constitutional sense. It is a legislated right that can be terminated by later legislation. But as long as that legislation stands, the goals statute conveys the right to that outcome.

This helps explain a great part of the disappointment and frustration Americans have begun to express against their government. First, goals statutes have put tremendous pres-

---

[24]David Schoenbrod, "Goals Statutes or Rules Statutes: The Case of the Clean Air Act," *UCLA Law Review* 30 (April 1983): 740–828. For a more extensive argument regarding the use of systems analysis and experts therein, see Theodore J. Lowi, "Toward a Legislature of the First Kind," in William Robinson and Clay Wellborn, eds., *Knowledge, Power, and the Congress* (Washington, D.C.: Congressional Quarterly, 1991), chap. 1. For a more extended treatment of the distinction between rules statutes and goals statutes and an evaluation of the difference, see Theodore J. Lowi, "Risks and Rights: In the History of American Governments," in *Daedalus* 119, no. 4 (Fall 1990): 17–40.

sure on agencies to turn out rules, rules by the dozens, by the hundreds. Since Congress delegates the responsibility for a whole, abstractly defined, open-ended system, the agency is given no priorities or guidelines, so that everything becomes absolutely compelling for them to try. They keep shooting arrows in the air hoping that one will hit its target. The second effect is one that appears at first glance to be contradictory to the first: the tendency for agencies to engage in new research. The only way the agency can locate priorities and translate the systems concept into concrete situations for purposes of regulation is to do more research into the problem, no matter how much research was done prior to passage. This delays agency *action* even as it increases agency *activity*. People who have an interest in that agency tend to grow impatient and cynical when they compare the grandiose goals with what appears to be the dilatory tactics of poststatutory research; and impatience grows when they compare the grandiose goals with the flow of relatively trivial rules that the agency eventually begins to generate. As the agency constituency grows impatient, they begin to claim the legislated goals as a matter of right and proceed to sue in court for a remedy or demonstrate in public for more government action.

This, then, to a large extent explains not only the explosion in the production of rules but also the explosion of litigation during the past couple of decades that has so alarmed most students of the judicial process. It has particularly mobilized conservative critics, who attack the federal courts as "an imperial judiciary," operating under the influence of new "public interest" groups bearing an anticapitalist, left-wing program. The conservative argument appeared to be validated as the federal courts began to liberalize their rules of standing, class action suits, and third-party suits, making it easier and easier to sue the United States government even when the individual or group does not satisfy the Article III requirement that there be a real "case or controversy" before a person can sue. It would be impossible to prove that all federal district and appellate judges are power hungry and seek an imperial judiciary, and it would be extremely difficult to prove that these same judges, after their appointment, suddenly came under some kind of socialist spell. But it is easy to confirm the alternative explanation that federal judges are responding to their natural calling: when a right has been denied, there has to be a remedy. If the statute ordains an outcome, and if that outcome is a right as long as the statute stands, then what alternative do federal courts have except to allow the claim to be given its day in court?[25]

The Internal Logic of Rights. It is a normal political tactic to strengthen claims or protect gains by calling them rights. The purpose of the tactic is to elevate one's claim above ordinary majority rule and outside the reach of interest-group bargaining. For purposes of political analysis (and especially in a liberal context), a right can be defined as a claim to a remedy that cannot be denied except by an extraordinary decision-making process spelled out in advance—such as a constitutional amendment, a Supreme Court ruling, a special referendum, a two-thirds vote.[26] As Ronald Dworkin put it, "An individual has a right to some opportunity or resource or liberty if it counts in favor of a political decision . . . even when no other political aim is served and some political aim is disserved thereby."[27] To establish a claim as a right is to give it safe haven. But the very potency of a right and the difficulty of establishing a claim as a right will tend to limit the distribution of rights to those claims that appeal to something very fundamental and widely shared in the society.

Despite these severe practical limits, we have already seen some of the reasons why there was nevertheless an expansion of successful claims to rights beginning in the 1960s and continuing for more than a decade, to a point where the epoch

[25]These passages on the consequences of rules statutes versus goals statutes are a revised version of pps. 36–38 of Lowi, "Risks and Rights."

[26]More elaborate use of the definition will be found in Lowi, "The Welfare State," 216ff.

[27]Ronald Dworkin, *Taking Rights Seriously* (Cambridge: Harvard University Press, 1978), 91.

has been referred to as a "rights revolution." And this is the bridge to the completion of the story of liberal fragmentation and its consequences. For once the rights rhetoric had spread across the Democratic party and the entire liberal community, it intensified the fragmentation and rendered coalition building and coalition maintenance almost impossible by converting disputes from bargaining points to moral principles. Rights necessarily involve morality, and morality radicalizes. By its very nature morality radicalizes. It thus follows that rights radicalize. As Oliver Wendell Holmes observed, every right tends to become absolute: "All rights tend to declare themselves absolute to their logical extreme."[28] To the extent that a right imposes a duty on others, "on the level of duty anything like economic calculation is out of place."[29] In other words, as rights come in the door, accompanied by duty, the liberal ideal of avoiding morality in political discourse goes out the window.

During the 1960s in particular, mainstream liberal leaders were very susceptible to claims of rights, therefore to radicalization. After all, liberals had morality on their side because there is in fact something morally reprehensible about the American addiction to racial prejudice. There is something morally reprehensible about the second-class status of women and about the spread of poverty despite plenty. With the message of rights-based morality being showered on mainstream liberals from their left, it would have been difficult to maintain a genuinely liberal public posture of instrumental rhetoric and utilitarian methods. During its decadent decade, the Democratic party had been an interest-group liberal party, taking its agenda from the demands of affiliated interest groups without any grounding in the Constitution or in any sense of priority independent of the group process itself. As some of the affiliated groups became radicalized, so did the

---

[28]*Hudson County Water Company v. McCarter,* 209 U.S. 355 (1908). Quoted in Fuller, *The Morality of Law,* 29.
[29]Fuller, *The Morality of Law,* 44.

Democratic party. But the influence of the Left was minuscule and short-lived. What is more, liberalism did not need it. Liberalism was radicalized by its own movement through rights toward morality, followed by a fast descent toward uncontrollable fragmentation and collapse. Such is the nature of the tragedy that the best of liberalism was to be undone by a poor rendering into law of its highest ideals.

Act III: How Liberal Success Produced Its Own Opposition

Act III is a preface as well as a conclusion. It brings to a close one era and brings into clear focus the emergence of the next.

If politics followed physics, every action would produce an equal and opposite reaction. But politics is not physics. In politics, some reactions are more equal than others.

The interests wedged from the liberal/New Deal coalition did not fly off into their own separate orbits. The relatively limited radicalization of the Democratic party from the Left in the 1960s produced a much broader and more intensive radicalization of the Republican party from the Right; but it also produced enough energy to make possible a coalition of right-tending fragments within a party no more compatible with them than with the Democrats.

The center of gravity toward which the fragments were to be drawn was the mainstream Republican party and its tradition of Old Liberalism (box 3 of table 1.3). Like the Democratic party, the Republican party was a decadent liberal party. Except for Barry Goldwater, Republican candidates typically ran like Democrats claiming they could manage the Second Republic more cheaply than the Democrats. And Goldwater's ignominious defeat in 1964 proved mainly that the Republican party would continue to have to kowtow to the New Liberalism of the Democratic party for at least a while longer. Nevertheless, this decadent Republican party was the center of gravity for no better reason than that it was the only other game in town.

The resultant (returning to physics metaphors) was not merely an electoral reaction to Democratic decadence. It was a genuine reaction—an ideological realignment totally independent of electoral realignment. It began with a coming together of genuine conservative and radical Right elements hitherto parochial and dispersed. To amount to anything on a national scale, these ideological fragments would have to coalesce within a party not congenial to them, for no longer would conservatives be content as a passive minority wing. This meant that the Republican era, if there was to be one, would be built, just as the New Deal coalition was built, on a coalition of contradictory elements, only more so.

Karl Marx provides the best exit line for Act III of the Democratic era, as well as the entrance line for our curtain raiser for the Republican era: "The first time as tragedy, the second as farce."

Tragedy or farce, how long would the Republican coalition last, and what difference would it make before it broke apart? As the new era began, at least one thing, however, was clear, and that was that the New Liberalism of the Democratic era had undone itself and in the process had given the Republican party all it needed to become not merely a new majority but a genuinely new republic; what was to take place was not merely the swing of the liberal pendulum between Old and New but a change of "political time"[30] itself.

[30]Stephen Skowronek, *The Politics Presidents Make: Leadership from John Adams to George Bush* (Cambridge: Belknap Press of Harvard University Press, 1993), 30, 49–52.

CHAPTER 3

THE REPUBLICAN ERA

Covenants, without a sword,
are but words.
THOMAS HOBBES, 1651

THE DEATH AND LIFE OF THE GRAND OLD PARTY

THE REPUBLICAN PARTY was the dynamo of post–Civil War American politics. It was the party of emancipation and the union. It was the party of new interests and newly emerging social forces, many of them radical. Abolitionists, dispossessed farmers, new corporate capitalists, new working-class immigrants. But above all, the Republican party was the party of liberalism.

It was the party of Abraham Lincoln, the liberal. As a war president, Lincoln was all things to all people, transcending party and ideology. Precisely because of his greatness, he has been the object of capture by all varieties of interests, particularly conservatives, because of his wartime appeals to God and country and sacrifice and tradition. But as president and as a politician, Lincoln was a liberal. No better evidence of his liberalism can be found than his first approach to emancipation, which also amounted to his first effort to end the war.

MESSAGE TO CONGRESS   MARCH 6, 1862
I recommend the adoption of a Joint Resolution . . . as follows:
   "Resolved that the United States ought to cooperate with any
   state which may adopt gradual abolishment of slavery, giving to
   each state pecuniary aid, to be used by such state in it's [sic]
   discretion, to compensate for the inconveniences public and
   private, produced by such change of system"
. . . I hope it may be esteemed no offence to ask whether the pecuniary
consideration tendered would not be of more value to the states and

private persons concerned, than are the institution, and property in it, in the present state of affairs.[1]

This proposal for compensated emancipation came six months before the draft version and nine months before the issuance of the more famous Emancipation Proclamation declaring slaves "forever free," without compensating the owners. But it was not a trial run. Lincoln considered his first effort a "fit and necessary war measure," and he continued to keep alive the possibility of compensated emancipation.

The Republican party was also the party of immigration. Although the fight over immigration had a strong economic element, it was suffused with race, and the Republicans occupied the liberal side of that debate. The 1886 Republican platform for candidate William McKinley was directed to these new-immigrant voters with the appeal to "cultural pluralism."[2] Yet, as Gwendolyn Mink reports, their argument was based little on the "rights of humanity" and hugely on the labor market interests of advancing industrialism.[3] Meanwhile, in the platform of the Democratic party for the presidential election of 1896, "the labor plank and the party's platform made nativism a central principle, . . . declaring that 'the most efficient way of protecting American labor is to prevent the importation of foreign pauper labor,'" which is to say, European new-immigrant peasants.[4]

The Republican party of 1932 was still the liberal party, led by one of the most successful of liberals, Herbert Hoover. The depression defeated the party in 1932, but it remained the minority party for most of the next fifty years because it failed to adjust its electoral constituency and its ideology to chang-

[1]*The Collected Works of Abraham Lincoln,* ed. Roy P. Basler (New Brunswick: Rutgers University Press, 1953), 144–46. The editor notes that Lincoln himself substituted "inconveniences" for "evils" and "persons concerned" for "owners."

[2]Gwendolyn Mink, *Old Labor and New Immigrants in American Political Development: Union, Party, and State, 1875–1920* (Ithaca: Cornell University Press, 1986), 129.

[3]Ibid., 110.

[4]Ibid., 129.

ing economic and social realities. First, there was no longer a capitalist system with a single set of economic interests—if indeed there ever had been. The Roosevelt and Taft administrations had prosecuted business combinations in restraint of trade, but the party remained static on most of the emergent problems because of its steadfast antistatism, which was fast becoming *Old* Liberalism. The Republican party lost a sizable segment of American business because their economic interests were no longer purely antistatist and their outlook was no longer steadfastly and uniformly Old Liberal. As Thomas Ferguson and Joel Rogers report, while the big companies in the heavy industrial sectors with high labor costs and deep domestic involvements remained Republican, many of the smaller, fast-growing companies, especially those in capital-intensive business, were able to respond more positively to the victorious Democrats. The segment moving toward investment in the New Deal included such firms as General Electric, IBM, Pan Am, R. J. Reynolds, many major oil concerns, and a number of the most important commercial and investment banks.[5] This substantiates Benjamin Ginsberg and Martin Shefter's observation that "one legacy of the 1930s . . . was an important break in the political unity of American business."[6]

But economic interest was not all there was to it. The affinity of a segment of business with the New Deal also had its ideological element. In other words, there were reasons as well as causes for a realignment among capitalist and other middle classes. The Republican party had failed to incorporate, indeed it had refused to incorporate, the progressivist movements that had been in and had sought spiritedly to stay in the Republican party—precisely because it was the liberal party. Leaders of General Electric and Brown Brothers Harri-

[5]Thomas Ferguson and Joel Rogers, *Right Turn: The Decline of the Democrats in the Future of American Politics* (New York: Hill and Wang, 1986), 46–51.

[6]Benjamin Ginsberg and Martin Shefter, "A Critical Realignment?" in Michael Nelson, ed., *The Elections of 1984* (Washington, D.C.: Congressional Quarterly Press, 1985), 1–2.

man and Standard Oil of New Jersey and California did not suddenly become Socialists or Communists. They threw their support to the New Deal because it, too, was becoming a liberal party, a liberal party with a difference.

Most of agriculture also jumped the Republican ship. Always more politicized than the other sectors, agriculture had found satisfaction in the Republican party from its very beginnings in the 1860s. In 1862, a Republican president and Congress created the Department of Agriculture, the first genuine "clientele agency," with a mandate "to improve and maintain farm income and to develop and expand markets abroad for agricultural products . . . and to maintain our capacity by helping landowners protect soil, water, forest, [etc.]." That same year, Congress adopted the historic Morrill Land Grant Act providing for the establishment of "agricultural and mechanical colleges" through grants of public land for locating and financing these institutions. Land grant colleges were quick to be built and immediately began providing public-supported services for improvement of farm life through increased productivity.

This Republican legislation coming out of the years of war and Reconstruction, though small by modern standards, enabled the Republican party "to steal the Jacksonian thunder and give economic power an egalitarian cast."[7] Although the Interstate Commerce Act (1887) was adopted under the first Cleveland administration, with a Democratic majority in Congress, this was almost immediately followed in 1890 by the Republicans with the Sherman Antitrust Act, which was even more directly a response to the demands of agriculture to regulate the major trusts. The Sherman act was of additional significance for the Republican party because, being antitrust and procompetition, it helped the party respond to and neutralize the reputation it was developing of being the party

[7]That observation of Louis Hartz is quoted in Charles Hession and Hyman Sardy, *Ascent to Affluence: A History of American Economic Development* (Boston: Allyn and Bacon, 1969), 395.

of the rich.[8] When operating as an organized national movement, agriculture was at home in neither major party. It formed its own political party between 1888 and 1896 and for a while joined William Jennings Bryan in virtually taking over the Democratic party. But when operating as a set of organized interests, comprised of commodity organizations as well as umbrella interest groups like the Farmers Alliance and the Grange, agricultural interests outside the South tended largely to affiliate with the Republican party. For agriculture, realignment began in the mid-1920s. Though predominantly Republican, the famous Farm Bloc came together under the banner "Make the tariff work for agriculture," demanding protection equivalent to that offered by Republicans to business all during the late nineteenth century. Republican presidents Herbert Hoover and Calvin Coolidge vetoed these proagriculture (McNary-Haugen) tariff bills, and by the late 1920s a new agricultural leadership was on the trail of a more extensive domestic policy for solving agricultural problems. In this, they found their champion in the Democratic party.

SAME OLD PARTY, NEW FALSE LABEL

Roosevelt's programs seemed radical—radical Left—because Hoover and the Republicans in retreat called them radical and Left. But that charge had credibility only because there was no genuine Left in America to help define the difference between liberal and Left. As Hartz put it so well,

> What emerged was a movement, familiar now [1955] for 50 years in Western politics, which sought to extend the sphere of the state and at the same time retain the basic principles of Locke and Bentham. . . . Roosevelt was not seriously compared by many Americans with Norman Thomas and Earl Browder. . . . [H]e did not [even] need to *reply* to them. . . . What would Roosevelt have said [to them]? He would be defending private property, he would be assailing too much

[8]See, for example, William Letwin, *Law and Economic Policy in America: The Evolution of the Sherman and Antitrust Act* (Chicago: University of Chicago Press, 1965), 85–95.

"bureaucracy," he would be criticizing the Utopian mood in politics. . . . [He would be] a liberal who tried to break with Adam Smith but could not really do so.[9]

Quite early in his administration, Roosevelt "succeeded in putting American partisanship on a new footing by connecting it to the pragmatic liberal argument [that] conflict has . . . always been between progressives and conservatives, between optimists and pessimists, or between those who have the courage to experiment and those who are afraid of change."[10] Try as they might, the Republicans in retreat could not make the New Deal out to be anything other than what it was—a more statist brand of liberalism rather than the more orthodox Smithian brand of liberalism. (And by contemporaneous European standards, one should add, it was only a *slightly* more statist brand.) The 1932 Democratic party platform had denounced Hoover's deficits and promised to balance the budget with cuts of 25 percent, strengthening the antitrust laws and otherwise getting government out of the economy. FDR quickly appropriated the labels "liberalism" and "progressivism," contrasting these to the party in retreat, defending existing interests and privileges, and opposing the very kind of experimentation that his improvisations could appear to be. The Democrats called this opposition conservatism, and that is all the content the label had.

Hoover had fought valiantly to maintain the Republican claim to the liberal label as well as the progressive label. In fact, "the one major label with which Hoover did *not* identify in the 1920s was the conservative label. Ironically, it was the one that would later be thrust upon him, and which, after years of struggle, he would reluctantly accept."[11] FDR had

[9]Hartz, *The Liberal Tradition in America,* 259–62. Emphasis in original.

[10]Robert Eden, "On the Origins of the Regime of Pragmatic Liberalism: John Dewey, Adolph A. Berle, and FDR's Commonwealth Club Address of 1932," in Stephen Skowronek and Karen Orren, eds., *Studies in American Political Development* (Cambridge: Cambridge University Press, 1993), 129.

[11]David Green, *Shaping Political Consciousness: The Language of Politics in America from McKinley to Reagan* (Ithaca: Cornell University Press, 1987), 96–97.

been casting about for the label that would best convey the message he wanted to send while covering over that which he wished to avoid. Moving with his staff, especially with Adolph Berle, Roosevelt generously used the liberal label along with the labels progressivism and pragmatism.[12] All during the 1920s, leaders and candidates in both major parties had fought for possession of these labels because, aside from their halo effect, they were eager to attract some of the supporters of Robert La Follette's third-party candidacy while neutralizing La Follette himself.[13] And no one wanted to be saddled with the conservative label, not only because it implied pessimism and fear in regard to experimentation in domestic affairs but also because it was connected to opposition to the war and to Woodrow Wilson's postwar policies, to which the liberal label had been applied. As the New Deal advanced, liberalism stuck and the progressive label began to disappear from Democratic self-designation because La Follette was no longer a factor and because many of the prominent pre–World War I progressive activists had become critics of FDR after the 1932 election.[14]

As the New Deal found itself succeeding with the public but failing in the federal courts and as the 1936 presidential election approached, the Democrats, especially FDR himself, began intensifying their ideological appeals. By 1937, the Democrats had won a genuine electoral mandate, they had won the constitutional battle with the Supreme Court, and consequently they had also won the ideological high ground with full possession of the liberal label. The conservative label was irretrievably attached as a millstone around the neck of the Republican party, and it was associated, virtually as a synonym, with reactionism. Hoover continued to fight the New Deal and to

[12]Eden, "On the Origins," passim.

[13]For more analysis and evaluation of these tactics and parties, see V. O. Key, *Politics, Parties, and Pressure Groups*, 5th ed. (New York: Crowell, 1964), 259.

[14]Green, *Shaping Political Consciousness*, 123; see also Otis L. Graham, *An Encore for Reform: The Old Progressives in the New Deal* (New York: Oxford University Press, 1967).

fight to retain the liberal label. And Hoover was of course correct. The Republican party was the Smithian party of Old Liberalism but at a time when Old Liberalism appeared to have been discredited. Consequently, Republicans could not avoid the conservative label, as a simple term of opprobrium.

By 1945, Hoover had reluctantly and bitterly given up the liberal label, with the following public comment:

> We do not use the word "liberal." The word has been polluted and raped of all its real meaning. The fundamentals of political liberalism were established . . . in the 19th century in England. Liberalism was founded to further more liberty for men, not less freedom. Therefore, it was militant against the expansion of bureaucracy, against socialism and all of its ilk. The conservatives in America are akin to the 19th-century liberals of England. . . . The Socialists and Communists daily announce that they are "liberals." They have nested in this word until it stinks. Let them have the word. It no longer makes sense.[15]

Other Republicans were not yet ready to follow Hoover in this, because if they gave Roosevelt the liberal label, they could be branded as opponents of the very essence of the Republican party. Here is the defeated 1948 Republican presidential candidate Thomas Dewey in a postmortem on the subject.

> [The theorists] want to drive all moderates and liberals out of the Republican party and then have the remainder join forces with the conservative groups of the South. Then they would have everything neatly arranged. . . . The results would be neatly arranged, too. The Republicans would lose every election and the Democrats would win every election.[16]

LIBERAL CONSERVATIVE, CONSERVATIVE LIBERAL: THE EISENHOWER CONCORDANCE

It was for President Dwight Eisenhower to find the concordance with which the Republicans could live, and occasionally win, in

---

[15]Quoted in Green, *Shaping Political Consciousness*, 162–63. See also Grant McConnell, *Private Power and American Democracy* (New York: Knopf, 1966), 64–70.

[16]Quoted in Key, *Politics, Parties, and Presure Groups*, 221.

the 1950s and beyond. Eisenhower moved from his earliest tendency to agree with Taft in referring to the New Deal as "creeping socialism" to a position of accepting the New Deal as deserving of the liberal label. He accepted the conservative label for the Republican party but emphasized that he was not completely a conservative, believing instead in something he himself called "dynamic conservatism," "progressive dynamic conservatism," "progressive moderation," "moderate progressivism," and "positive and progressive." Adlai Stevenson responded with the observation, "I have never been sure of what progressive moderation means, or was it conservative progressivism? . . . [A]nd I am not sure what dynamic moderation or moderate dynamism means." Nevertheless, Eisenhower had found a formulation that was picked up by virtually every active member of the Republican party at that time. It appears that he worked out this formulation toward the end of 1954, after he had lost control of Congress but retained his own immense personal popularity. His formulation was that his administration "must be liberal when . . . talking about the relationship between the Government and the individual, conservative when talking about the national economy and the individual's pocketbook."[17] It was hard to know exactly what came under the rubric of fiscal and economic affairs and what came under the rubric of human affairs, but whatever the case, it meant that most of the programs of the New Deal would be left in place but would be more frugally and rationally administered by Republicans. As Eric F. Goldman observes, most of the people close to President Eisenhower were "basically conservative," but all of them had spent the previous twenty years learning to operate their businesses and other affairs within the context of the Roosevelt government. "They were part of the new, more adaptable managerial class."[18]

[17]Stevenson and Eisenhower quotes in Eric F. Goldman, *The Crucial Decade—And After* (New York: Random House, Vintage Books, 1960), 282–83.
[18]Goldman, *The Crucial Decade*, 268–69. It was this very willingness of capitalists to adapt to the New Deal that so angered the novelist/philosopher Ayn Rand, leading her to attack them with such venom in her writings.

Since the Eisenhower concordance between liberal and conservative proved to be a formula for electoral success, it became Republican strategic doctrine. What it meant was that henceforth Republicans would run like Democrats. The socialist label was used primarily to tie Democrats to softness toward Soviet foreign policy. Of domestic matters it was "Yes, but." And as a consequence, the Republicans made no serious attempt to terminate any New Deal programs. There were revisions of the National Labor Relations Act (NLRA) with Taft-Hartley (1947) and Landrum-Griffin (1959), but the basic principle of the NLRA was not affected. There was a serious effort to reduce farm price supports, but farm programs and laws themselves were not changed. There were actual expansions of certain welfare programs and public works (principally highways), and there was, of course, the beginning of federal aid to education—the first federal aid to secondary and primary schools in U.S. history (following the Sputnik embarrassment). But if foreigners had looked back on the Eisenhower administration from the perspective of the 1960s, they would not know it had been a Republican administration. It was attacked bitterly by genuine conservatives, such as the intellectuals writing for the *National Review*. But they were genuine conservatives, and their label had been appropriated by the Old Liberals. These genuine conservatives saw early what it took three decades for others to discover, and some have not discovered it yet. Acceptance of the Eisenhower formula, although it produced electoral victories, was the beginning of Republican decadence: from electoral defeat to electoral victory to ideological decadence to the degradation of democratic discourse.

After 1952, Republicans won the presidency more often than they lost it, and occasionally they won it by smashing margins. But they could not win Congress (except for 1953–54 and the Senate in the period 1981–86), and they could not get an electoral realignment. Since there had been national electoral realignments properly so-called after 1896 and after 1932, political scientists and many others began a realignment watch at least by 1968 and, to my knowledge, have not given up yet. There are varieties of theories about why voters split their tickets rather than realign, preferring Republicans for president and Democrats for Congress. All these theories are correct in some part. My own favorite is one that is consistent with the strategy of Republican presidents described above: Voters, including hordes of committed, partisan Democratic voters, bought the argument that the Republican party could give Americans their liberal, positive state—including their welfare state—but at lower cost. Even after the New Liberal coalition collapsed and the liberalism label became stigmatized, Democrats continued to carry Congress while Republicans won the presidency. The polls consistently confirmed American support for New Deal liberal programs and for members of Congress associated with them even as Congress as an institution declined to historically low levels of popularity. The persistence of the phenomenon of split party control of the two political branches was initially called *de*alignment, to distinguish these outcomes as clearly as possible from *re*-alignment and to sustain the argument that ticket splitting was basically the behavioral manifestation of the decline of party organizations and of the overall weakening of the two-party system.[19] But the decline-of-party thesis did not blind observers to the policy and ideological implications of split voting. The splitting of government control that arose out of split ticket voting came to be called "divided government."

Divided government was a concept developed in the late 1980s in recognition of the institutionalization of split control, whereby the Democrats consistently controlled Congress and the Republicans almost as consistently controlled the White House. We needed some way to explain not only the historically high budget deficits of the 1980s but the fact that they

[19]The probable inventor and clearly the best analyst of the dealignment thesis is Everett Ladd; for example, "On Mandates, Re-Alignments, and the 1984 Presidential Election," *Political Science Quarterly* 100, no. 1 (Spring 1985). See also Howard Reiter, *Parties and Elections in Corporate America* (New York: Longman, 1993).

persisted and the rate of increase actually increased, regardless of the state of the economy. This came to be called "gridlock"—a dramatic but not inaccurate means of indicating an inability of the government to respond to the economy, especially its inability to reduce the deficit during the relatively prosperous years following the 1981–83 recession. Divided government was seized on as an explanation for gridlock, despite the fact that we had operated with divided government for most of the time since World War II and that during most of those years the policy output of Congress and the national government was quite high.[20] This is not to approve of every piece of legislation and every presidential decision. It is only to suggest that all during those years the national government was in fact able to take actions that were responsive to changes in the economy and the society. For some reason, although David Mayhew[21] and many others have demonstrated that divided government did not make a great deal of difference in the passage of important legislation, Americans had come to the conclusion that the national government was gridlocked. In other words, the very bipartisan agreement that had helped perpetuate the New Deal for nearly half a century came to be denounced as a disgrace to democratic government.

THE RECONSTITUTED REPUBLICAN PARTY: RALLYING ROUND NEGATION

The Reagan Policy Legacy

Gridlock was virtually a policy of no policies. To say the very least, gridlock was a function of policy decisions made early in the Reagan administration, which effectively eliminated all policy options available to Reagan and to his successors George Bush and Bill Clinton. Reagan's decisions were popular decisions. They can be considered his electoral mandate:

---

[20]See David Mayhew, *Divided We Govern: Party Control, Lawmaking and Investigations, 1946–1990* (New Haven: Yale University Press, 1991).
[21]Ibid.

(1) cut taxes drastically; (2) do not meddle substantively with the two major categories of expenditure, defense and welfare; and (3) impair all the New Deal programs but do not dismantle them. Every time President Reagan mentioned the Evil Empire or did something aimed at it, his poll ratings went up. Every criticism of welfare expenditure depressed his ratings so consistently that he had to make widespread public reassurances that he was committed to maintaining the "safety net"—a term he invented. And although deregulation was popular and he sought deregulation in his own way, by impoverishment, President Reagan did not seek the termination of a single major regulatory program.

This three-tiered package was a package of fundamental policy decisions, the farthest thing from gridlock. Many of the most radical members of the Reagan White House felt betrayed by the combination of decisions, because they knew that "supply side" economic theory was precisely the voodoo economics that candidate George Bush had called it in his 1980 primary campaign against Reagan. They knew that it was a lie to argue that lower taxes would produce higher revenues. David Stockman had revealed their awareness of the lie from almost the beginning of the Reagan administration in what became a spectacular exposé published in *Atlantic Monthly* by William Greider in early November 1981.[22] Stockman survived the exposé, although he continued to feel betrayed by the Reagan administration's refusal to move against the New Deal. ("After November 1981, the administration locked the door on its own disastrous fiscal policy jail cell and threw away the key.")[23] Stockman stayed with the administration as Office of Management and Budget (OMB) director until the summer of 1985. But far more significant than his resignation from his job was his psychological resignation about the

[22]William Greider, "The Education of David Stockman," *Atlantic Monthly,* November 1981; and Greider, *The Education of David Stockman and Other Americans* (New York: New American Library, 1986).

[23]David Stockman, *The Triumph of Politics: Why the Reagan Revolution Failed* (New York: Harper & Row, 1986), 13.

ideology and public policy of the Republican era. Below are three brief passages from the final chapter of his autobiography.

> The Reaganites were, in the final analysis, just plain welfare state politicians like everybody else. . . . The only thing the Reagan administration could do about federal spending was: fake. (385–386)

> I finally saw . . . the awesome staying power of the Second Republic. (388)

> The abortive Reagan Revolution proved that the American electorate wants a moderate social democracy to shield it from capitalism's rougher edges. (394)[24]

In other words, Reagan left all of the New Liberal state intact but made it almost impossible for it to work. Drastic tax cuts coupled with maintenance of defense and welfare commitments effectively killed governmental capacity.

At first, President Bush seemed comfortable with this Reagan policy legacy. After all, Bush was a genuine Old Liberal with sincere faith in the self-perfecting capacities of the free market and sincere opposition to government interference. He soon had to break his no-new-taxes pledge with one of the weightiest tax increases in our history, blaming it on the failure of Congress to cut government expenditures, and that contributed to the spreading sense of gridlock.

But gridlock turned out to be a manifestation of something still more profound: beyond the mere inability of liberal government to make timely decisions, gridlock meant *negation of government itself.* Gridlock was in the nature of a self-fulfilling prophecy. Policy decisions deliberately designed to incapacitate government were used to prove that government was innately incapable and thus a mischievous force—a parliament of whores living off the self-governing and otherwise perfectible market system.

---

[24]Ibid., from the epilogue; page references in parentheses.

Reagan had brought the attitude of negation with him from California. Adopted in 1978, California's Proposition 13 (which became Article XIIIA of the state constitution) set an absolute constitutional limit on the power of state and local governments to tax their citizens. Since 1978, the ceiling on property taxes has remained the same, and no tax can be increased except by a two-thirds vote of all citizens in the principality to which the tax applies. And the Proposition 13 mentality swept the country, along with Ronald Reagan's popularity, as twenty-two other states followed California with taxation limits of equal or greater severity.[25]

Just as significant as Proposition 13 was its adoption in California and elsewhere by initiative and referendum. Whenever Americans are fed up with government, they do not go after the allegedly hated and feared bureaucracy but after representative government itself. And after 1980, this mentality focused on the national government. That is what President Reagan meant when he said government is the problem, not the solution. Congress bashing reached epidemic proportions thereafter. All powers to the president, making right decisions, supported directly by "the people." Indictments of public officials at all levels reached unprecedented numbers, with use of the courts to supplement direct democracy with "politics by other means."[26]

Congress attempted to doctor this epidemic attack of illegitimacy with the 1985 Balanced Budget and Emergency Deficit Control Act, known by the names of two of its sponsors, Senators Phil Gramm and Warren Rudman (its third sponsor was Senator Ernest F. Hollings). The law set up a five-year program of deficit reduction, to culminate in 1991 with a zero deficit. If in any intervening year Congress did not meet that year's budgetary target, the budget would be cut across the board by the necessary amount. Since some programs would

[25]For a thorough evaluation of the impact of Proposition 13, see Richard Reeves, "The Tax Revolt that Wrecked California," *Money*, January 1994, 90–103.

[26]Benjamin Ginsberg and Martin Shefter, *Politics by Other Means: The Declining Importance of Elections in America* (New York: Basic Books, 1990).

be exempted, including interest on the debt and the so-called entitlement programs, the mandatory cuts, called "sequestrations," would require virtual 10 percent cuts in all other programs and agencies, including the Department of Defense and the FBI. No one genuinely expected it to work. But without being able to raise taxes or substantially cut individual programs, Congress chose the Gramm-Rudman approach as their best effort to indicate to the nation an intention to respond to the widespread sense of the crisis of public authority.

And it did not work. Not only did Gramm-Rudman not produce the legislated deficit reductions but deficit increases continued to mount at alarming rates. At that point gridlock became an almost universal expression, and other reform demands also began to mount. Favored with special intensity by President Reagan was the proposal to give the president constitutional "line-item veto." The theory is that the president is forced to accept the worst kinds of pork barrel hidden away in appropriations bills because at present he can only get at those costly evil items by vetoing the entire appropriation bill, bringing a whole department or program to its knees. The underlying assumption is that presidents would have the courage lacked by members of the House and Senate to take the responsibility for cutting out those very juicy items. In any event, the significance of the proposal for the line-item veto is not that it would actually bring the budget deficits into line but that, like Gramm-Rudman, it would indicate that Congress is institutionally incapable of dealing with serious policy decisions. To the supporters of the line-item veto, deficits are simply a way of keeping score on Congress's incapacity.

Fed by the failure of Gramm-Rudman and the lack of progress toward a line-item veto amendment, public clamor mounted in favor of term limitations of twelve years—six successive two-year terms for members of the House and two successive six-year terms for senators. Although this proposal draws its justification in part from the term limit put on the president of the United States by the Twenty-second Amendment, there has not been a sustained campaign to adopt a constitutional amendment for congressional term limits. There were instead unprecedented adoptions by initiative and referendum in fourteen states in 1992—out of fourteen states in which such an attempt was made. And although these states cannot constitute a nationwide sample,[27] a national poll taken in April 1992 indicated that 80 percent of Americans did favor term limits, and as of the end of 1993 six additional states had joined.

These results almost certainly sent a powerful message to Washington that Americans may have come to feel that "their liberty is being threatened . . . by a class of self-perpetuating professional politicians" and that the solution is simple and elegant.[28] And there was probably a supplementary message that Americans are so distrustful of government institutions, in particular, national government institutions, that they demand more opportunity for direct democracy. There is serious doubt that the adoption of term limits by states on members of Congress is constitutional, not because it was done by referendum but because it seems to violate Article I, Section 5 of the Constitution: "Each House shall be the judge of the Elections, Returns and Qualifications of its own Members." In 1969, the Supreme Court ruled that although the power of Congress to judge the qualifications of its members was absolute and did exclude Supreme Court review, this power was limited to qualifications already provided in the Constitution and that Congress could not add any new ones. This could easily and logically be extended to the states, because it would make no sense if the states could add qualifications for Congress that Congress itself could not add.[29] However, even if the term

[27]Two states were in the South, two were in the Midwest, and the other ten were west of the Mississippi.

[28]Richard P. Hiskes, "Why Did Americans Back Term Limits?" *The Public Perspective: A Roper Center Review of Public Opinion and Polling* 4, no. 2 (January/February 1993): 31.

[29]*Powell v. McCormack,* 395 U.S. 486 (1969). The qualifications in the Constitution are in regard to age, citizenship, and place of residence. The qualification to be added is "prior congressional service," in the sense that any service beyond twelve years would constitute a *dis*qualification.

limit qualification proves unconstitutional, the message to Congress in the meantime is no less strong and clear.

Still other reform efforts send the same message. There are campaign finance reforms, providing especially for public financing in return for severe limits on political action committee (PAC) involvement. There are also moves afoot to take internal congressional administration out of the hands of Congress, by putting the House Post Office, banking services, and so on, under outside and independent management.

It is doubtful that any of these reforms will, if adopted, achieve what the proponents seek. Meanwhile, there will, as always, be serious unanticipated consequences. But the purpose here is interpretation, not criticism. Each reform proposal can and should be taken as a political expression much more profound and troubling than the reform demand itself. Most people become attached to a particular reform because they like the sound of the appeal (e.g., "put the people in," "throw the rascals out") or because it may seem to fit a particular grudge they may have. Few supporters of term limits, for example, have really thought through the implications of the proposal, nor have they listened carefully to the arguments made by the opponents. Few are troubled over the inconsistency between their support for term limits in general and their support for their own incumbent in particular. But taken together, all of these reforms and all of the enormous sentiment favorable to them provide an indication far better than any polling can provide that national government is suffering a severe case of illegitimacy.

The question of whether and what reforms is out of the Congress's hands. As the veteran Mike Synar, Democrat of Oklahoma, put it, Congress had to continue to try to enact some kind of campaign finance reform. But why? "We have to, because Perot is a nightmare for all of us if we don't take that weapon out of his hands."[30] The Perot phenomenon was

---

[30]Quotation from Adam Clymer, "Stirrings of Self-Restraint on Campaign Spending," *New York Times*, 20 June 1993, p. 3, sec. 4.

indeed an expression of the illegitimacy of the national government. And there is no question that this belief went well beyond the large constituency supporting Ross Perot. Perot may not want to be president, and he did not want a third party to participate regularly in the government of the nation. He was riding on a sentiment that would favor shutting the government down. He simply did not know how far he wanted to go.

Pulling Up the Curtain on Radicalized Old Liberalism

Perot did not create the phenomenon that bears his name. One could say that it created him. As we shall see in the next two chapters concerning Reagan and the Right in the 1980s, Perot gave form and timeliness to a widespread attitude already in existence. Beyond that, the Reagan phenomenon made the Perot phenomenon possible. But something else prior to Reagan made both possible. This was the revival and the radicalization of Old Liberalism.

Just as New Liberalism was coming to its end, there was a resurgence of the brand of liberalism that, most everyone thought, had died with Herbert Hoover. It is this resurgence in the late 1970s as one of the two major responses to the collapse of New Liberalism that will not only help explain the success of Ronald Reagan in the 1980s but will also help explain the sense of immobility, illegitimacy, and decline in the 1990s noticed even more by foreigners than by Americans themselves. The following is an excerpt of the theme of a major conference on post–cold war American government sponsored by the Center for North American Studies in Göttingen, Germany, in July 1993 written by the German hosts.

> This conference will focus on the contrast between rapid changes in the global system on the one hand and the—apparent or real—immobility in American domestic, social and foreign policy on the other. With regard to the significance to the worldwide changes generated by the end of the communist regimes . . . it is striking to see how little enthusiasm the

United States developed. Problems stemming from domestic social and economic crises soon replaced any triumphal feelings about the end of communism. [We note, for example,] the intensity of the debate on the decline of America which can be observed both in academic literature and in the mass media. . . . Never before has the contrast between a radically changing international context and a rather static or inflexible approach to policymaking in the U.S. been wider than in the end of the Bush administration. This striking discrepancy is at the center of the questions which shall be addressed at the conference.

The question is, why now? The answer does not lie in the decline of American resources, because they are no less ample today than in the past. Nor does the answer lie in the collapse of our political institutions. The answer will be found in the actual policy decisions made in the 1980s which have effectively eliminated options available to political institutions, thereby creating the impression of declining resources and institutional immobility. But that repetition only leads to the next question: Once it was clear that the annual deficits were putting government in a cage, and once it was clear that Reagan policies, despite short-term recovery, were going to mean long-term disaster if left in place, why did all of the presidential candidates, the political leaders in Congress and elsewhere, and even the Democrat elected president in 1992 capitulate to Reagan policies and accept the absence of options, even if that meant the end of positive government?

THE END OF OLD LIBERALISM

The answer lies in the realm of public philosophy rather than objective conditions. The Republican era of the 1980s was caught between the end of two liberalisms and the resurgence of genuine conservatism. All three of these important public philosophies, despite the conflicts with each other, have contributed to a significant, catastrophic decline in the confidence Americans have always had that people through their government can have a positive effect on their economic and social environment. All three public philosophies, pushed to their radical extremes, have had a deeply caustic effect on representative democracy. Having already looked at the influence of one of those, New Liberalism, we now turn to look at the influence of the other liberalism, the Old. A confrontation with conservatism will be held over until the next two chapters.

From 1932 into the 1960s, the Democrats ran against the ghost of Herbert Hoover even while Hoover was still alive and was being resurrected by the Democrats themselves, with Truman's appointment of Hoover to head the biggest modern effort at administrative reform, the Hoover Commission. But the purpose of the Hoover Commission, and of the Second Hoover Commission appointed by President Eisenhower, was to help make the positive, liberal state more efficient as well as more responsible, not to emasculate it. Hoover's acceptance of this important Truman appointment and Eisenhower's extension of the Hoover Commission are indicative of Republican acceptance of the New Deal and the public philosophy of the New Deal and the New Liberalism. They could call it "yes, but"; they could call it, as Eisenhower often did, the middle of the road. But it was a genuine acceptance of the programs of the New Liberalism.

Revival through Radicalization

Yet Old Liberalism as an ideology was alive, not, as they say, in Argentina but in Chicago. The story of its survival and revival is testimony to the strength of the liberal tradition and also to the power of theory in the affairs of state. Its persistence despite widespread mislabeling and misunderstanding was also a strong confirmation of the truth of Keynes's observation that

> the ideas of economists and political philosophers, both when they are right and when they are wrong, are more powerful than is commonly understood. . . . Practical men, who believe themselves to be quite exempt from any intellectual influences, are usually the slaves of some defunct economist. Madmen in authority, who hear voices in the air, are

distilling their frenzy from some academic scribbler of a few years back.[31]

Even at the height of the Keynesian hegemony in America, the spirit of Adam Smith and his followers was alive and beginning to stir.

There had already been F. A. Hayek, whose *Road to Serfdom*, written during World War II, was widely read and criticized by defenders of the new American state, even though Keynes himself took only moderate exception to Hayek. After all, the book was aimed not at Keynes but at socialism.[32]

However, given the willingness of the Eisenhower Republicans to go along with Keynes and to accept the conservative label, one would almost have to say that the novelist/philosopher Ayn Rand triggered the revival of Old Liberalism as well as its radicalization. Although her first novel, *The Fountainhead* (1943), with its worshipful approach to the acquisitive individual as hero, became immensely popular after the film starring Gary Cooper appeared (1949), the cult of radical liberalism (called "Objectivism" by Rand) probably came together around her 1957 book, *Atlas Shrugged*, which, along with the interminable narrative, contained a "speech" of over one hundred pages by the main character John Galt laying out a modern and highly radicalized, manifesto version of *The Wealth of Nations*.[33] It is for intellectual historians to dig out more precise causes. What seems clear to those of us who were college teachers in the early 1960s, few students began to get

[31]John Maynard Keynes, *The General Theory of Employment, Interest and Money* (New York: Harcourt 1953), 383.

[32]The economic historian Robert Heilbroner reports that Keynes sympathized and liked the book but complained in a letter to Hayek that there should be more planning rather than less, so long as the planning took place in a community in which people shared Hayek's own moral position. Heilbroner, *The Worldly Philosophers*, 5th ed. (New York: Simon and Schuster, Touchstone Book, 1980), 275–76.

[33]In the conversation referred to earlier, I asked Hayek what he thought of *Atlas Shrugged*, and he retorted sheepishly that he thought her story was engrossing enough but that he "couldn't get through the John Galt speech."

interested in the short and highly readable *Road to Serfdom* or in individualist ideas at all until after *Atlas Shrugged,* when there began to appear actual cults of serious readers not only of Rand's writings and lectures but of the virtually unreadable *Human Action* by Ludwig von Mises, which had sat gathering dust since its publication in 1949. In the context of the radical liberalism of Rand and von Mises (who had been a teacher of Hayek back in Vienna), Hayek appeared indeed to be a compromiser.[34]

Gaining Academic Respectability

During the 1950s and 1960s, many serious economists were still writing and teaching in the classical tradition of Adam Smith, and there were frequent direct confrontations between them and the, usually younger, Keynesians. At Harvard, "the launching pad for the Keynesian rocket in America,"[35] opposition to Keynes was at first so intense that the Department of Economics was investigated by a visiting committee on behalf of Harvard's Governing Board. The committee found that a Keynesian bias definitely existed. This finding was eventually rejected by Harvard's president, but "there was much bad blood."[36] At Yale, there was a crisis over adoption of Paul Samuelson's *Economics: An Introductory Analysis,* a Keynesian-oriented textbook that eventually dominated the introductory

[34]According to Stephen Newman in the best book on Old Liberalism, the dogmatic liberals found Hayek's position obnoxious, largely because of Hayek's willingness to acknowledge that freedom is not absolute but can exist only when it is "properly bounded as well as protected by law." Newman, *Liberalism at Wit's End: The Libertarian Revolt Against the Modern State* (Ithaca: Cornell University Press, 1984), 134. Newman is also one of the few who appreciates the radicalism of Old Liberalism, which he quite accurately calls libertarianism. In his preface he reports that as a graduate student he began to study eighteenth-century British radicalism but then switched to modern libertarianism when he discovered its similarities to the older radicalism.

[35]Quoted in John Kenneth Galbraith, "Came the Revolution: Rise of Unorthodoxy," *New York Times Book Review,* 16 May 1965. Reprinted in Theodore J. Lowi, ed., *Private Life and Public Order* (New York: W. W. Norton, 1968), 148–49.

[36]Lowi, *Private Life and Public Order,* 149.

course for decades throughout the United States.[37] But despite the numbers of classical economists and despite the popularity of Ayn Rand and the boost from the Goldwater candidacy for president in 1954, intellectual leadership was to come from the pen and tongue of Milton Friedman. Already on the way to an eventual Nobel Prize for his fundamental work in monetary theory, Friedman published *Capitalism and Freedom* in 1961, a decidedly ideological work written for wide popular distribution.[38] The Austrian school of economics that had spawned (among others) von Mises and Hayek found its new home at the University of Chicago (with Hayek, Friedman, and a number of other distinguished libertarian economists), and from there it spread to a number of other "fresh water" schools, including the University of Rochester, Washington University/St. Louis, and Virginia Polytechnic Institute.[39] Another boost came from the Harvard philosopher Robert Nozick in 1974.[40] Since Friedman's *Capitalism and Freedom* and his later *Free to Choose*[41] were unabashedly ideological works, Nozick's work was important for the respectability it contributed. Others of Nobel and near-Nobel quality came along in quick succession, and their work, though not well known beyond narrow academic circles, added intellectual strength and respectability to the revival of Old Liberalism.[42]

[37]An account of the Yale crisis will be found in William Buckley's *God and Man at Yale* (Chicago: Henry Regnery, 1951), discussed in chap. 4.

[38]Samuelson received his Nobel Prize in 1970, the second Nobel Prize for economics to be awarded. Hayek received his in 1974, Friedman in 1976.

[39]The category of "fresh water" universities comes from Peter Johnson, "Unpopular Measures: Translating Monetarism into Monetary Policy in the Federal Republic of Germany and the United States, 1970–1985," Ph.D. dissertation, Cornell University, 1991.

[40]Robert Nozick, *Anarchy, State, and Utopia* (New York: Free Press, 1974).

[41]Milton Friedman and Rose Friedman, *Free to Choose* (New York: Avon Books, 1979). This was associated with a widely circulated series on capitalism presented on public television.

[42]In fact, their influence created a new ideological atmosphere in which a number of Old Liberal ("classical") economists won Nobels: Hayek (1974), Friedman (1976), Theodore Schultz (1979), George Stigler (1982), Ronald Koase (1991), and Gary Becker (1992), all of the University of Chicago, and James Buchanan (1986), then of Virginia Polytechnic Institute. Their influence brought

What seemed most to inspire the revival of Old Liberalism was its radicalism—or, more specifically, its radical antistatism. A favorite radical libertarian pamphlet widely circulated in the 1960s and 1970s was by Lysander Spooner, an obscure mid-nineteenth-century lawyer embittered by having been forced out of a successful private postal service by the federal government. His comparison of government to the highwayman is worth quoting at length because of its emotional value to the reawakened Old Liberals.

> The highwayman takes solely upon himself the responsibility, danger, and crime of his own act. He does not pretend that he has any rightful claim to your money, or that he intends to use it for your own benefit. . . . Furthermore, having taken your money, he leaves you, as you wish him to do. He does not persist in following you on the road, against your will; assuming to be your rightful "sovereign," on account of the "protection" he affords you. He does not "keep protecting" you, by commanding you to bow down and serve him; by requiring you to do this, and forbidding you to do that . . . and shooting you down without mercy, if you dispute his authority, or resist his demands. He is too much of a gentleman to be guilty of such impostures, and insults, and villainies as these. In short, he does not, in addition to robbing you, attempt to make you either his dupe or his slave.[43]

Thus, to Spooner and to his followers, the state is theft. This is no less radical a statement than the contention of the socialist Pierre-Joseph Proudhon that "property is theft."

There is a long tradition of rebellion in the United States, reaching back to the original one against its mother country. It runs through the popular Henry David Thoreau (a contempo-

---

about the adoption of monetarism as the basis of monetary policy in the two most important banking systems of the world, the United States Federal Reserve and the German Bundesbank, along with the appointment of Paul Volcker as chairman of the Federal Reserve by Jimmy Carter, anticipating the Old Liberal policies that were to prevail in the Reagan administration. See also Johnson, *Unpopular Measures.*

[43]From *The Collected Works of Lysander Spooner,* as quoted in Newman, *Liberalism at Wit's End,* 24.

rary of Spooner). But the purpose of rebellion, whether viewed by Thoreau or by the Students for a Democratic Society or by the civil rights movement in the 1960s, is to redeem the system. To the rebel, the laws are to be broken in order to demonstrate and dramatize the gap between what people in authority believe and what they are actually doing. This is not true of libertarian antistatism. Its purpose is not to redeem the state. The state, by its very nature, is not redeemable. This is what makes Old Liberal or libertarian antistatism radical.

In the previous chapter, one direction of radicalization of liberalism was exposed: the direction taken by the New Liberalism, leading to a form of totalitarianism, step by step through the lengthy chains of causation of injury, for which the modern liberal state holds itself responsible. Now we have another direction of liberal radicalization, of whose influence we have not yet seen the end. For example, the more recent developments in public choice theory, associated with James Buchanan, have substantially reinforced and further legitimized this radicalizing influence with the argument that inefficiency, irrationality, irrational growth, and exploitation are sewn into the very nature of government, even the most beneficently oriented government. One version of this, William Niskanen's, holds that in government there are two types of actors, bureaucrats and politicians, and that, assuming they act on the basis of their individual rationality, bureaucrats are the sole suppliers of goods and politicians are the only buyers. The rational objective for the bureaucrats is to maximize their agency budget; the rational goal for the politicians is to maximize votes. "The outcome of this relationship between bureaucrats and politicians is the oversupply of public goods and services when compared to what would be optimal according to citizen preferences." In other words, regardless of forms, constitutions, traditions, or rules of law, the governmental outcome is innately irrational.[44] In this

---

[44]This version is provided by Desmond S. King, *The New Right: Politics, Markets and Citizenship* (Chicago: Dorsey Press, 1987), 102–4. The quote is King's, p. 103.

context, democracy may be the most irrational of all forms of government. This is the contribution of Old Liberalism to the end of the republican as well as the Republican era.

REFLECTIONS ON THE TWO ENDS OF LIBERALISM

Some would argue that libertarianism came into its own in response to the exposure of the real Richard Nixon as a New Liberal. For them, the last straw was dropped on the elephant's back with Nixon's acceptance and vigorous implementation of wage and price controls.[45] I am sympathetic to this analysis and have already expressed an appreciation of the role of wage and price controls in defining Nixon as a New Liberal—perhaps the last New Liberal president. But that only validates what Nixon and the 1970s Republican party had, in their decadence, become. Something more was needed to validate the radical antistatism of the Old Liberalism that was to have such an extraordinary influence on the 1980s.

Politics not being physics, it is generally true that when political authority collapses and God fails, the reaction is disproportionate to the action. But the positive liberal state did not need the reaction of the genuine Right to endanger its enormous accomplishments. As with New Liberalism, its friends made enemies unnecessary.

The positive liberal state was thus caught between the two ends of liberalism. Although an obituary would be premature, the frustrations with late New Liberal policies coupled with the impossibly high political standards of radicalized Old Liberalism rendered American government as immobile as the Russian bear with feet of clay. Note again what has happened in America since the collapse of the USSR. If we won, why do we feel so bad? What won? Certainly not democracy. The victory seems to have gone to a radical view of market-based capitalism. American government has been immobilized by a renewed public philosophy that is fundamentally antagonistic to government in general (Old Liberal-

---

[45]An account of this will be found in Newman, *Liberalism at Wit's End*, 29.

ism) and national government in particular (Old Liberalism in coalition with genuine conservatism).

Representative government itself is in danger as a consequence. The market economy, properly understood in the real world rather than in its radically idealized form, is compatible with democratic political regimes. However, market systems are compatible with many other types of regimes as well. Friedman joyously consorted with the Chilean dictatorship. U.S. business long maintained positive relationships with South Africa and continues to do so with China, having faith, with no immediate validation whatsoever, that a little more free market will create a lot more political democracy. Authoritarian Singapore, Taiwan, and Korea are shining examples of the Free World. Everywhere there is an assumption that if left to its own devices and not "interfered with" by an irrational and self-aggrandizing government, the free market will emerge spontaneously, will prosper rationally, and will in fact produce a democratic political system compatible with it. There is just as much economic determinism among libertarians as there is among Marxists.

History is repeating itself, this time as farce rather than tragedy. Radical libertarian antistatism, far from producing the ideal political regime, can undermine the modest movement toward the ideal political system we have been able to attain. Hayek was the one libertarian wise enough to recognize that markets must operate within "the rule of law," which for him meant a particular kind of constitutional, stable, predictable political regime. But this meant *good* government, not *no* government.

This locates precisely the intersection of the two liberalisms where the national government of the United States was caught and immobilized. The New Liberals recognized that markets—capitalism—could not exist without a state, but they lacked a sense of the Constitution such a state ought to have. Old Liberals, holding steadfastly to the other end of liberalism—that the state itself was at issue—contributed to the very conditions that could bring down liberal democracy and with it, capitalism itself. It seems appropriate to close this chapter with the moral of one of James Thurber's fables: "You might as well fall flat on your face as lean over too far backward."

CHAPTER 4

THE CONSERVATIVE ERA

The Patrician Right and the Struggle for a
Concordance Between Capitalism and Christianity

> *Not many conservatives would be*
> *happy to enlist under the banner*
> *of one abstraction, Capitalism,*
> *against another abstraction,*
> *Communism—or to die, absurdly,*
> *for "a higher standard of living."*
> RUSSELL KIRK, 1982

IF RONALD REAGAN left no other legacy, he will be long remembered for Europeanizing American national politics. Before Reagan, the national political dialogue was between two variants of liberalism. With Reagan, a new participant joined, bringing with it ideological polarization not experienced in the United States in this century. The new participant is genuine conservatism. Not the ersatz conservatism that is actually Old Liberalism erroneously labeled conservative but genuine conservatism—a substantive ideological confrontation with liberalism per se on the nature of government and the individual, rather than a difference between two liberalisms on the degree of government involvement. If it is ironic that a modestly educated small-town boy from Eureka, Illinois, could internationalize anything, it is doubly ironic for this same person to succeed in stamping liberalism as extreme Left, since the American tradition of liberalism, being procapitalist, is well to the right of center in every other country except the United States. In 1961, Daniel Bell could publish *The End of Ideology*[1] and President Kennedy could in

[1] Daniel Bell, *The End of Ideology: On the Exhaustion of Political Ideas in the 50s* (New York: Collier Books, 1961).

effect endorse it in his 1962 Yale commencement address. Events would prove that news of its demise was a trifle exaggerated.

CHARACTERS IN SEARCH OF A PLOT

In the 1960s, conservatism was indeed in retreat. But it had been advancing during the previous fifteen years. Names such as Hoover (J. Edgar), McCarthy, and MacArthur come immediately to mind, personifying widespread fears of the imminent victory of communism among the war-ravaged countries of the Northern Hemisphere, the underdeveloped countries in the Southern Hemisphere, and inside the United States as well. There is no need to go into the causes, because the reasons are more important. And in so many respects, the best reasons offered for the advance of conservatism are to be found in the voice and prose of Whittaker Chambers.

Whittaker Chambers—Turncoat Hero

Chambers joined the Communist party in 1925, was openly active in Communist party activities for several years, and became a member of the Communist underground in the spring of 1932. He spent the next six years as an underground courier for the party, using a variety of aliases. His cover was his work as a writer and editor for the Communist newspaper, *The New Masses*, working toward what Chambers considered the attainable goal of a "Soviet America."[2] Chambers always emphasized to friends and associates that he was a member of the Russian, not the American, Communist party. He was fluent in Russian, traveled to the USSR on a fraudulent passport, trained as an agent at the Lenin School, and apparently received extensive briefing by Soviet military intelligence (Fourth Branch) officials, who became Chambers's contact after he joined the underground.[3]

---

[2]Details of his activities will be found in Allen Weinstein, *Perjury: The Hiss Chambers Case* (New York: Random House, Vintage Books, 1978), chap. 3.
[3]Ibid., 115–16.

Chambers served as a spy for Soviet intelligence from at least mid-1934 to 1938, "primarily as an organizer among covert Communists within Washington and as a conduit for their stolen documents."[4] He apparently left the Communist party in 1938 and claims that at the same time he left his second double life as a roving homosexual—his "darkest personal secret," which he had never divulged to his family or to his friends. He claims also that he left both underground lives largely "with God's help, embracing, for the first time, religion."[5] But since his affiliation with organized religion did not happen until several years later and since the letters from that period do not indicate any interest in religion whatsoever and since he continued casual homosexual attachments after he broke with communism, the more likely explanation for his break with the Communist party seems to be one of self-preservation. His break with the party and his escape into hiding in 1938 are closely associated with the Stalin purges and the fact that even some American agents like himself had disappeared without explanation. Thus when Chambers was summoned back to the Soviet Union in mid-1937, he managed to postpone responding to the invitation while continuing to work regularly for the party as an agent. A second invitation to Moscow was arranged, along with passport and visas to facilitate the trip. At that point he began to make his plan for breaking away from the party and finding a secret haven in the United States.[6] After some hesitation, Chambers decided to follow a public appeal from Leon Trotsky himself to defectors from Stalinism to speak publicly and fully of their defection.

After trying some versions of his experience on several of his ex-Communist friends, Chambers went to Roosevelt adviser Adolph Berle with an offer to provide details, including names of underground associates, in return for immunity

4Ibid., 131.
5Ibid., 119.
6Ibid., 310–15.

from prosecution. Although he did not get such immunity, he did provide Berle with a considerable amount of information, including names; but after the death of still another close friend within the Communist party, Chambers decided to discontinue his efforts to expose former underground associates. He feared that such cooperation would be not only fatal but futile, and he developed a very interesting theory of conspiracy to explain this futility. In his own words, his theory was that most of the New Deal agencies were packed with CP persons, that this would expand when the Soviet Union became an ally in the war, and that after the war the American government officials would be "stirring up data for a great Moscow Trial in which it would completely whitewash itself. . . . The sufferers in this perjury were people like you and me, . . . but the big CP's would remain in control of the show; only then they would be completely disguised, having proved publicly that they are anti-CP. So I have become increasingly reluctant to have anything to do with this filth."[7]

This was 1942. Chambers had become an editor at *Time*, had become an Episcopalian and then joined a Quaker meeting, and was building a conspiratorial view of world communism based on his Communist experience, his defection, and his conversion to the Christian religion.

So here we have one of the heroes of modern conservatism: Whittaker Chambers, born Jay Vivien Chambers, user of a dozen aliases, a genuine converted Communist, a member not of the American but of the Russian Communist party, an underground agent and courier in a Soviet spy network, and a traitor to his country and his family, sustaining a belief even after his defection in the ultimate goal of Soviet America—a symbol and an inspiration for American conservatism. Chambers, a gifted writer much admired at *Time*, can speak best for himself, in a passage chosen as inspirational by William Rusher, publisher of the *National Review* and one of the most respected and influential conservatives from the 1950s through the 1980s.

[7]Quoted in Weinstein, *Perjury,* 331–32.

[Communism] is not new. It is, in fact, man's second oldest faith. . . . It is the great alternative faith of mankind. Like all great faiths, its force derives from a simple vision. Other ages have had great visions. They have always been different versions of the same vision. The vision of God and man's relationship to God. The Communist vision is the vision of Man without God. . . .

The crisis of the Western world exists to the degree in which it is indifferent to God. It exists to the degree in which the Western world actually shares Communism's materialist vision, is so dazzled by the logic of the materialist interpretation of history, politics and economics, that it fails to grasp that, for it, the only possible answer to the Communist challenge: Faith in God or Faith in Man? is the challenge: Faith in God.

Economics is not the central problem of this century. It is a relative problem and can be solved in relative ways. Faith is the central problem of this age. The Western world does not know it, but it already possesses the answer to this problem—*but only provided that its faith in God and the freedom He enjoins is as great as Communism's faith in Man.*[8]

William Rusher, National Review, and the Plot

In his autobiography, Rusher praises the Chambers analysis as establishing an opposition to communism not merely as a by-product of America's cold war "but a bold stand against the latest and deadliest form of the atheist materialism so often associated with the 18th-century Enlightenment: The last chance for the Western world to regain its bearings and save itself from moral—and therefore ultimately physical—destruction."[9]

Then Rusher goes on to make a very curious connection: "In *Witness,* Chambers demonstrated that philosophical anti-Communism was a full and worthy partner of classical liberalism in the arsenal of the American right."[10] Although nothing

[8]Quoted in William Rusher, *The Rise of the Right* (New York: William Morrow, 1984), 25. Emphasis added.
[9]Rusher, *The Rise of the Right*, 25–26.
[10]Ibid., 26.

could possibly be more atheist or materialist than classical liberalism, Rusher is typical in his urgent insistence on associating the deeply moral and religious basis of the American Right with the—let us be generous—nonreligious and non-moral position of classical liberalism and market-driven capitalism. As we shall see time and again, the association of conservatism with classical or Old Liberalism is coalitional, not organic. The effort of conservative intellectuals and practitioners to associate the two in a philosophically organic way has to be seen as strictly tactical, a generally successful political tactic. But it is important here at the outset to maintain a clear sense of the truth—that these are two quite separate and at bottom quite contradictory public philosophies.

To this mixture of God and anticommunism has to be added the view, shared by virtually all of the conservatives of the 1950s, that the world they opposed was a highly conspiratorial one. Even those liberals who were not and had never been Communists were engaged in a conspiracy with Communists and fellow travelers and other atheists to undermine God, to elevate Man, and thereby to help usher in the victory of communism over freedom. Belief in conspiracy is generally easy to confirm, and confirmation was not long in coming. They found conspiracy in the job that was done to discredit Joseph McCarthy. They even found conspiracy in the bored reaction to the founding of the *National Review.* Arising out of the ashes of other failed right-wing journals, the *National Review* had put together an extraordinary group of talented authors. But when it first appeared in 1955, the response was negative in the three publications that bothered to recognize its founding at all; and response was nonexistent in all other publications. The three publications that reviewed the *National Review* were *Harper's, Commentary,* and *The Progressive.* Though different in so many ways, they were cataloged as identical "liberal publications." Further proof of the conspiracy was found in the fact that "America's liberals abruptly shifted their tactics and subjected [the *National Review*] to a treatment that threatened to be far more effective: silence."[11] However, William Buckley, founder and managing editor, insisted in his response to the rather pale reception of his journal, "It is to be expected that They should set the hounds on us."[12] Thus, even to the very sophisticated William Buckley, there had to be a conspiracy, and it had to be a concerted, intensive, and aggressive one, even if it took the form of a cold shoulder.

Buckley did say something else in his initial response to his critics that is much more accurate in its characterization of the response of liberals and others who opposed the emergent conservatism.

> For several years, the dominant intellectual agitators in the United States have got away with the fiction that those who substantially disagree with them do so because they suffer from serious diseases of one kind or another. The theory holds that not intellectual, but social or psychic difficulties are responsible for the perversity of Right-wing dissent.[13]

We shall soon see the accuracy of Buckley's observation here. If there was a conspiracy against the Right, it was not a conspiracy of active opposition or sabotage, but it was a conspiracy in the form of a consensus view that the Right was an aberrant belief system that only occasionally and temporarily brought attention to itself and would then disappear once again under the rocks of political pathology. This will become a key issue later in the chapter.

Rusher is, like Chambers, a useful personification of the conservatism of the 1950s, because he is an unabashed ideologue who writes well enough and explicitly enough to identify quite clearly the package of beliefs that comprise the patrician Right not only in the 1950s but in the 1980s and 1990s as well. Having started political life as a mainstream Republican, Rusher was pulled away from Eisenhower and the middle

[11]Ibid., 52.
[12]Quoted in Rusher, *The Rise of the Right*, 52.
[13]Ibid.

of the road first by the likes of Whittaker Chambers, whose writing gave him the philosophical and religious reasons (rather than the liberal instrumental reasons) for opposing communism. This would also give Rusher and the Right a stronger basis for tying liberalism to communism despite the fact that liberals were, in their own way, just as anti-Communist as the Right. True, liberals (and many others) had been friendly with the USSR when we were all allies against fascism and nazism. And liberals may have gone too far, trusting Russians as well as cooperating in the conduct of the war. But it is indeed indicative of the character of the Right that they were insistent on tying liberalism to communism yet were perfectly capable of forgiving and embracing genuine traitors like Chambers so long as they were willing to confess to the error of their ways and to proclaim their rejection of the secular Communist God for the sacred Judeo-Christian God. It would seem, then, that the real basis of the tendency of the Right to define liberalism as far Left is the refusal of liberalism to bring religion and morality into public discourse; communism itself did not have much to do with it.

Rusher reports in his autobiography a second influence leading him to reject the Republican party and turn to genuine conservatism: Hayek's *Road to Serfdom*. This, too, is an interesting insight into the Right, because there is absolutely no logical connection between Hayek and the outlook personified by such people as Whittaker Chambers and William Buckley. It is obvious that Rusher felt he needed a religious/moral argument favoring capitalism, and somehow Hayek's ardency against socialist planning was close enough to a moral equivalent of religion.[14]

---

[14]It is worth referring back once again to Stephen Newman's account of Hayek's appreciation of a statist framework for the market and how that made him a problem, indeed an anomaly, for radical, purist libertarians. But it made Hayek more acceptable to the Right, because the statist element was for them just an aspect of the moral dimension that made market capitalism an acceptable feature of their overall public philosophy of "capitalism rightly understood."

The third influence in the making of Rusher's right wing was the work of Russell Kirk. So moved was Rusher by Kirk's *The Conservative Mind* (1953) that he reproduced in the first chapter of his autobiography (as part of his "personal word") an almost verbatim list of Kirk's "six canons of conservatism." In drastically condensed form, they are (1) belief that a divine intent rules society and individual conscience and that political problems are at bottom religious and moral problems; (2) belief that civil society requires orders and classes, and all attempts at leveling lead to despair; (3) belief that property and freedom are inseparable; and (4) belief that human appetites must be controlled. As Rusher himself puts it, "By mid-1954 I could no longer be satisfied merely with being a 'Republican'—whatever that meant. I was something else: something with a longer tradition, a richer heritage, a deeper significance. I was a *conservative*."[15]

Sorting Out the Two Branches—Patrician and Populist

Rusher was quite accurate and precise in his contention that conservatism is older and richer than the Republican party. But he was incomplete. There is still more to conservatism than Burke through Kirk plus Christianized capitalism.[16] One could say that Rusher's conservatism, though genuine, authentic, and deeply American, was the *patrician* upper-class version. There was also a lower-class, or *populist*, version—

[15]Rusher, *The Rise of the Right*, 31. Emphasis in original.

[16]It is significant that a genuine philosophical conservative like Russell Kirk had almost nothing to say about Adam Smith. Smith comes up only twice in *The Conservative Mind:* first, in Kirk's assertion that *The Wealth of Nations* was "founded upon faith in Providence" (90), and second, that Smith echoed Locke's "utilitarian extreme" view, putting work above piety and contemplation (372). Kirk was certainly aware, though did not make it explicit, that this instrumental view of work truly severs property, and therefore civic order, from Providence. Both Locke and Smith were religious individuals, but they were genuine liberals to the extent that their "faith in Providence" had no direct bearing on their analysis and theories of the condition of society or economy, or, for that matter, the polity. Providence totally aside, the *right* to property comes from the work (or labor) the individual mixes with property (Locke); and the *value* of the property comes from the market, or exchange (Smith).

just as genuine, just as authentic, and perhaps even more American. Both are genuinely conservative, and both comprise important dimensions of the American Right, but they come from different parts of society. As Richard Hofstadter observes, "The United States has not provided a receptive home for *formal* conservative thought or *classically* conservative modes of behavior. Lacking a formidable aristocratic tradition, this country has produced at best patricians rather than aristocrats, and the literature of American political experience shows how unhappy the patricians (for example, Henry Adams) have been in their American environment."[17] Hofstadter goes on to recognize that in addition to this patrician Right, there is what he referred to as "the extreme Right wing" who are antagonistic to the patricians while sharing most of their conservative outlook. "Such conservative institutions as the better preparatory schools, the Ivy League colleges and universities, the Supreme Court, and the State Department—exactly those institutions that have been largely in the custodianship of the patrician or established elements of American society—have been the favorite objects of Right-wing animosity."[18]

Hofstadter is correct in his characterization of the class position and the antipatrician attitude shared by the populist Right. But he is incorrect in suggesting that the religious-based populist conservatism is by nature any more "far Right" or "radical Right" than the upper-class Burkean version. Rather than personify this segment of conservatism with a single individual, I will try to project this point of view and its social location through that most activist and observant segment, the Evangelicals. According to Gallup polls, nearly 20 percent of Americans were evangelicals at the begin-

[17]Richard Hofstadter, "Pseudo-Conservatism Re-Visited: A Postscript—1962," in Daniel Bell, ed., *The Radical Right* (Freeport, N.Y.: Books for Libraries Press, 1963), 84. Emphasis added. Although I reject much of Hofstadter's analysis, I fully accept his distinction between patrician (upper-class) and populist (generally lower-class) conservatives. I will utilize this distinction in my analysis.
[18]Ibid., 84–85.

ning of the 1980s; by the end of the 1980s, Gallup reported that one white in three belongs to a denomination considered evangelical. These polls report that the basic profile of evangelicals is relatively low in socioeconomic status, rural, southern, older, and more religiously observant. Certainly there are affluent evangelicals in business and managerial positions, but the general profile is on the lower socioeconomic side.[19]

Evangelicals and related fundamentalist Christians have from time to time been prominent in social reformist movements that can only be understood as coming from out of the left side of the ideological spectrum—fitting into the Old Left box 1 of the original definitional table 1.3 in chapter 1. For example, evangelicals were active in the movement for abolition and for women's suffrage as well as for prohibition. As one of the most intelligent students of populist ideologies, Allen Hertzke, puts it, "[The] blending of moral traditionalism with economic radicalism was not uncommon in the American past. In contemporary politics, however, the populist heritage is split. Both sides of the political spectrum must contend with the discontents in the ranks. . . . Jesse Jackson champions the dispossessed and afflicts the comfortable, [and] Pat Robertson trumpets moral renewal and chastises cultural elites for flouting traditional values."[20] Yet far and away the largest element of this Christian populism, especially since the 1950s, has been on the Right. As Jerome Himmelstein observes, in the early part of this century there was a "Great Reversal," during which evangelicalism and social reform were separated. "Evangelical beliefs, religious fervor, and the quest for individual salvation, once the source of reform movements, became more and more indifferent or

[19]Data reported in Jerome Himmelstein, *To the Right: The Transformation of American Conservatism* (Berkeley, Los Angeles, and Oxford: University of California Press, 1990), 109; and Ted Jelen and Clyde Wilcox, "The Christian Right in the 1990's," *Public Perspective* 4, no. 3 (March/April 1993): 10.

[20]Allen Hertzke, *Echoes of Discontent: Jesse Jackson, Pat Robertson, and the Resurgence of Populism* (Washington, D.C.: Congressional Quarterly Press, 1993), 21.

even hostile to them. The reform tradition, in turn, became more and more secular."[21]

These so-called ultraconservatives and their churches began in the 1940s and further resolved in the 1950s to form their own alternative coordinating institutions, in response to the mainstream National Council of Churches and the World Council of Churches. Led by the archconservative and highly conspiracy-oriented Carl McIntire, the conservative denominations formed the American Council of Christian Churches (ACCC) and the International Council of Christian Churches (ICCC), not only as alternatives to the mainstream ones but named to indicate the precise sense in which they were alternatives. Other organizations, more fundamentalist than evangelical, were also formed in the 1950s and came within the ambit of the ACCC and the ICCC. These included the Rev. Billy James Hargis and his Christian Crusade, Edgar Bundy and his Church League of America, and Verne Kaub and his American Council of Christian Laymen. Another important organization of that period was the Christian Anti-Communism Crusade, founded and led by Dr. Fred C. Schwartz. Picking up where Gerald L. K. Smith and other populist radical Christians had left off before World War II, these evangelical and fundamentalist groups made particularly vigorous and effective use of radio transmission and were fairly quick to learn how to use television. While the more moderate Billy Graham drew more attention with his mass public meetings, the far Right populist religious leaders and their organizations made tremendous headway not only through radio and television but also through their Bible colleges, journals, and book publishing houses. It was also in this period that the most conspiracy oriented and probably the most right wing of the right-wing religious-based groups was formed: the John Birch Society (1958). Although not a religious group itself, the John Birch Society helped intensify the focus of these populist religious groups on the evils of the

[21]Himmelstein, *To the Right*, 113.

more mainstream and liberal churches and church organizations.[22]

The results are the next best thing to dramatic. As the mainstream churches were losing membership in the 1960s and 1970s, the evangelical and fundamentalist churches were growing. For example, in the decade between 1970 and 1980, the United Presbyterian Church lost 21 percent of its members, the Episcopal Church lost 15 percent, the United Church of Christ lost 11 percent, and the United Methodist Church lost 10 percent. Meanwhile, the Southern Baptist Convention grew by 16 percent, and the Assemblies of God grew by 70 percent. These latter percentages are drawn from a smaller base, but the growth pattern is nevertheless impressive. Moreover, the conservative evangelical and fundamentalist churches were drawing more affluent members, so that "by the mid-1970s evangelicalism and fundamentalism were no longer a marginal religious force in retreat. They were growing in organization, followers, and resources."[23] The mainstream churches were simply too liberal, or not conservative enough for the likes of most American Protestants.

Both paths to conservatism will be pursued in this chapter, but the latter, populist path gets more attention in chapter 5.

EXPLAINING CONSERVATISM—AND WHAT WAS WRONG WITH THE EXPLANATION

Nothing should be striking about the account up to here. It confirms what we could and should know about ideology and the geography of ideology in America. There was always an equal basis for a conservative tradition in opposition to the

[22]For accounts of these religious organizations, I depended on the following sources: Himmelstein, *To the Right*, 108–15; Bell, *The Radical Right*, especially chapters by Richard Hofstadter (3 and 4), Peter Viereck (7), and Alan Westin (11); and Steve Bruce, *The Rise and Fall of the New Christian Right: Conservative Protestant Politics in America, 1978–1988* (New York: Oxford University Press, 1988), chap. 2.

[23]Himmelstein, *To the Right*, 115; some of his materials are drawn in turn from A. James Reichley, *Religion in American Public Life* (Washington, D.C.: Brookings Institution, 1985).

liberal tradition within the U.S. Constitution, as demonstrated already in chapter 1. And not only would state government be hospitable to conservatism, the radical tendency of
the Right was also in hospitable territory. It is worth repeating
here that, cleansed of its many self-serving and pejorative
uses, radicalism means "of or pertaining to roots." As in
mathematics, so in politics, radical has to do with questioning
fundamentals, therefore seeking to understand and criticize
things at their foundations. Although *radical* in the United
States came to mean extremism bordering on violence, radical
is a suitable adjective for conservatism in the United States,
not because all conservatives are extremists but because the
tendency of conservatives to introduce morality into political
discourse radicalizes the discourse. Thus, conservative, Right
(fitting it into the European modality), and radical Right are
as natural to the American ideological terrain as is liberalism,
and far more solidly grounded in American territory than the
Left and the radical Left. Yet each time conservatism imposes
itself on national consciousness, the reaction is one of surprise, downright alarm, as though conservatism was nothing
more than a momentary disequilibrium or, for some, a pathology.

Liberal Explanation—Using Science as a Weapon

To political analysts and intellectual historians, being mostly
academics and liberals, conservatism is likely to be treated as
a particular social phenomenon to be subjected to precise
explanation rather than as a historical presence. Moreover,
their explanation is likely to be drawn from the social structure or changes in the social structure or in values, such that
the phenomenon itself would disappear once the causal conditions for it subside. In one sense this is a scientific approach
to the phenomenon of conservatism, inasmuch as, scientifically, all phenomena can be treated as effects that are the
product of causes. Put another way, each phenomenon is
treated as a *dependent* variable, to be explained by one or more
independent variables. What is suppressed in this scientific

structure is the fact that there is an ideological leap involved here, which permits the observer to treat a particular phenomenon as *dependent*. This points directly back to an observation made earlier, that the suppression of conservatism in the United States was not the result of an organized conspiracy to suppress conservatives but the unplanned result of a consensus among liberal intellectual historians and social scientists that conservatism is not natural to the United States, that it is a caused phenomenon. It is but a short step, then, to treating it as pathological. This consensus and the analysis derived from it can go a long way toward explaining the lack of appreciation of the role conservatism has played in American political history.

It is useful to refer once again to Louis Hartz, who asserts early in his classic work that "we have never had a real conservative tradition."[24] Later in the book he confronts "conservatism in a liberal society," identifying (or defining) it exclusively as southern. This is in a chapter he entitles "The Reactionary Enlightenment," in which some of the best minds ever produced in America (Calhoun et al.) are being used in the impossible philosophic defense of slavery. Hartz concludes that indeed a book ought to be written "about the Southern search for a cultural code before the Civil War" but that it "is a book to be written in the psychiatric vein."[25]

Henry Steele Commager, the historian to Hartz's political scientist, in a book published five years before *The Liberal Tradition in America*, had a broader definition of conservatism but no richer appreciation of it as a "conservative tradition" equal or comparable to "the liberal tradition." Commager begins his analysis with ample recognition.

The strength and persistence of fundamentalism well into the 20th century is one of the curiosities of the history of American thought. That a people so optimistic and self-confident should accept a theology which insisted on the depravity of man, that

[24]Hartz, *The Liberal Tradition in America,* 57.
[25]Ibid., 149.

a people so distrustful of all authority could yield so readily to the authority of the Scriptures as interpreted by men like themselves, that a people so inclined to independence should take their religious ideas at secondhand, that a people so scientific minded should resolutely ignore the impact of science in the realm of religion—all this is difficult to explain, except on fundamentalist grounds.[26]

He goes on to try to explain the phenomenon.

Perhaps it was because religion meant, on the whole, so little: because, divorced as it was from the intimate realities of daily life and excused from active participation in the affairs of business, politics, or society, it could be regarded as a thing apart. . . . Because they rarely subjected their religion to the test of experience and application, they could cherish it as they might cherish some museum piece. . . . For what is striking about fundamentalism is not alone the zeal with which it was maintained or the general acceptance it commanded but the superficiality with which it was observed.[27]

But Commager seemed bothered by this characterization because he also recognized a contradiction in the treatment, inasmuch as "geographically, fundamentalism and lynching seemed to go together." It was a very broad and important movement before World War I, after which it "lost much of its driving force"; and yet even afterward it continued to appeal broadly to "the uneducated and the half-educated," and it fueled much of the energy and influence of Left as well as Right populism in the Klu Klux Klan, William Jennings Bryan, and the militant opposition to the Democratic presidential candidate, Al Smith.[28] Thus Hartz might well have cited Commager to support his assertion that the book on the conservative tradition be written "in the psychiatric vein." And they could have agreed that a broadly based conservative tradition was out of place, erratic, and sporadic in America.

[26]Henry Steele Commager, *The American Mind* (New Haven: Yale University Press, 1950), 178.
[27]Ibid., 179.
[28]Ibid., 180–81.

Few sociologists and even fewer political scientists have systematically studied conservatism, historically or contemporaneously, as ideology, as movement, or as electoral phenomenon. Moreover, when they are not mixing conservatism together with Old Liberalism as an indistinguishable mélange, they are engaging in wishful thinking that even excels that of the historians. The prize for wishful thinking probably goes to Bell for *The End of Ideology* (1965). The subtitle is also interesting: *On the Exhaustion of Political Ideas in the 50s.*[29] Bell also organized and served as editor of the most systematic effort to direct attention of leading sociologists toward the conservative phenomenon of the 1950s. Titles are once again interesting. First published under the title *The New American Right,* it was revised, expanded, and updated with a new title, *The Radical Right.*[30] The contributors numbered among the most important social scientists in the United States, all having made lasting and significant contributions to knowledge about American society and politics. But on the matter of the American Right, it seems to me that they were peculiarly myopic.

As one younger sociologist observed, "Liberal sociologists in the early 1960s spent considerable time on what they called the 'radical Right,' but largely to stress how peripheral it was to the dominant directions of social and political change."[31] Being radical, conservatism was, as observed earlier, considered pathological and a "dependent variable" that could be explained and, ultimately, controlled by controlling its causes. In fact, in his revised chapter in the second, enlarged edition, Hofstadter conceded, "One of the facets of my own essay which I am disposed to regret is its excessive emphasis on

[29]Daniel Bell, *The End of Ideology: On the Exhaustion of Political Ideas in the 50s* (New York: Free Press, 1965).

[30]Daniel Bell, ed., *The New American Right* (New York: Criterion Books, 1955); Bell, *The Radical Right.* Contributors to this volume were Richard Hofstadter, David Reisman, Nathan Glazer, Peter Viereck, Talcott Parsons, Alan Westin, Herbert Hyman, and Seymour Martin Lipset.

[31]Himmelstein, *To the Right,* 1.

what might be called the clinical side of the problem."[32] But despite this extraordinarily candid admission, he immediately went on to say, "A good deal more might have been said on purely behavioral and historical grounds to establish the destructive and 'radical' character of pseudo-conservatism."[33] In other words, conservatism was not a genuine part of the American tradition. If American at all, it was sporadic and played a distorting part. David Riesman, probably the best known of the Bell contributors at that time, put it this way:

> Without the Cold War and the revolutionary ferment in the world . . . the radical Right would have far less of a colorable focus for its resentments. . . . Nevertheless . . . the more we read American history, the more we are struck by the persistence of a secularized crusading spirit, seldom managing to seize power but frequently distorting the political spectrum and creating a climate in which the range of discussion and the possibilities for peaceful change had been foreshortened.[34]

This woeful underestimation of the conservative tradition by leading intellectuals helps explain why conservatism was misunderstood and underestimated by the public at large as well as by other social scientists and by mainstream politicians. But what explains *their* underestimation? As Byron once said of Wordsworth, "Explaining metaphysics to the nation, I wish he would explain his explanation," so should we try to explain the explanation of these social scientists. That would go a long way toward a more complete evaluation of the conservative phenomenon in our own time.

Explaining the Explanation   To begin, it is worth repeating that the consensus among liberal intellectuals to relegate conservatism to the level of pathology is itself part of the explanation. In a way, the prevailing (largely Hartzian) explanation for why there is a liberal tradition and why there is no socialist

[32]Hofstadter, in Bell, *The Radical Right*, 84.
[33]Ibid., 84. For Hofstadter, "true conservatism" was the aristocratic tradition of Europe, especially in England.
[34]Riesman, in Bell, *The Radical Right*, 116.

tradition was just too neat to permit theoretically the existence of a conservative tradition. Hartz is his own best critic,
all the more powerfully because he did not recognize that his
criticism was best directed to himself and to the other liberal
colleagues who were sniffing at the conservative phenomenon in the 1950s: "I believe that this is the basic ethical
problem of the liberal society: not the danger of the majority
which has been its conscious fear, but the danger of unanimity, which has slumbered unconsciously behind it: the 'tyranny of opinion' that Tocqueville saw."[35]

But now to more substantive aspects of an explanation for
why conservatism has been so unappreciated and misunderstood in America. The first element of this is the parochialism
of conservatives. Conservatism, especially American conservatism, is by its nature parochial. The *OED* defines parochial
as referring to matters of the parish, with a second and more
recent definition, that of being narrowly local in orientation.
Parochial has come to have negative connotations, especially
when pitted against such words as *cosmopolitan, sophisticated,*
and *urbane.* The latter are the characteristics necessarily associated with the nation, where conflicting values were likely to
call forth toleration, if not downright relativism. The former,
parochialism, takes on more positive connotations when
associated with such words as *local, decentralized,* and *communitarian.* In fact, as a general rule, *community* is a conservative's
code word; *communities* is for the liberals. American conservatism finds its true expression when matters such as religion
and morality are seated in real localities with real families,
identifiable institutions, real and bounded histories, real and
definable traditions. With parochialism a virtue, conservatives tend also to follow Burke in a disdain for abstraction and
a resistance to philosophy. At the risk of extending this
discussion of parochialism too far, I draw a delicious quote
from Russell Kirk.

[35]Hartz, *The Liberal Tradition in America,* 11.

Innovation . . . comes from the cities, where a man uprooted
seeks to piece together a new world; conservatism always has
had its most loyal adherents in the country, where a man is slow
to break with the old ways that link him with his God. . . .
Thus it was that while [Burke] believed in the rights of English-
men and in certain human rights of universal application, he
despised the "Rights of Man" which Paine and the French
doctrinaires were soon to proclaim inviolable. Edmund Burke
believed in a kind of constitution of civilized peoples. . . . But
the exercise and extent of these rights can be determined only
by prescription and local circumstances.[36]

Parochialism rendered conservatives less concerned, perhaps
even complacent, about public affairs beyond their bailiwick.
For example, although they became fierce anti-Communists in
the 1940s and 1950s—to such an extent that they supported
McCarthyism and were willing to embrace even the most
treasonable former Communists, such as Chambers (once he
invoked such key words as *God* and *home*)—conservatives
were basically isolationist. But isolationism itself can be understood as

the wishful preservation of an old order, which allegedly need
never have been disturbed but for the willful interference of
malevolent elements, Communists and their sympathizers.
The nationalistic overtones center on a phantasy of a happy
"American way" where everything used to be all right. . . .
Also it tends to spill over into a kind of irritated activism. On
the one hand we want to keep out of trouble; but on the other
hand, having identified an enemy, we want to smash him
forthwith. The connection between the two can be seen, for
example, in relation to China, where the phantasy seems to be
that by drastic action it would be possible to "clean up" the
Chinese situation quickly and then our troubles would be over.[37]

But the parochialism and narrower frame of reference did
not render conservatives apolitical. Nor were they antigovernment—a mistaken impression conveyed by the melding of con-

[36]Kirk, *The Conservative Mind*, 19–20.
[37]Talcott Parsons, "Social Strains in America—1955," in Bell, *The Radical Right*,
190–91.

servatism with Old Liberalism. Their perspective on politics and their location within the American Constitution were laid out already in the definitional treatment of conservatism in chapter 1. That could be extended to explain more substantively why conservatism went unnoticed by students of national political and intellectual forces. Liberalism found its natural habitat in the national government, and since presidents, journalists, and political scientists have mostly been liberal in this century (until 1980), liberalism has gotten almost all the attention. There was never a shortage of conservatives. But going to Washington would have been a waste of time for them. You do not go to Washington to change the divorce laws or to clarify adoption or custody of children. You do not go to Washington to tighten compulsory education requirements or to regulate sexual practices or abortion and the status of women.

Take, for example, the Catholic church. Until the 1960s, organizations for or sponsored by the Catholic church were not much seen or heard in Washington. The National Catholic Welfare Conference (NCWC) was the most important Catholic lobby in Washington, and the representation of Catholic institutional interests "was really the Conference's reason for being."[38] However, although it was a potential vehicle for national political activity, NCWC was not strongly supported by the American Catholic bishops; not all bishops attended annual meetings, its statements were rarely presented as the collected pronouncement of the entire Catholic hierarchy, and "bishops often paid their tax to the national office in the quiet hope that their fealty ended with the mailing of a check." Important metropolitan archbishops and cardinals had such a modest opinion of the Washington operation that they rarely permitted their priests to work there.[39] It was not until the

[38]Luke Ebersole, from his book, *Church Lobbying in the Nations' Capital* (New York: Macmillan, 1951); quoted in Timothy Byrnes, *Catholic Bishops in American Politics* (Princeton: Princeton University Press, 1991), 47.

[39]Byrnes, *Catholic Bishops in American Politics*, 47–48; the quote is that of George A. Kelly, *The Battle for the American Church* (Garden City: Doubleday, 1979), 370, as quoted in Byrnes, p. 48.

mid-1960s that the bishops formally established the National Conference of Catholic Bishops (NCCB) as their official national body for the purpose of taking solidary and authoritative positions on national political issues. *Commonweal*, an important Catholic lay journal, wrote approvingly that the "unwieldy and largely voluntary association of bishops [was] being shaped into a viable instrument with power adequate to national problems."[40] But all the while, the Catholic church and various organizations sponsored by the Catholic church had been a powerful presence in every state capital and in most of the big cities. It is neither accidental nor gratuitous that the headquarters of the archbishop in New York City, located in the shadow of St. Patrick's Cathedral, was traditionally referred to, by *local* politicians, as "the powerhouse."

Conservatives and the New Deal

This gives rise to a separate, fascinating question: If there was a genuine conservative tradition in America, why did it not surface and organize against allegedly the greatest assault on conservatism, the New Deal? This is not a tangential question, because the answer to it will advance the explanation we seek for why conservatism went so long unappreciated and lost inside somebody else's party and somebody else's definition of conservatism.

In the first place, the question just posed is based on a false premise, that the New Deal was a particular assault on conservatism. If it was an assault on anything, it was an assault on Old Liberalism, not on conservatism. Since conservatism is a statist public philosophy, there was nothing about the expansion of the national government in the 1930s that would, in itself, be an assault on conservatism. But it is possible to be a good bit more specific than that. The traditional view of conservatives toward capitalism ranges from deep moral antagonism to practical sociological concern, with rarely more than two cheers in its favor. We have already confronted the

[40]Quoted in Byrnes, *Catholic Bishops in American Politics*, 49.

profound opposition of conservatism to unrestrained wants and to the purely voluntary and individualized notion of contract. The long passage drawn from Edmund Burke in chapter 1 to help define the conservative point of view could be reiterated here to document more specifically conservatism's view of capitalism as problematic at best, motivated by greed, caustic to community values. We shall see later how dedicated many American conservative intellectuals have been to make a philosophic and moral concordance between conservatism and capitalism; but we shall also see that the best they can accomplish is a coalition, not a concordance. This being the case, conservatives could well view many, if not most, of the policy efforts of the New Deal as a defense of community and family values.

Another choice quote comes from former Congressman John Rankin, Democrat of Mississippi, known throughout the country in the 1930s, 1940s, and 1950s as a rabid right-wing reactionary. But on matters involving national politics during the New Deal, Rankin sounded more like a Bolshevik. Speaking in 1933 to an assembly of disabled World War I veterans, Rankin said,

> I am for taxing profits of the late war in order to take care of the deficit, care for our disabled veterans, redistribute the wealth of the nation, and lift the burden of taxation from those least able to bear it. I am told that Andrew W. Mellon himself has an income of $30 million a year. If I had my way we would put a wound stripe on his purse big enough to be seen from Pittsburgh to Philadelphia.[41]

Rankin was a genuine conservative with a conservative's concern about capitalism and a national elite of wealth, combined with a conservative's willingness to use the state to defend community and family values. Practically the entire conservative wing of the Democratic party shared Rankin's view, and they were generally stalwart supporters of Roose-

[41]Quoted in Denis W. Brogan, *The American Political System* (London: Hamish Hamilton, 1943), 12.

velt in Congress — as long as Roosevelt stayed away from racial issues and trod lightly around race and class (labor) issues.

An important recent study statistically confirms these observations. On four of the six categories of public policy at the very core of the New Deal, southern Democrats voted with the nonsouthern Democrats in support of FDR roughly 87 percent of the time. By contrast, Old Liberal Republicans opposed these measures with almost equal consistency. The opposition of southern conservatives to expanding the authority of the national government "focused very specifically on interventions into the region's race relations and labor markets."[42] Using the national government to regulate capitalism and to put a floor under poverty would hardly have gotten through Congress without the cooperation of the many Southerners who not only contributed their votes but chaired most of the key legislative committees. Even on questions of labor regulation the southern conservatives cooperated with Roosevelt as long as agriculture and domestic labor were excluded from the jurisdiction of the new regulatory agencies.[43]

Conservative acceptance of the basic New Deal programs was not limited to the southern Democratic conservatives. Although the bulk of the Republican party opposed the New Deal domestic legislation, as many as 20 percent of Republican members of Congress could be expected to defect on particular roll calls, and one could be sure that most of these defectors were conservatives. Many years later, George Will gave the relevant reasons for the willingness of many conservatives to support the basic principles of the American welfare state.

> Two conservatives (Disraeli and Bismarck) pioneered the welfare state, and did so for impeccably conservative reasons: To

[42]Ira Katznelson, Kim Geiger, and Daniel Kryder, "Limiting Liberalism: The Southern Veto in Congress, 1933–1950," *Political Science Quarterly* 108, no. 2 (Summer 1993): 292–94.

[43]See also Suzanne Mettler, "Dual Citizenship: Gender, the State and the New Deal," Ph.D. dissertation, Cornell University, 1994.

reconcile the masses to the vicissitudes and hazards of a dynamic and hierarchical industrial economy. . . . A welfare state is certainly important to, and probably indispensable to, social cohesion, and hence the national strength. A welfare state is implied by conservative rhetoric. A welfare state can be an embodiment of a wholesome ethic of common provision.[44]

This kind of conservatism—Burkean or patrician—was not prominently promoted by the Republican right wing in the 1930s and 1940s, because they were so few in Congress and had so little institutional power, whatever their specific views of the New Deal policies might have been. That becomes more interesting in the context of the role and influence of Republican conservatism when the country voted in a Republican Congress in 1946—the famous Eightieth Congress.

The most important action by the Eightieth Congress was, of course, the Taft-Hartley Act of 1947. Denounced vociferously by organized labor as a reactionary effort to "turn the clock back" to pre-1933, or for that matter pre-1905, and vetoed at labor's urging by President Truman, Taft-Hartley was far from a labor-busting law or a repeal of the Wagner Act (NLRA). Taft-Hartley was a step in the right direction for Old Liberals in the GOP, but it did not go far enough for them precisely because it did not turn the clock back to pre-1905.[45] This is because Taft-Hartley was more conservative than Old Liberal. The act did not even seek seriously to alter the basic provisions of NLRA.[46] It added provisions defining certain

[44]Will, *Statecraft as Soulcraft*, 126–27.

[45]The year 1905 was the year the Supreme Court gave us *Lochner v. New York*, which provided that government could not intervene between an employee and an employer because that would violate the doctrine of "liberty of contract," which is between free and equal individuals. Although *Lochner* was a case involving the power of state governments under the Fourteenth Amendment, it did most clearly articulate the attitude prevailing at that time that to protect the individual worker either by laws regarding hours and working conditions or by laws providing the opportunity for laborers to organize into unions would be unconstitutional as well as contrary to rational economic practice.

[46]It did amend NLRA by narrowing the definition of employees to be covered by NLRA, but it did not alter the status of the vast majority of American workers that were covered by NLRA.

unfair practices engaged in by unions to balance the unfair management practices in sections 7 and 8 of the original NLRA. A second genuine conservative feature—and the most famous or infamous feature of the act—was section 14(b) amending NLRA to give states the power to outlaw union shop agreements in plants within the physical boundaries of that state. This is typical conservatism—making it possible to have forty-eight (at that time) different labor statutes rather than one national statute covering the whole "free market." Nevertheless, the principle of government intervention on behalf of labor was not altered but strengthened by Taft-Hartley. The Supreme Court had only barely validated this principle ten years before, and it can only have been strengthened by bringing labor into some equivalent restraints.[47]

But all things considered, the Eightieth Congress will be better remembered for what it did *not* do. It did alter the income tax structure to ease the burden on higher brackets; but it did *not* seek to alter the structure or philosophy of progressive income taxation. It did cut appropriations for soil conservation and the crop storage aspects of agriculture price support policies; but it did *not* seek to alter the basic structure of the most important and costliest of policies, the Agricultural Adjustment Administration (AAA) price support/acreage control program itself. It rejected President Truman's request to extend Social Security and public housing; but it did *not* produce any bills confronting any New Deal welfare state policies head-on. And all this was in the context of an Eightieth Congress that had demonstrated its ability to pass legislation over a weak president's veto.

Robert Taft's loss of the 1952 Republican presidential nomination and General Eisenhower's eventual victory was an important turning point for conservatism. Taft had become Senate majority leader and had managed to put his most

---

[47]*NLRB v. Jones and Laughlin Steel Corporation* and four companion cases were all decided by 5–4 votes. For good coverage of the Taft-Hartley Act in relation to Wagner, see Charles O. Gregory and Harold A. Katz, *Labor and the Law*, 3d ed. (New York: W. W. Norton, 1979), chap. 12.

conservative allies into strategic committee and parliamentary posts, pushing many Eisenhower friends to the periphery.[48] But this produced no efforts to eliminate the basic New Deal system. What galled the Taft conservatives was not Eisenhower's willingness to go along with the fundamentals of the New Deal but the peripheral aspects of his program—to be blunt, the pork barrel stuff. Taft was apoplectic when informed by President Eisenhower that the $9.5 billion deficit in the 1954 budget (the last drawn up by the Truman administration) could only be cut to $5.5 billion. This confirmed the view he had expressed personally to Eisenhower during the 1952 campaign, that it "would be more difficult to combat a Republican New Deal than a Democratic one."[49] Taft died toward the end of 1953, too early to witness confirmation of his fears, with Republican sponsorship of the vast Interstate Highway System, made more palatable with the change of title to "National Defense Highway System."

Conservatives Against the Republican Party

One after another, the conservatives were leaving the Eisenhower camp. The split was expressed publicly in a 1956 editorial debate in the pages of the *National Review* on the very significant and indicative question, "Should conservatives vote for Eisenhower-Nixon?"[50] By the end of the 1950s, most of the genuine conservatives within the Republican party were about ready to do as Rusher had already done in 1954, to put conservative first and Republican second, or nowhere at all. There was one final provocation, the straw that broke the elephant's back: the Compact of Fifth Avenue, 1960.

On Manhattan's Fifth Avenue, slightly to the north of all the fancy shops, Nelson Rockefeller had his New York lodging, a thirty-two-room apartment, to which he summoned Richard Nixon on July 23, just two days prior to the opening of the 1960

---

[48]William Manchester, *The Glory and the Dream* (Boston: Little, Brown, 1974), 655.

[49]Quoted in Green, *Shaping Political Consciousness*, 224.

[50]Reported in Green, *Shaping Political Consciousness*, 227–29.

Republican presidential nominating convention. Nixon was fearful of a divisive fight over the nomination or the platform, and his willingness to meet Rockefeller on Rockefeller's terms indicated his vulnerability. The compact they signed was more in the nature of a Nixon capitulation. The two men virtually rewrote the Republican platform to include fourteen Rockefeller provisions, all of which committed Nixon and the Republican party to a much more positive—that is, Demo-cratic—government. They phoned the provisions to Chicago to be incorporated into the platform even though the platform committee had already finished its work.[51]

The conservatives immediately reacted with expressions of disgust and threat of revolt. Senator Goldwater, who was just becoming the darling of the conservatives, denounced the compact as "the Munich of the Republican party." This pro-jected Goldwater before the convention as an alternative presidential candidate for 1960. Eventually Goldwater permit-ted his name to be placed in nomination by his own state of Arizona, and then, by prearrangement, he addressed the convention and requested that his name be withdrawn in favor of solidarity behind the Nixon ticket in November. (This was a courtesy not returned by the liberal Republicans four years later when it was Goldwater's candidacy.)

Another, more lasting response to the compact was the formation of the Young Americans for Freedom (YAF) in September to capitalize on the thousands of conservative activists still in or just out of college, "who were now furious at the GOP and unwilling any longer to confine their politick-ing to the Young Republican Federation."[52] Their program, referred to as the Sharon Statement, named for the Buckley family estate in Sharon, Connecticut, where the conservative youth organization was founded, was probably the first sus-tained and systematic statement of a political platform strictly

[51]The account of the compact comes from Peter Collier and David Horowitz, *The Rockefellers,* 338–43; and Theodore H. White, *The Making of the President 1960* (New York: Atheneum, 1961), 208–25.

[52]Rusher, *The Rise of the Right,* 89.

for genuine conservatives. It stressed "this time of moral and political crisis," and it played hard on the dependence of political freedom on economic freedom and the dependence of economic freedom on "the preservation of internal order."[53] It continually stressed the virtues of "the market economy," but this was framed within a Constitution that gave "primacy to the several states." Thus the document, though full of verbal fealty to the market economy, was also full of morality and order, and victory, seeing no logical problem between them. It insisted on the market economy and on the primacy of the states without any sense that a market economy (to a genuine libertarian) would choke on the idea of primacy of *any* state. It concluded on the conservative's strongest foreign policy belief, that "the United States should stress victory, rather than coexistence with, [international communism]."[54]

A related post-1960 reaction by the conservatives was of equal import for the future of conservative politics: the formation of the Conservative party in New York. The Conservative party was never designed to be a national third party. Its purpose was to organize New York conservatives to deal with Governor Rockefeller. Organizations like the New York Conservative party and YAF were particularly significant because they were genuinely political organizations, indeed electorally oriented ideological organizations, that would provide conservatives with political channels that would encourage sustained activity in the national political discourse.

There was greater incentive to remain formally within the GOP after Nixon's loss to Kennedy in the 1960 election, because that left the Republicans without any recognizable national leadership. With a vacuum in the national Republican organization and with a nascent organization, the conservatives returned with renewed interest to reformation from within.

Goldwater was the perfect conservative candidate: a "Sunbelt Republican," Episcopalian but with ties to a Jewish family

[53]Quoted in Rusher, *The Rise of the Right*, 90–91.
[54]Ibid., 91.

back in New York which had been active in Democratic machine politics (a Goldwater relation was a partner in the law firm of Goldwater and Flynn, that is to say, Ed Flynn, Democratic boss of the Bronx), and a loyal Republican despite his dissidence. Goldwater's conservative leadership was established with the publication of his book, *The Conscience of a Conservative,* which was cobbled together out of Goldwater's speeches written by Buckley brother-in-law Brent Bozell and others. Ultimately it allegedly sold 3,500,000 copies.[55] Goldwater sincerely embraced a combination of genuine, Old Conservatism and radical Old Liberalism. His faith in free market competition existed within an overlay of the Goldwater that was remembered best for the aphorism in his speech accepting the presidential nomination in 1964: "I would remind you that extremism in the defense of liberty is no vice! And let me remind you also that moderation in the pursuit of justice is no virtue!" That little ditty was composed by one of the archconservative philosophers in academia, Harry Jaffa of Claremont Men's College.

Goldwater had kept faith with the mainstream Republicans by urging everyone to pull together for Richard Nixon in 1960, but he also inspired the populist conservative distrust of eastern Republicanism and the conspiratorial way in which the Old Guard Republican liberals controlled the party. The following example is an allegation by one of the most ideological of conservatives, Phyllis Schlafly, explaining how liberal Republicans had defeated conservative Republicans for presidential nominations in the previous series of elections.

> It wasn't any accident, it was planned that way. In each of the losing presidential years, a small group of secret king makers, using hidden persuaders and psychological warfare techniques, manipulated the Republican national convention to nominate candidates who had sidestepped or suppressed key issues.[56]

[55]Ibid., 88.

[56]Quoted in Seymour Martin Lipset and Earl Rabb, *The Politics of Unreason: Right-wing Extremism in America, 1790–1970* (New York: Harper & Row, 1970), 258–59.

Barry Goldwater went down to ignominious defeat at the hands of Lyndon Johnson in 1964. But in his own way, Goldwater was victorious, in that he was the link or the bridge that made the Reagan Revolution possible. The following is Rusher's evaluation of 1964, and it is accurate enough to deserve extensive quotation.

1. It handed the Republican party over—permanently, as matters turned out—to a new and basically conservative coalition based on the South, the Southwest, and the West, ending the long hegemony of the relatively liberal East in the GOP's affairs.
2. It sensitized large numbers of previously dormant conservatives, turned them into political activists, and introduced them to each other through direct-mail techniques.
3. It launched the political career of Ronald Reagan and thereby provided the conservative movement with its most important political leader.[57]

Those linkages between the Republican party and the Right were personal, organizational, and institutional. But still another linkage had to be forged—the ideological one. Some kind of concordance—an ideological or philosophic concordance—would have to be made between Old Liberalism and the genuine conservatism with which we are concerned here. Without that concordance, there would be hell to pay, because, as observed earlier, the Republican party could not maintain a coalition among its contradictory partners on the basis of patronage alone. Being the Old Liberal, antigovernment party, the Republican party was not as free as the Democratic party of New Liberals to rely on patronage—particularly if it meant expanding government in order to expand the patronage base.

THE STRUGGLE FOR CONCORDANCE BETWEEN
OLD LIBERAL AND CONSERVATIVE

Almost all people wish to believe that their motives and their morality are in agreement; almost all people would like to

[57]Rusher, *The Rise of the Right*, 161–62.

believe that their heroes and leaders are, like themselves, acting according to their beliefs. And although most Americans also espouse the ideal of separation of church and state, they persist in the expectation that the state accepts the teaching of the church (however that is defined) and has church blessing. But among all Americans, conservatives have had the strongest urge for concordance between morality and motive and thus between church and state. Moreover, even if it is basic to their conservative nature and not to that of the Old Liberals to seek this kind of concordance, they would eventually get every kind of encouragement from the mainstream Old Liberal segments of the Republican party to demonstrate that God loves the market and that to God the market is not greed but giving, not selfishness but service. Why should any genuine capitalist object to such an effort? Why should any leader within the mainstream of the Republican party say anything against any effort that could make their collaboration with the Right stronger than merely a coalition?

Concordance—Early Efforts, Deep Chasm

Long before the conservatism of the current era, there had of course been efforts to make ethical concordances between capitalism and morality. Social Darwinism might be considered the most prominent as well as the most systematic effort to make such a concordance. Evolution was tied to progress, and the fittest who survived bitter economic competition were by implication morally as well as physiologically superior, because their survival advanced civilization. It is no wonder that Herbert Spencer considered Andrew Carnegie one of his closest friends as well as his patron.[58]

But the efforts most relevant to building concordances between Old Liberals and conservatives today are of somewhat more recent vintage. One notable and instructive example is the effort of Bruce Barton. A staunch, highly partisan

[58]Hofstadter, *The American Political Tradition*, 168.

Republican who served for a time in Congress, Barton is probably best remembered for his isolationism and its recognition by President Roosevelt in his attack in 1940 against "Martin, Barton and Fish." Perhaps his most lasting accomplishment was the founding of the great advertising firm of Batten, Barton, Durstine and Osburn (BBD&O). In 1925, Barton published a book entitled *The Man Nobody Knows,* in which he argued that Jesus himself was a businessman, indeed "the founder of modern business." Jesus "sold" a new religion by applying the "principles of modern salesmanship." Barton argued further that if Jesus had lived in the 1920s he would have preached, along with Barton, the message that satisfaction should be placed above self-denial, that luxury should be placed above hardship, and that spending should be placed above thrift. As a "great Companion, a wonderful Friend, a kindly, indulgent, joy-loving Father," Jesus would have been a great capitalist in the twentieth century.[59]

Many in active political and journalistic life who considered themselves genuine conservatives operated as though the connection between capitalism and Christianity were so logical and natural that little if any effort at concordance was really necessary. Ronald Reagan, from about the time he became the major public spokesperson for General Electric in the 1950s, believed in the natural concordance of capitalism and Christianity as a self-evident truth. Many more thoughtful people agreed. Beginning with his inaugural book, *God and Man at Yale,* William Buckley threw the two together. Here is an approving account of Buckley by Rusher.

> The [Yale] Department of Economics, he demonstrated, not to mention those of politics and sociology, was awash with "collectivists" and all but devoid of advocates of "individualism," while the Departments of Religion and Philosophy were largely in the grip of avowed atheists and agnostics. . . . Buckley openly suggested that if Yale was indeed supposed to be a

[59]Bruce Barton, *The Man Nobody Knows* (New York: Bobbs-Merrill, 1925).

fundamentally Christian institution and a pillar of the free-enterprise system, its alumni were not, to put it mildly, getting their money's worth.

"Individualism" (i.e., free-enterprise economics) and the Christian tradition! Here, in this first book by a 25-year-old graduate of Yale, one sees an early example of the meshing of two of the three principal strands of post-war conservative thought: traditionalism and classical liberalism.[60]

Rusher was not unaware of the tension between the two "principal strands of post-war conservative thought." For example, he included in his autobiography a long excerpt from an article by Murray Rothbard, the most orthodox of libertarian intellectuals, denouncing the conservative movement of the 1950s. The following is a small portion of Rothbard's article.

[The modern conservative movement] . . . combined a traditionalist and theocratic approach to "moral values," occasional lip service to free-market economics, and an imperialist and global interventionist foreign policy dedicated to the glorification of the American state and the extirpation of world Communism. *Classical liberalism* remained only as rhetoric, useful in *attracting business support, and most of all as a fig leaf for the grotesque realities of the New Right.* . . .

In a few brief years the character of the Right wing had been totally transformed: Once basically classical liberal, it had become a global theocratic crusade.[61]

According to Rothbard, the chasm between liberalism and conservatism could hardly be wider or deeper. Yet all Rusher could do was to denounce Rothbard's treatment as "a grotesque caricature." Rusher then turned to Russell Kirk, of all people, for his defense.

These two bodies of opinion [conservative and libertarian] share a detestation of collectivism. They set their faces against

---

[60]Quote from Rusher, *The Rise of the Right*, 39. The third was anticommunism.
[61]Quote of Rothbard from Rusher, *The Rise of the Right*, 83–84. My emphasis. The full text of the Rothbard article will be found in *Inquiry*, 27 October 1980, "Requiem for the Old Right," 24–26.

the totalist state and the heavy hand of bureaucracy. That much is obvious enough.[62]

Not content with that much of Kirk's argument, Rusher went on with just enough Kirk to hang himself.

What else do conservatives and libertarians profess in common? The answer to that question is simple: nothing. Nor will they ever have. *To talk of forming a league or coalition between these two is like advocating a union of ice and fire.*

The ruinous failing of the ideologues who call themselves libertarians is their fanatic attachment to a simple solitary principle—that is, to the notion of personal freedom as the whole end of the civil social order, and indeed of human existence. . . . [On the contrary, the] great line of division in modern politics . . . lies between all those who believe in some sort of transcendent moral order, on one side, and on the other side all those who take this ephemeral existence of ours with a be-all and end-all—to be devoted chiefly to producing and consuming. In this discrimination between the sheep and the goats, *the libertarian must be classified with the goats—that is, as utilitarians admitting no transcendent sanctions for conduct.*[63]

Rusher included the Kirk passage without appearing to recognize that Kirk's argument was deepening the chasm between genuine conservatism and classical liberalism (libertarianism). Compare it with the presumably more profound and self-conscious William Buckley.

I had always been taught . . . that an active faith in God and a rigid adherence to Christian principles are the most powerful influences toward the good life. I also believed . . . that free enterprise and limited government had served this country well. . . .

These two attitudes were basic to my general outlook. One concerned the role of man in the universe; the other . . . the role of man in his society. . . . I therefore looked eagerly to Yale University for allies against secularism and collectiv-

[62]Quote from Russell Kirk in Rusher, *The Rise of the Right,* 84. My emphasis. The full text of Kirk's article will be found in "Libertarians: The Chirping Sectaries," *Modern Age* (Fall 1981): 345.

[63]Kirk, in Rusher, *The Rise of the Right,* 85.

ism, . . . against those who seek to subvert religion and individualism. . . .

I contended that the trustees of Yale, along with the vast
majority of alumni, are committed to the desirability of fostering both a belief in God, and a recognition of the merits of our
economic system. I therefore concluded that as our educational
overseers, it was the clear responsibility of trustees to guide the
teaching at Yale toward those ends.[64]

This was going to make the concordance between the two all
the more difficult, but also all the more necessary. With such
founding fathers as Rusher and Buckley throwing the two
elements together without feeling the need to construct a
concordance, the job was going to have to fall to activists with
a stronger philosophic commitment than that of Rusher or
Buckley. Two such candidates are George Gilder and Michael
Novak.

George Gilder and a Protestant Effort

In a title worthy of the great nineteenth-century economic
theorists, *Wealth and Poverty,* George Gilder sought valiantly
to make the concordance once and for all between capitalism
and morality (we ought to say capitalism and Protestant
morality) by reducing Adam Smith himself to the status of a
thinker of limited imagination, full of mechanistic fallacies.
As John Diggins put it, "Gilder boldly revises 2,000 years of
intellectual history, rendering wrong-headed not only Jesus
and Marx but Adam Smith himself. . . . Gilder tells us that
Smith was wrong to assume that behind the 'invisible hand'
of the marketplace were the motives of 'selfishness,' 'avarice,'
and 'greed.'"[65] And as Gilder puts it eloquently for himself,

Adam Smith was at once an intellectual who shared all the
typical prejudices against the business class and a libertarian
conservative who knew the value of freedom and enterprise.
His solution was to locate the source of wealth not in the

[64]Buckley, *God and Man at Yale,* xiii–xiv.
[65]John P. Diggins, *The Lost Soul of American Politics: Virtue, Self-Interest, and the
Foundations of Liberalism* (Chicago: University of Chicago Press, 1986), 337.

creative activities of businessmen but in the "invisible hand" of the market. Smith believed that capitalism worked not because of the virtues of capitalists but because of the "great machine" of exchange that converted their apparent greeds and vices into economic value.[66]

As though gritting his teeth, Gilder goes on to quote from Smith:

Not from benevolence do we expect bread from the baker . . . but from his self-love. . . . In spite of their natural selfishness and rapacity, though they mean only their conveniency, though the sole end which they propose from the labors of all the thousands they employ, be the gratification of their own vain and unsatiable desires . . . they are led by an invisible hand . . . without intending it, without knowing it, to advance the interest of society.[67]

Gilder continues, "In essence, Smith and his followers believe that the wealth of nations springs from a kind of Faustian pact: a deal with the devil through which humans gain wealth by giving in to greed and avarice."[68]

Gilder moves from there to his own position with a linking observation that "such a vision . . . is unattractive to most religious or otherwise idealistic thinkers and simply unbelievable to the average man. It seems preposterous to most people to say that the way to create a good and bountiful society is to give maximum freedom to a group of predatory philistines. But to intellectuals this theory had the crucial advantage of praising capitalism without exalting capitalists."[69]

According to Gilder, Smith's error was in founding his theory "on the mechanism of market exchanges" rather than on the capitalists. What Smith, according to Gilder, takes as self-interest is not avarice at all but simply a "mutual transfer of information." Smith's analysis fails because it was stuck on greed and subordinated a "higher and more complex level of

---

[66]George Gilder, *Wealth and Poverty* (New York: Bantam Books, 1981), 35–36.
[67]Adam Smith, as quoted in Gilder, *Wealth and Poverty*, 36.
[68]Gilder, *Wealth and Poverty*, 36.
[69]Ibid.

activity—the creation of value." Smith had put his faith in mechanism when man "is at the heart of capitalist growth." Gilder then goes on with his more positive argument, which is based on the simple assertion that "capitalism begins with giving. Not from greed, avarice, or even self-love can one expect the rewards of commerce, but from a spirit closely akin to altruism, a regard for the needs of others, a benevolent, outgoing, and courageous temper of mind."[70]

This is the concordance according to Gilder—a leap of faith over the chasm. He is not trying to say that for two hundred years we have all misunderstood and misinterpreted Adam Smith. Quite the contrary. To Gilder, Smith has been properly interpreted and he is all wrong. The capitalist system is not based on self-interest at all, or greed or avarice, as Smith argued. According to Gilder, capitalism is based on altruism, Christian charity. Gilder not only grounds this in Western, Judeo-Christian notions of God and the sacred sources relating to that but also in the anthropology of primitive societies that engage in various forms of giving—for example, "pot-latch"—as an essential feature of economic distribution and redistribution.

It is not my intention here to engage in an elaborate refutation of Gilder's effort. I cite and draw extensively from his argument to document the boldness and strenuousness of the efforts on the part of the Right to establish this concordance between capitalism and Christianity, or capitalism and morality. My personal opinion is that Gilder is his own refutation. But what is more important is the political question of whether the argument is convincing to the many hundreds of politicians and millions of voters who are seeking such a concordance in order to find comfort in the relationship between the apparent greed of "the pursuit of happiness" and the counsels of the major Western religions.

---

[70]This is a refrain repeated in several instances; see Gilder, *Wealth and Poverty*, 23 and 37.

Michael Novak and a Catholic Concordance

Finally, by far the most dedicated and systematic effort at concordance is that of Michael Novak.[71] Novak not only recognized and appreciated the chasm; he saw beyond the need to make the traditionalist conservative more comfortable with capitalism and looked toward a larger constituency that needed more than the smoothing out of logical glitches. The need was to meld capitalism and Christianity in a way that could bring together the disparate and antagonistic elements of Christianity — within the Catholic church, between Catholics and Protestants, and between mainstream Protestants and populist Protestants ("populist" in this instance being a euphemism for lower-class).

Although most observant Protestants have tended toward the Right in politics, especially in their support for state laws concerning social status and moral conduct, they have on occasion been turned toward a strong statism of the Left, as if to confirm the old contention that "Christianity is the religion of which socialism is the practice." And as we shall see directly below, the very concept of "social justice" came out of an important papal encyclical of 1933, and many see the Sermon on the Mount as socialist. To a conservative like Novak, a concordance with capitalism would be a great contribution to social order in America. Others might be able to use such a concordance to cement more tightly the Republican party coalition. For Novak, the stakes were even larger than that.

To accomplish his mission, Novak had to take on virtually everybody who had ever tried to discover and develop a wholly scientific, internal dynamic of capitalism. Adam Smith's *Wealth of Nations* and its complete reliance on the internal dynamic, which Smith called the invisible hand, demonstrates how this dynamic transforms private vice into public virtue. Novak tried first to counter Smith's market theory

[71]Novak, *The Catholic Ethic and the Spirit of Capitalism*. Page references to Novak are in parentheses in the text.

with Smith's own *Theory of Moral Sentiments,* as though Smith's
recognition that "man" has morality and sympathy means
that capitalism is driven by morality rather than by greed and
rational calculation (8). But it turned out that there is really no
way morality can shake hands with the invisible hand; in
Smith's *Wealth of Nations,* there is an undeniable and un-
bridgeable chasm between morality and capitalism. So, in
effect, Novak resigned himself to this genuine lack of concordance in Smith by tossing Smith in among the other intellectuals in a section of his book entitled "The Anticapitalist Bias
of Intellectuals," suggesting that people like Smith could not
truly appreciate the morality of capitalism because, as an
eighteenth-century student of theology (and recall that virtually all university students then were students of theology),
Smith was subjected to the theology of his time, with its roots
in the land, the landholders, and rural peasants—therefore in
a time that was "adversarial to both commerce and manufac-
turing" (105). To Novak, Smith's education gave him a primor-
dial prejudice. In sum, Novak's is a bold confrontation with
the whole tradition of classical economics, in which it is the
very amorality of capitalism that makes an economic science
possible and an economic system efficient.

Just over one hundred years after *Wealth of Nations,* Pope
Leo XIII issued his famous encyclical, *Rerum Novarum* (1891),
in which he tried to modernize Church teaching and to bring
the Church out of the isolation into which Leo's predecessor,
Pius IX, had pushed it by his "hostility to the world of his
time" (37). Although Pope Leo, according to Novak, "pre-
dicted with remarkable accuracy the futility of socialism"
(60), he also judged (consistent with Catholic views before
and since) that liberal-capitalist society was also to be condemned (1) for misconceiving humans as radically individualist and isolated from others (except through contract) and
(2) for assuming that all human beings are equal and are
expected to compete with others on equal terms (50). Capitalism thus left too many at the mercy of the few and "handed
over the workers, each alone and defenseless, to the inhu-

manity of employers and the unbridled greed of competitors" (50).

So, beyond what Novak asserts, Pope Leo's extraordinary document of 1891 seemed prescient on both socialism *and* capitalism. But in Novak's view, the pope was mistaken about capitalism. Granted, capitalism might inculcate habits of choice based solely on profit and loss, hard-heartedness, and cruelty (in a word, greed); but Leo, according to Novak, was resting his judgment on a

> hidden premise [that] liberal capitalism is a single-minded, unrestrained system, subject to no checks and balances (from the civil law and from the political and moral systems, for example). In such a tripartite system, instrumentalist thinking may be restricted to those aspects of life for which it is appropriate. It should be vigorously repelled when it encroaches on other spheres. This institutional pluralism disrupts rationalism; it encourages practical wisdom. The rationalist conceit [is] at the heart of socialism. (53)

It is amazing that Novak would attribute rationalism ("the rationalist conceit") only to socialism, because rationalism, or to put it in modern terms, rational choice, is at the heart of capitalism. This is precisely what makes capitalism generally antagonistic to government—any government, socialist or otherwise.

Novak attempts to get around Pope Leo's problem by use of some intellectual sleight of hand with the invisible hand. He sneaks in moral order and "checks and balances" as forces that restrict "instrumentalist thinking . . . to those aspects of life for which it is appropriate." In other words, capitalism can be saved from its "rationalist conceit" by morality and democracy. But, of course, that is no longer capitalism; it is the imposition of moral and political constraints *from the outside* that, from the perspective of capitalism itself, must be considered irrational.[72] In this matter, Novak is behaving not as a

[72]For views by serious Old Liberal or "laissez-faire" economists of politics as the source of irrationality in the economy, see James Buchanan, *The Limits of*

philosopher but as a raw ideologist to the extent that he is suggesting that capitalism has internalized the morality that has been imposed on it by society, by law, *and by government* from the outside. All genuine conservatives and all liberals (New as well as Old) agree that certain moral and legal constraints must be imposed from the outside on capitalism and that the successful imposition of these constraints does produce a capitalism with which a society can survive and thrive. Here in fact is the essential dividing line between liberals and socialists—for whom no mere moral or ethical restraints on capitalism would be enough. But this connection between capitalist rationality and *any* morality imposed on it from the outside does not amount to "moral capitalism." It is a matter of competing principles and competing institutions, not integration and concordance.

Novak's Failure, Pope John Paul II, and the Shades of James Madison

Novak's search for a conservative and Catholic capitalism took him also to the great sociologist and economic theorist Max Weber and his renowned book, *The Protestant Ethic and the Spirit of Capitalism.* The significance of this book for Novak can be seen in Novak's choice of title for his own book. Here in brief is Weber's own statement of the ethic.

> [The] bourgeois businessman . . . as long as his moral conduct was spotless and the use to which he put his wealth was not objectionable, could follow his pecuniary interests as he would and feel that he was fulfilling a duty in doing so. The power of religious asceticism provided him in addition with sober, conscientious, and unusually industrious workmen, who clung to their work as to a life purpose willed by God.
>
> The peculiarity of *this philosophy of avarice* appears to be the ideal of the honest man of recognized credit, and above all the idea of a duty of the individual toward the increase of his

Liberty: Between Anarchy and Leviathan (Chicago: University of Chicago Press, 1975); James Buchanan and Gordon Tullock, *The Calculus of Consent* (Ann Arbor: University of Michigan Press, 1962); and William Niskanen, *Bureaucracy and Representative Government* (Chicago: Aldine-Atherton, 1971).

capital, which is assumed as an end in itself. Truly what is here preached is not simply a means of making one's way in the world, but a peculiar ethic. The infraction of its rules is treated not only as foolishness but as forgetfulness of duty. That is the essence of the matter. It is not mere business astuteness, that sort of thing is common enough, it is an ethos. This is the quality which interests us. (Weber, quoted in Novak, 3–4; Novak's emphasis)

Novak then asks, do many real human beings actually share in such an ethos? (3) He answers, no; and he is correct. But one must bear in mind that Weber always liked to deal with what he himself called "ideal typical" categories. Today these might be called models or paradigms. As with his famous definition of bureaucracy, his definition of this ethos, being idealized, is not supposed to fit particular persons or situations. Moreover, there is absolutely nothing new in Weber's definition or the list of characteristics that abstractly define the spirit of capitalism: the sense of duty toward acquisition of wealth for its own sake; willingness to risk one's wealth by buying cheap and selling dear to beat the competition; asceticism in avoiding luxury; and a sense of calling, such that work is undertaken conscientiously. Whether that characterization is correct (as I believe) or incorrect (as Novak and others seem to believe), Weber's is a pretty straightforward extension or application of Smith. What is new is Weber's grounding *in religion* of his explanation for the spirit of capitalism. But bear in mind also that this for Weber was a *functional* explanation, not an argument that there is an ethical or spiritual concordance between religion and capitalism.

No treatment of Weber can serve the purpose that Novak seeks to fulfill. In fact, as Novak and others have demonstrated, Weber's thesis taken liberally is rather silly. But what is even sillier is Novak's argument that a disconfirmation of Weber confirms the converse: "By Weber's own testimony, the Calvinist ethic imposed many moral constraints upon capitalist behavior" (6–7). The ethic Weber described was an ethic of pure selfishness or avarice; *but since it is an ethic,* that seemed to be enough linkage for Novak's proposition later on that "without the daily practice and conscious legitimation of certain moral habits . . . the objective institutions of capitalism would be hollow sepulchers" (108). And in his eagerness to establish a concordance between religion and capitalism, Novak reaches out and cites in his favor an observation made by the Nobel Prize-winning economist and radical libertarian, James Buchanan: "The political economy is already *artifactual;* it has been constructed by human choices" (quoted in Novak, 109; emphasis in original). How this supports an argument favoring concordance is beyond me, but it is a recurrent point in Novak's effort.

This provides the linkage at last to Pope John Paul II and his important 1991 encyclical, *Centesimus Annus.* Most of Novak's treatment of John Paul is in a chapter entitled "Capitalism Rightly Understood," as though we had all been waiting two hundred years for this revelation. I do not wish to sound mean-spirited, but we are being told in effect that the Catholic church has the most convincing proof of the morality of capitalism precisely because John Paul II suddenly converted from Church theology and teaching that had explicitly been in the opposite direction for two hundred years. Here is Novak on that very point.

> No other religious tradition has wrestled so long with, or been so reluctant to come to terms with, the capitalist reality. So it should not be too surprising that many of the hard-won—and now most useful—terms for understanding capitalism spring from the struggles of [the Catholic] tradition against itself. (xvii)

And thus we have another case like that of Whittaker Chambers, whose endorsement of conservatism and the decline of the liberal West was rendered self-evidently true by the fact that Chambers had, before his conversion, been a Communist, a traitor to his country, a systematic and extensively promiscuous bisexual traitor to his wife and family, and an informant on his friends in return for a promise of leniency. Conversion, not confession, is good for the soul—and everybody else's.

Desiring "to end the divorce between religion and economics once and for all" (106), Pope John Paul II in *Centesimus Annus* declared "personal economic initiative" central to Catholic social teaching and a "fundamental human right, second only to the right of religious liberty" (ibid.). So, after two hundred years, the Catholic church ratified the U.S. Constitution and the Bill of Rights. And by plugging this ratification of the Bill of Rights into Genesis, the pope had "found a way to heal the breach between religion and economics from which the West has suffered for 200 years" (ibid.).

And just how did he do it? By following James Madison, not Genesis. Here is Novak's analysis of how this was done.

> To be sure, a new economy was not—is not—enough; it must be checked and balanced by a *democratic* polity, since a fully humane free economy requires a sound juridical system rooted in the consent of the governed, and also requires the guidance of disciplined, compassionate, and realistic cultural institutions. But here the classical liberal economists made a mistake. They tried to describe economic reality . . . in objective *scientific* terms, while neglecting to state explicitly the sort of *moral* habits required to make those institutions work. (107)

> Pope John Paul II proposed a tripartite social structure composed of a free political system, a free economy, and a culture of liberty. After living through the great political debate of this century, he is in favor of democracy; after living through the great economic debate, he is in favor of capitalism rightly understood (that is, not *all* forms of capitalism). (115; all emphases Novak's)

Virtually everything I can discern from Novak's loyal and careful exposition of *Centesimus Annus* confirms that the Church's solution to the antithesis between religion and capitalism is no concordance at all but a Madisonian equilibrium *between opposing principles*. Novak explicitly associates the pope with Madison and Hamilton in *The Federalist*. (See, e.g., Novak, 123.) But the pope seems to go beyond Novak in this, essentially to reject a concordance by pitting the state against capitalism—a state powerful enough to maintain the "tripartite social structure composed of a free political system, a free economy, and a culture of liberty" (115). According to Novak, this is "capitalism rightly understood," but in fact, it is the pope's restatement of American constitutional theory, which resides in competition, not concordance.

In spite of this, Novak insists that through it all he has found or has constructed "capitalism rightly understood" and that it is confirmed by the presence of his and the pope's concept of "ordered liberty," which is a special kind of liberty that "does not mean libertinism, laissez-faire, the devil take the hindmost" (116). But this is merely an arbitrary personal assertion unsupported by anything in the book. Moreover, it flies in the face of any standard definition of liberty, which actually comes very close to "libertinism, laissez-faire, the devil take the hindmost." ("Liberty: exemption or release from captivity . . . ; freedom from bondage . . . ; exemption or freedom from arbitrary, despotic, or autocratic rule or autocratic rule or control" [*OED*].)

In fact, Novak and the pope have appropriated "ordered liberty" from Justice Benjamin Cardozo and have redirected it, quite irresponsibly, toward novel and unintended usage. Ordered liberty, Cardozo's invention, is a juridical construct designed as a standard to help determine when a particular right or liberty granted by the Bill of Rights was so fundamental that it had to be incorporated into the Fourteenth Amendment and applied without exception to all citizens regardless of the state wherein they reside. Thus ordered liberty is not a grant of liberty at all but a standard to help determine *when liberty can be denied*. By 1937, when the concept was fully articulated, only two provisions of the Bill of Rights had been considered sufficiently fundamental as to be considered a liberty possessed by all Americans regardless of residence: protection against the taking of property without due process (1897) and, more or less, the entire First Amendment (1925, 1931, 1937). All other liberties specified in the Bill of Rights were in fact denied, including immunity from double jeopardy, which Cardozo was in the process of denying in the 1937 case using "ordered liberty" as the standard.

"Ordered liberty" was in no way intended to be—nor has it come to be accepted as—"the Anglo-American definition of liberty" (Novak, 95). Nor is there is any warrant in the concept as defined and used by Justice Cardozo for Novak's assertion that liberty in America means "the liberty to do what we *ought* to do" (ibid.; Novak's emphasis). That is a private, self-serving conservative definition of liberty, as observed earlier, with implications far beyond the simple dictionary definition of liberty, which is a lot closer to "the liberty to do what we *wish* to do" (taken by Novak to mean the opposite of ordered liberty; p. 95).[73] In fact, if "what we ought to do" is made uniform for everyone, then it is the very opposite of liberty— as noted by Roger Williams as early as 1644: "God requireth not an uniformity of religion to be enacted in any civil state. . . . Uniformity sooner or later is the greater occasion of civil war, ravishing of conscience, . . . hypocrisy."[74]

CONCORDANCE: WHO WANTS IT, AND WHY?

Many people in the world should be able to celebrate Pope John Paul II's discovery of the American liberal/pluralist method of getting the best of religion and of capitalism. But there is no concordance between the two. And who really wants one?

A concordance could provide a short-run solution to the problem of maintaining the Republican coalition. But the costs would be cumulative. Moral capitalism would define any political interference (even in the name of morality) as not only irrational but downright immoral, tantamount to treason. Who would ultimately want that except those who have gained power with it and can use it to justify the power of law to maintain their personal power? Although many worship at the altar of Christian capitalism or capitalist Christianity, I offer the hypothesis that most educated elites do not believe in the existence of a concordance but will encourage others to

[73]Cardozo developed the concept of ordered liberty in two cases: *Snyder v. Massachusetts*, 291 U.S. 97 (1934); and *Palko v. Connecticut*, 302 U.S. 319 (1937).

[74]Quote from Lawrence Herson, *The Politics of Ideas* (Homewood, Ill.: Dorsey Press, 1984), 25.

believe in its existence if and when it serves their interest. All groups, institutions, parties, and nations have ideologies. The obligation of a political scientist is to ask, Of what use is the ideology to the advocate?

Virtually everyone could celebrate Novak's report that Pope John Paul II has come up with a way to get the best of the competing worlds of religion and capitalism. But that is not what Novak and his fellow travelers are after. They are after a concordance, and a concordance between the two has not been accomplished, by the pope or anyone else. If this had been a match between religion and capitalism, we would have to call it a draw. If it had been an effort to synthesize the antitheses, we would have to call it a flop.

But that is only my contention, and it is the contention of a doubter, while Novak and others are preaching to the converted. Only time will tell how successful their text has been, especially in the arena of concern here, the political. If the presentation of a concordance between Christianity and capitalism proves convincing to the people who really count in politics, then morality and capitalism will march undisturbed within a stable Republican coalition. It will be a stable coalition between genuine conservatives and Old Liberals, and it will for a long time be the dominant ideological influence, whether in the electoral majority or not. But to be successful and stable, this coalition has to do more than keep the patrician conservatives (and neoconservatives) happy. That is not too difficult, because the really sophisticated members of this coalition based on a Christian/capitalist concordance do not actually have to accept and believe in the concordance. They can in fact *privately* reject it and still embrace it publicly; and for political reasons, they have every incentive to do so. Just as there can be (and probably have been) atheist popes, there can be atheist or agnostic political leaders, who themselves do not believe in the concordance but believe it is important that "the people" believe. Will it work on the people, and for how long? More specifically, will it work on the populist conservatives, who, unlike the patricians, really need to believe? Patricians may believe but do not really need to. Patricians know about the Noble Lie and that they have Plato on their side. That is the greatest benefit of their classical education. But lies in public, however noble, are calculated risks. The risk may be to democracy itself. If capitalism is to remain compatible with democracy, it cannot deny its liberalism and put itself beyond the reach of democracy. Moral capitalism, like moral socialism, would signal not only the end of liberalism and the end of conservatism but also the end of the republican era.

CHAPTER 5

THE END OF CONSERVATISM

> *In the United States even the*
> *religion of most of the citizens is*
> *republican, since it submits the*
> *truths of the other world to private*
> *judgment, as in politics the care of*
> *their temporal interest is abandoned*
> *to the good sense of the people.*
> ALEXIS DE TOCQUEVILLE, 1835

INTRODUCTION TO THE FOUNDER

Ronald Reagan, the Theology

ON MARCH 8, 1983, President Reagan delivered a formal address to the National Association of Evangelicals, meeting
in Orlando, Florida. He opened with an affirmation of his
belief in prayer and of his belief that "freedom prospers only
where the blessings of God are avidly sought and humbly
accepted." For confirmation, he turned to the wisdom of
Tocqueville.

> Not until I went into the churches of America and heard her
> pulpits aflame with righteousness did I understand the great-
> ness and the genius of America.

President Reagan continued,

> This administration is motivated by a political philosophy that
> sees the greatness of America in . . . the institutions that fos-
> ter and nourish values like concern for others and respect for
> the rule of law under God.
>
> Now, I don't have to tell you that this puts us in opposition to,
> or at least out of step with, a prevailing attitude of many who
> have turned to a modern-day secularism, discarding the tried
> and time-tested values upon which our very civilization is

158

based. No matter how well intentioned, their value system is radically different from that of most Americans.[1]

Immediately following that passage, the president turned to a specification of "the nation's political agenda," including support for state criminalization of abortion and support for state power to control prayers in the public schools, adultery, teenage sex, pornography, and hard drugs. His commitment to highly coercive government controls of many areas of conduct did not seem to cause him any embarrassment despite its contrast with the often-repeated proposition that "government is not the solution to our problem; government is the problem."

Reagan returned then to the main theme of his address with a concept unusually abstract for standard Reagan rhetoric: "the phenomenology of evil, or, as theologians would put it, the doctrine of sin." Making one of his earlier allusions to "the Evil Empire," he went on to distinguish the two systems as examples of good versus evil and warned the audience and the nation not to yield to "the temptation of blindly declaring yourselves above it all and label both sides equally at fault . . . and thereby remove yourself from the struggle between right and wrong and good and evil." President Reagan called on Whittaker Chambers, "whose own religious conversion" qualified him to report to us that "the crisis of the Western World exists to the degree to which the West is indifferent to God." Perhaps most curiously of all, he closed his address with a quote from Thomas Paine: "We have it within our power to begin the world over again." Immediately following this was the last sentence of his speech, a perfect juxtaposition to Paine and Tocqueville: "We can do it, doing together what no church could do by itself. God bless you, and thank you very much."

[1]Source for Reagan address quoted here and below, Paul Boyer, ed., *Reagan as President: Contemporary Views of the Man, His Politics and His Policies* (Chicago: Ivan R. Dee, 1990), 165–69.

Ronald Reagan, the Prose

The speech to the evangelicals was a great success in Reagan's effort to cement the Christian Right to the Republican party. He, or his speech writers, knew they had a fundamental problem to overcome. On the one hand, the national Republican party was a liberal, eastern, Wall Street party. On the other hand, the most numerous elements of the conservative wing—deserving the term "populist"—were antielite, anti-eastern, anti-Wall Street, and antiliberal (to the extent they understood liberalism). Wherever possible, Reagan had to demonstrate that Republican versus Democrat meant good versus evil and that this was truly God's work.

In drawing on Tocqueville, Reagan conveniently avoided Tocqueville's worries about the relationship between religion and the state. Quick review of the passage already quoted in chapter 1 will indicate that to Tocqueville, "the peaceful dominion of religion" in the United States is attributable in fact to the clear separation of church and state. The earlier Tocqueville passage can be reinforced by the epigraph opening this chapter and by still another:

> The church cannot share the temporal power of the state without being the object of a portion of that animosity which the latter excites. (vol. 1, 321–22)

Even the *New Republic* was dumbfounded by Reagan's address to the Evangelicals. By 1983, the *New Republic* had already become thoroughly neoconservative and fairly consistently pro-Reagan, but editorially, this influential periodical expressed alarm at Reagan's "slander of secularism," making it the collaborator of communism. It was equally alarmed by Reagan's wrongful representation of certain important authors. They quote at length from Reagan's construction of the views of the Founding Fathers. Here is Reagan:

> When our Founding Fathers passed the First Amendment, they sought to protect churches from government interference. They never meant to construct a wall of hostility between government and the concept of religious belief itself.

Leave aside the fact that the First Amendment was adopted by the First Congress of the United States and not by the Founding Fathers. The key point at issue is the founding attitude toward church and state. While the president is correct that the Founding Fathers did not design "a wall of hostility," no sane person ever believed that that was their intention. As the *New Republic* put it, their purpose was to maintain and protect a separation between the two, not a hostile attitude toward churches or toward religion. That was the very aspect of the Constitution that Tocqueville so appreciated. Another wrongful reference to the Founders is to their "respect for the rule of law under God." The rule of law is an entirely secular concept; "the rule of law need not be under God, as long as it is over man." They objected also to Reagan's use of Thomas Paine, which, for them, was "exactly the opposite of the Devil quoting Scripture."[2]

The *New Republic* was hitting on a practice that other analysts have also noticed, Reagan's regular use of famous opposing views as supportive of his own position. In fact, Reagan possessed an uncommon ability to confuse his adversaries and critics with such rhetorical cross-dressing, to such an extent that he was giving rhetoric itself a bad name.[3] Among all his various references to his opponents as supporters, his favorite was Franklin Roosevelt. This is wonderfully ironic, since Roosevelt used a similar device to confuse his adversaries by, among other things, stealing the label of liberalism from Herbert Hoover. But more than Roosevelt, Reagan's claiming his opposition as his supporters was quite sincere. As the Roosevelt/Truman scholar William Leuchtenburg put it, Reagan's usage of Franklin Roosevelt was so "contrary . . . to reality that one might register it as the greatest sleight-of-hand of modern American politics, save for one thing. No one believed it more sincerely than Ronald

[2]All quotes in this paragraph are from the *New Republic*, "Reverend Reagan," 4 April 1983. I relied on the version reprinted with permission in Boyer, *Reagan as President*, 172–75.
[3]David Green, *Shaping Political Consciousness*, 256.

Reagan."[4] His cross-dressing included mixing conservatism with Old Liberalism as though they were one. And he threw in anticommunism versus communism as a dichotomy parallel to conservatism versus liberalism.

Reagan's success left New Liberalism and the Democratic party opposition with a tiny island of public philosophy to stand on, and the smallest wave might inundate it. All of this politics of language helps explain how it was possible for the liberal label to be stigmatized. It became the "L-word" with which nobody wanted to be associated; in Ronald Reagan's own terms, the Democrats were "so far Left, they've left America."

Behold Ronald Reagan. Ronald Reagan, the prose. Some find truth in "Ronald Reagan, the Movie."[5] But there is a deeper truth behind the movie's images. The prose of Ronald Reagan *is* Ronald Reagan, the man who would reconstitute the Right, the Republican party, and the American political dialogue. And, if necessary, English language and literature.

RECONSTITUTING THE REPUBLICAN PARTY—THE LAST ELEMENTS

Populist Christianity—Rendering Nothing unto Caesar

Mobilization of patrician conservatism was necessary but not sufficient. It provided the intellectual finesse to close the gap between Old Liberalism and genuine conservatism. In fact, it gave capitalism a moral claim it had not had since Social Darwinism and *Lochner.* But just as the concordance between capitalism and Christianity would not completely bond in the old days, so it would not completely bond in the 1970s. If "all politics is local," all politics is also ephemeral.

But patrician conservatism was insufficient mainly because it lacked the numbers and the passion. For conservatism to be

[4]Quoted in Green, *Shaping Political Consciousness,* 256–57.
[5]Michael Rogin, *Ronald Reagan, the Movie—And Other Episodes in Political Demonology* (Berkeley, Los Angeles, and London: University of California Press, 1987).

a genuine force in national politics, the numbers and the passion would have to come from another source: populist conservatism, or, one could say, populism turned conservative.

The primary source of populist conservatism, which came to be known as the New Christian Right (NCR), was evangelical Protestantism. As reported earlier, polls estimate that approximately one white American in three belongs to a denomination considered evangelical, which regards the Bible as containing the absolute truth and whose adherents bear witness to having been "born again." A definition with a higher threshold, requiring that the individual evangelical accept the Scripture as the whole truth *and* testify to having been born again, constitutes approximately 20 percent of white Americans.[6]

Moreover, populist Protestantism has been growing while mainstream Protestantism has been shrinking. This pattern was reported in chapter 4 in percentages for the 1960s and 1970s. Impressive as those figures are, the absolute numbers, including the 1980s, may be still more impressive to political candidates. Between 1965 and 1992, membership in the Presbyterian faith dropped from 4.2 million to 2.8 million. During the same period, Lutheran membership dropped from 5.7 million to 5.2 million; United Methodist, from 11 million to 8.7 million; United Church of Christ, from 2 million to 1.5 million; Episcopal, from 3.6 million to 2.4 million; and Disciples of Christ, from 1.9 million to 1 million.[7] Meanwhile, according to *Newsweek* religious editor Kenneth Woodward, there is "an evangelical church opening somewhere almost daily."[8]

However, size and growth do not make populism politically significant. National mobilization does. The story of popu-

[6]Figures and definitions from Jelen and Wilcox, "The Christian Right in the 1990s," 10. A still larger percentage of African-Americans meet these criteria, but although many African-Americans hold conservative positions on certain issues, few were counted on by those who were mobilizing the New Christian Right.

[7]Gallup Polls, as reported in Kenneth Woodward, "Dead End for the Mainline?" *Newsweek*, 9 August 1993, 46–48.

[8]Woodward, "Dead End for the Mainline?" 46.

lism and its right turn has been told often, and I have profited from these accounts.[9] But my own interpretation will be at variance with most of them, because for me, populism did not disappear and suddenly come to life again a generation later. It was mobilized on a national scale but not from scratch. All the elements were there and ready.

According to the account of Kenneth Wald, one of the more careful historians of the politics of populist religion, evangelical Protestantism "was an animating force in American life" until the 1920s.[10] It had been greatly influential on both sides of the slavery issue, supporting abolition in the North and supporting equally the slave economy in the southern states. It provided a large source of the energy behind the reform era of the 1890s, and it was a driving force behind national and state agriculture programs, national and state labor legislation, and national antitrust legislation as well as women's suffrage and prohibition. Evangelical Protestantism was strengthened and enrichened after 1910 with publication of the famous pamphlet *The Fundamentals* and the spread afterward of fundamentalism. One of the leaders in the fundamentalist segment of populist Christianity was William Jennings Bryan, who was both a religious conservative and a genuine harbinger of the Roosevelt Revolution.

According to this account, the political influence of populist Christianity seemed to come to an abrupt end with the accomplishments of the immediate post–World War I period. As Wald put it, "Evangelical Protestantism was displaced from its perch as a major cultural force by a series of major social developments that culminated in a virtual social revolu-

[9]The sources on which I have relied most heavily are Bruce, *The Rise and Fall of the New Christian Right*; Hertzke, *Echoes of Discontent*; Matthew C. Moen, *The Transformation of the Christian Right* (Tuscaloosa: University of Alabama Press, 1992); Reichley, *Religion in American Public Life*; Kenneth D. Wald, *Religion and Politics in the United States* (New York: St. Martin's Press, 1987); and George M. Thomas, *Revivalism and Cultural Change: Christianity, National Building and the Market in the Nineteenth-Century United States* (Chicago: University of Chicago Press, 1989).

[10]Wald, *Religion and Politics in the United States*, 183.

tion."[11] Factors behind this displacement of populist Christianity as a political force were rapid urbanization, the spread of science and technology, and non-Protestant immigration.

Rich as such accounts are, each is, like Wald's, an example of the underestimation of the solidity and continuity of populist Christianity, as already witnessed in the previous chapter with regard to the treatment by social scientists of the so-called radical Right sentiment in the 1950s. While it is true that national tastes and mores did in fact change drastically, giving the 1920s a special place in cultural history, that says nothing of the reality of populist Christianity at the same time. To be overshadowed is not to be eliminated, or even displaced.

What had actually happened was that, as with anticommunism for a scant few years in the 1950s, there were two or three national moral issues that required national decisions, and as soon as Christian interest mobilized and dealt with those, they returned home to their normal pursuits. But "normal" here does not mean disappearance from politics. The relatively lengthy reform period involving populist Christians between roughly 1890 and 1920 *continued in a different form*. In historical context, it continued in a more normal form, with concentration on city, county, and state politics.

Take the case of prohibition. Prohibition of the distribution and sale of alcohol required a constitutional amendment and therefore mobilization on a national scale to achieve extraordinary majorities in the Senate and in the House of Representatives. But it also required ratification in three-fourths of the state legislatures and, beyond that, required additional implementing legislation in all of the same legislatures if the goal of a "dry state with dry counties" were to become a reality. Making prohibition a reality was a goal that would drastically reorient all morally motivated political activists. Is there any wonder, then, that populist Christianity seemed to have been "displaced from its perch as a major cultural

[11]Ibid., 183.

force" in the 1920s? It had gone back to being a cultur-
al/political force in each state, not particularly concerned
about the national culture or the national climate of opinion.
The state was its natural habitat. Parochialism was its inborn
virtue.

Other students of the politics of populist Christianity or
evangelicalism are of the opinion that the experience with the
Scopes trial of 1925 caused evangelicals and fundamentalists
to retreat from the political scene and "to seek refuge in their
spirituality."[12] In other words, populist Christians became
unpolitical as well as demobilized. They speak of "political
abstinence [that] made their awakening in the late 1970s all the
more compelling."[13] In fact, "of all the shifts and surprises in
contemporary political life, perhaps none was so wholly un-
expected as the political resurgence of evangelical Protestantism in the 1970s."[14]

It should already be clear that this is a mistaken interpretation. What shall become clear below is that populist Christianity not only did not disappear and did not engage in
political abstinence but was in fact more active than probably
ever before. As a localized political force, populist Christianity, especially evangelicalism, took a distinctively right
turn.

Populist Conservatism/Conservative Populism

The last genuinely leftward-looking commitment of populist
Christianity was also its last national mobilization before the
1970s—the Nineteenth Amendment giving women the right
to vote and the Equal Rights Amendment, a vain attempt in
1920 and 1921 to extend the Bill of Rights to women. After that,
populist Christianity opposed the Equal Rights Amendment
in each of the ensuing twenty years that it came before

[12]Moen, *Transformation of the Christian Right,* 2.
[13]Ibid.
[14]Wald, *Religion and Politics in the United States,* 182. Quoted with approval by
Moen, *Transformation of the Christian Right,* 2.

Congress[15] and at the same time turned its attention toward still more conservative directions.

Even at the time of the Equal Rights Amendment, the "war on crime" — a concept that was actually coined at that time — was much higher on the agenda of populist Christians. Response was immediate, with establishment of crime commissions in at least twenty-four states before, not after, the various Capone-like mobs had formed to exploit the opportunities provided by the prohibition laws. The orientation of these crime commissions was not merely to fight indulgence in forbidden liquids but to render more severe the definition of crime and punishment. State laws reversed many of the leftish reforms of the pre–World War period involving rehabilitation and prison reform. The whole liberal idea of criminal justice came under strong attack in the 1920s, and most liberal programs were terminated. Many states adopted new laws abolishing indeterminate sentences; other laws were adopted requiring consent of the prosecuting attorney and presiding judge of the court before granting parole to an offender. According to one student of the period, there was a notable "trend in the period from 1917 to 1927 towards more severe penalties, longer prison sentences, increased use of the death penalty, and more opposition to the trend towards humane treatment of the criminal."[16] No signs here of conservatives seeking refuge in their spirituality.

Another area heavily laden with morality that called for the energy and concentration of conservatives in general and Evangelicals in particular was secondary education. The principle of compulsory education was well established by the 1920s, but there were by then widespread currents and influences of "liberal" or "progressive" education that centered on

---

[15]Jane J. Mansbridge, *Why We Lost the ERA* (Chicago: University of Chicago Press, 1986), 8–9.

[16]Material for most of this paragraph, including the quote, comes from Nathan Douthit, "Police Professionalism and the War Against Crime in the United States, 1920s–30s," in George L. Mosse, ed., *Police Forces in History* (Beverley Hills, Cal.: Sage, 1975), 318–25.

the individual child, stressing voluntarism and the individual pupil, expression versus rote learning, and freedom versus regimentation. In his account of educational policy, Lawrence Cremin, a recognized expert on the subject, noted that "one looks in vain for the reformism that had been the leitmotif of the movement before 1919." Another historian observed of the same period that "progressive education lost its momentum as a reform movement."[17] Along with alteration of the status of the child and the concept of good pedagogy, there was also a great deal of energy directed toward state and school district legislation altering the substance of school teaching. This was especially true in such areas as patriotism, nativism, the Christian religion, and aspects of moral conduct. The most spectacular issue coming out of the period was the proposal for laws prohibiting the teaching of evolution in the schools. This was part of a still larger movement to oppose the teaching of science in general—not merely to require that science teaching be balanced with the teaching of the biblical version of Creation. Legislation banning outright the teaching of evolution in the schools was adopted only in five states, all southern, but campaigns for such legislation were seriously mounted in a much larger number of states. Populist Christian opposition to teaching evolution in the schools, made famous by Bryan in the Scopes trial, was motivated not only by defense of Scripture but also by their opposition to the Social Darwinism that had been key to the late nineteenth-century liberal effort to establish a concordance of morality, science, and capitalism.[18]

Although it may be true that Evangelicals voted less regularly than other white Americans, it is also true that religious leaders—Catholic, Jewish, and Protestant—were politically active and drew on their flocks for local political influence. It

[17]The latter quote is Henry J. Perkinson, *The Imperfect Panacea: American Faith in Education, 1865–1965* (New York: Random House, 1968), 199. The quote of Lawrence Cremin is from the same source, p. 199.
[18]My thanks to Professor Elizabeth Sanders for contributing this refinement to my analysis of the 1920s populist Christian opposition to evolutionary theory.

is also true that the influence of religious leaders, both clerical and lay, was conservative.[19] Anyone following politics in the cities, including the big cities, in the 1920s would see that underneath the freewheeling culture that gave the decade its reputation was a regular, vigorous, and constant effort by religious conservative leaders to maintain their influence in local and state politics. Some homely case studies will illustrate the intensity of religious interest in state and local political affairs and of the character of their influence on political elites, including machine politicians.

The first anecdote is told by New York mayor George McClellan, on taking office in 1904. It indicates not only the political influence of the Catholic church in New York City politics but also the prominence and richness of organized religion in its vocabulary.

> I called on [Archbishop] Farley and consulted him in reference to the three departments in which he would presumably have been most interested, Charities, Correction and Tenement Houses. I asked him if he had any candidates to propose or any suggestions to make. He replied, "I have no candidate for any of these offices and only one suggestion to offer: that is, that in making these appointments you do not name Catholics. I should much prefer that you appoint fair-minded Protestants. All that the Church wants is a square deal . . . ; on the other hand, Catholics of the kind you should appoint will lean over backwards in their effort to avoid appearance of favoring their own church, and the church will suffer as a consequence."[20]

The second anecdote also involves Mayor McClellan. He is an interesting case because he was considered a strong and independent mayor, albeit closely associated with the Democratic machine until late in his administration.

> Dr. Charles Parkhurst [a crusading reformist Protestant minister] came to see me with a delegation of his admirers. He said to me, "We are not satisfied with the way [Commissioner] McAdoo

---

[19]Reichley, *Religion in American Public Life,* 226.
[20]Quoted in Theodore J. Lowi, *At the Pleasure of the Mayor* (New York: Free Press, 1964), 15.

is running the Police Department, and demand that you do not retain him." I replied much to the good doctor's surprise, "I quite agree with you. . . . If you gentlemen will submit the name of a candidate for the office who is qualified for the job I shall be very happy to appoint him." Thereupon Parkhurst replied, "It is not our duty to find you officials. Our duty is to see that they do their work after you have found them."[21]

Another story, this one with a bit of data, ought to make absolutely clear the intensity as well as the regularity of religious leadership involvement in local politics. In 1917, largely in response to the demands of leaders of local religious groups, the city of New York created a genuine, authoritative board of education composed of seven members, with considerable powers over the city's primary and secondary school system. Since no division of the number seven could provide an equal distribution of appointments among the three major religious groupings and since there were constant complaints about the equitability of the distribution, a system worked itself out over the ensuing years. And with seven-year staggered terms, agreements made by one mayor were binding on successive mayors, to make the distribution work. The first appointments to the board were three Catholics, three Protestants, and one Jew. The first two vacancies (1920) were of the same religion as their predecessors: Protestant replaced Protestant and Jew replaced Jew. In 1921, the "Protestant vacancy" was filled by another Protestant, but in 1922 and 1923, Protestant vacancies were filled by Catholics, with the next vacancy in 1924 returning to a Protestant. Thus during the first ten years, the new board's membership shifted from three Protestants, three Catholics, and one Jew to 2:4:1, 3:3:1, and 1:4:2, respectively. The ratio for the total period was 9:14:5, roughly responsive to the numbers and influence of the three religions within the Democratic party organizations of the city of New York. Although the insurgent Republican reformer Fiorello LaGuardia cooperated in his pattern of appointments to the

[21]Ibid., 15–16.

Board of Education, the process was so complicated that in 1948, New York City got from Albany a law increasing board membership to nine members. From that point on, the membership ratio of the board became 3:3:3.[22] And, whatever the substantive qualification of each candidate, the key parameter was their contribution to the board's religious balance.

This three-way balancing pattern needs no interpretation beyond two fairly simple propositions. First, the political stakes were high enough to make it impossible for the religious leaders or church organizations to avoid local and state political involvement. The "great school wars" of the nineteenth century were still with us, albeit in new form. Along with school wars were virtual political wars over changes in divorce laws, adoption laws, delinquency and other individual child problem laws, sabbath closing laws, laws concerning services by charitable and philanthropic organizations, and so on and so forth. All of these arrangements required state legislation and then had to be implemented by city and county agencies that were given enough discretion by state law to require constant interest-group surveillance. A second contention—repeated so as to avoid losing the point—is that religious group involvement was constant but tended to get notice on the front pages of the newspapers or in the articles and books of the academic analysts only when national political campaigns were mounted—which, until the 1970s, were sporadic and short-lived, like most social movements. In most instances, the major religions were competing against each other, which kept their involvement all the more intense. It is not until the 1970s that Protestants and Catholics were able to make common cause over a number of issues. This is all the more important because the cooperation was not to be between Catholics and Protestants at large but between *conservative* Catholics and conservative *populist* Protestants.

[22]Ibid., 32–33. A couple of decades later the size of the board was once again reduced to seven members. But that is another story.

MOBILIZATION: CAUSES AND REASONS FOR THE NATIONALIZATION OF PAROCHIALISM

Causes — Social Movement Theories

Although it is patently incorrect, as I hope previous pages have demonstrated, to say that populist Christianity is apolitical or at any time has "taken refuge in its spirituality," it is accurate to say that this large segment of American life is too dispersed to be treated as a unitary interest group in the ordinary political sense of the term. The conservative base in America is large and diffuse but not atomized. There are many organizations, but no organization. As one observer put it, during the 1970s there was a "political awakening of evangelical Protestants [including] the spectacular growth rates of theologically conservative churches."[23] But that was a far cry from a modified movement. Mobilization would require a lot more energy and drive.

Within the account in this chapter alone, it is easy to locate several factors that inhibited the conversion of conservatism into a genuine movement with a focus on and an influence in national politics. First, there is the parochialism, theirs by nature and embraced as a virtue. Parochialism separates; parochialism decentralizes. Second, there is a cultural gulf between populist and patrician conservatives. For example, although patrician conservatives may revere religion and speak of religion as a necessary component of the political community, they do not rely on Scripture in their arguments. In the Burke tradition, they may take pride in being nonphilosophical; nevertheless, their writing is too philosophical for observant Christians, who prefer the passion of Scripture to the rather clinical style of the intellectuals. Third, Protestants are traditionally split North from South, which would tend to reinforce parochialism. Fourth, there has traditionally been an even deeper split within Christianity between Protestant and Catholic. Protestants, especially southern Protestants,

---

[23]Wald, *Religion and Politics in the United States*, 182.

saw fealty to Rome as un-American. (Southerners in years past referred to the pope as the Pope of Rome. It came out as one word, poparome.) And despite the papacy in Rome, Catholics and their clergy are politically just as parochial as Protestants; well into the 1960s issues of greatest interest to Catholics and the Catholic church were, as with Protestants, issues at the local and state level. But mutual distrust was still the reality of their relationship. Finally, conservatism as a national movement had no leadership. Thus to make a genuine national conservative Christian movement, conditions must be favorable, including a class of entrepreneurs with experience in national affairs and in mass politics.

Political sociologists look to social conditions for the cause or causes of social movements. This apparatus of explanation is called social movement theory, and there is quite a lot of literature on the subject. The best of the literature is a rich body of empirical case studies, detailed accounts of actual social movements. Abolition, the temperance movement, the women's suffrage movement, the civil rights movement, the women's rights movement, and so on. But the literature gets weaker as the authors attempt to generalize about the causes of social movements.

Probably the most widely embraced theory of social movements is that associated with Talcott Parsons and associates. This is appropriately called a "structural strain" theory, based on Parsons's assumption that "neither individuals nor societies can undergo major structural changes without the likelihood of producing a considerable element of 'irrational' behavior."[24] What Parsons calls irrational is picked up by his students as radical or social movement behavior. Neil Smelser

[24]Quoted in Steve Bruce, *The Rise and Fall of the New Christian Right*, 9. References to the works of other sociologists will be drawn from Bruce's book rather than directly from the original authors, because Bruce has made the most serious recent effort to focus social movement theory on the contemporary Christian Right as a social movement in America and elsewhere in the world. Page references to Bruce's volume will be put in parentheses in the text where appropriate.

converts this into a kind of model of social movement genesis, in three steps: (1) social strain produces widespread anxiety; (2) those sharing the anxiety discover a specific cause for their strain; and (3) they designate a specific solution, without which there would be no movement but only a kind of wish fulfillment (Bruce, p. 9). At first blush this seems to be a credible model. But, as Steve Bruce observes, what social groups are *not* under social strain and *not* suffering from widespread anxiety? Some may be suffering from lack of status, but other groups with high status can be suffering equally from their fear of losing status. Those who have enjoyed recent success in improving their status may suffer particularly intense anxiety about the future. As Tocqueville observed of France of the late 1780s, the French found their position the more intolerable the better it became. Thus it would seem that the structural strain theory explains too much and at the same time not enough. For, as one study of the John Birch Society demonstrates, California Birchers were "for the most part, well educated, reasonably young individuals with substantial family incomes . . . employed in upper-status occupations, [etc.]" (quoted in Bruce, p. 11). So much for structural strain.[25]

Bruce is not alone in finding structural strain theory inadequate, and he shares with others an interest in an alternative approach referred to as "resource mobilization" theory. Resource mobilization theory was a healthy reaction against the overly deterministic structural strain theory, which took too

[25]Another objection I have to "structural strain" is that it is post hoc. Reasoning backward from an event, it is not difficult to locate a set of conditions that might well have caused or given rise to it. However, in theorizing about the event, such as a social movement, the theorist is never quite clear and definitive as to how long the lag time can be and still constitute an explanation for the event in question. Thus, for example, the conditions of structural strain in the U.S. economy favoring a movement toward a larger and stronger national government existed for at least fifty years prior to the New Deal. The conditions of structural strain and of cultural change had been around for a good while before the successful national mobilization of the Christian Right in the 1970s. Is a general set of conditions a cause no matter how long it exists before the effect in question takes place?

literally and gullibly the connection among strain, grievance, and the movement response (21). But positing merely a set of skilled "issue entrepreneurs" (ibid.) as the sufficient explanation for a movement was not novel to resource mobilization theory; moreover, if taken literally and in the extreme, resource mobilization is as mechanistic as the theory it abandons, and if taken permissively, it is virtually truistic.

This is not to say that strains and grievances are irrelevant, or that leadership and entrepreneurial skills are inessential, but that they can only be taken as predispositional. And this moves the analysis away from the search for causes toward a more interesting question: What are the *reasons* for a particular movement, this or any other? Even if people need provoking, they still need to choose. From Minutemen to Moral Majority, from abolitionism to abortion, people have more than one grievance, more than one source of strain, and more than one network of people who share their status or their values. They choose; they have reasons for choosing to accept their lot or to dedicate their time, sometimes their life, to a movement. The reasons can be inappropriate in the eye of the outside observer and thus can be called irrational. But reasons are necessary, and they can be sufficient.

Reasons—An Alternative Theory

The reasons for the nationalization of a populist conservatism in America at this particular moment are all reasons of state, that is, normal human reactions to government policies that were perceived as violating the values and expectations of a whole category of individuals spread throughout the United States. Table 5.1 is a pictorialization of the reasons, and it deserves some elaboration. The most important feature of the items in this table is that they all go beyond the New Deal-type economic regulation about which conservatives were positive or apathetic. As reported earlier, the items in table 5.1 were given the informal name "social legislation." For many people these were code words for race and for the poor, but even as a neutral designation, "social legislation" made a

Table 5.1

Focus for Nationalization of Conservatism

Type of Action—Major Initiatives Only	Action Taken by	Date of Initiative	Unit Acted on	Restrict (R) or Expand (E)
1. Civil rights–school segregation	Supreme Court	1954	State	R
2. Civil liberties–sedition	Supreme Court	1956	State	R
3. Civil liberties–rights of accused	Supreme Court	1961, 1963, 1964, 1966, 1969	State	R
4. School prayer	Supreme Court	1962	State	R
5. Civil rights–voting	Congress and Supreme Court	1957, 1960	Federal State	E R
6. Food Stamp Program	Congress	1964	Federal State	E E
7. Reapportionment	Supreme Court	1962, 1964	Federal	E
8. Civil rights–schools, public facilities, employment, etc.	Congress	1964	State Private	R R
9. Welfare-Medicare, Medicaid	Congress	1965	Federal State	E E
10. Elementary and secondary education	Congress	1965	Federal	E
11. Civil rights–voting	Congress	1965	Federal State	E R
12. Birth control	Supreme Court	1965	State	R
13. Comprehensive health services	Congress	1966	Federal State	E E
14. Welfare rights	Supreme Court	1970	Federal State	E R
15. Privacy rights–women and abortion	Supreme Court	1973	State	R
16. Removal of tax exemption	Internal Revenue Service	1977	Local Private	E R

certain amount of sense in that it distinguished these post-1954 initiatives from the policies of the New Deal. Although all of these initiatives had important economic implications, their formal jurisdiction and informal reach went far beyond the typical government policy of pre-1954. The items in table 5.1 are "societywide," coextensive in scope with the welfare state even when the item in question is on a specialized topic.

Another feature of the table that is both obvious and significant is the extensive involvement of the Supreme Court in extending the reach of the national government and in restricting the powers of state and local governments. This only proves what most genuine conservatives already appreciated but what came as a great surprise to so many Old Liberals: Courts, including the Supreme Court, are instruments of the state and not mere umpires operating as a third party between competing private parties. But it was only in this recent epoch that critics began to attack the courts as engaging in "judicial legislation." That was the basis of the still more potent charge of "the imperial judiciary." For those who did not like the direction of the decisions made by the Supreme Court under Chief Justice Earl Warren, it made no difference whether these initiatives came from the judiciary or from the legislature. This is why bumper stickers proclaiming "Impeach Earl Warren" and "Impeach Bill Douglas" spread like wildfire in the 1960s. Even the distinguished minority leader Gerald Ford submitted a formal motion to Congress for an impeachment proceeding against Justice Douglas; ironically, it was that very same Gerald Ford who would, less than three years before his own selection as vice president by Richard Nixon, articulate the key criterion for impeachment: "whatever a majority of the House of Representatives [decides] at a given moment in history."[26]

From the constitutional standpoint, the Supreme Court initiatives as shown in table 5.1 were virtually all to be

---

[26]From the *Congressional Record*, as quoted in David M. O'Brien, *Storm Center: The Supreme Court in American Politics*, 2d ed. (New York: W. W. Norton, 1990), 133.

understood as the step-by-step "nationalization of the Bill of Rights," which means that most of the major clauses of the Bill of Rights were "incorporated" into the Fourteenth Amendment and were applied as restrictions on the powers of state legislatures just as they already were restrictions on the powers of the federal government. These Supreme Court decisions did severely restrict state powers in each of the categories of action to which the case referred, but *they did not directly expand national power*. Nevertheless, it was viewed by the opposing forces as evidence that federalism was dying and that the national government was growing at the expense of the states.

Further evidence to support their fears can be drawn from those parts of the table that involve initiatives by Congress. In each of the congressional initiatives shown, there was either an expansion of federal power coupled with a restriction on state power or an expansion of both levels at the same time, as in the case of certain welfare programs. Thus putting Supreme Court initiatives in the same table with congressional initiatives makes a great deal of sense from the standpoint of the perspectives of the emerging right-wing movement in the United States.

This requires a closer look. First of all, the grievance of the genuine conservatives was only against the expansion of the *national* government. Most of the conduct covered by the items in table 5.1 *was already subject to some kind of government control*. The purpose of many of the initiatives shown in the table—especially the court decisions—was to *free up*, not to increase, government control. Thus what must have been particularly irksome to conservatives was not the expansion of national government power itself—since conservatives are generally statist—but the reduction of the power of the state governments. In other words, although many initiatives in the post-1954 epoch amounted to the expansion of national power, it was the actual loosening or weakening of state government control that was particularly irksome to the Right. In some areas, such as reapportionment, criminal justice, and race relations, the cumulative result of these initiatives was "principally the imposition of national standards on the states."[27] Nevertheless, control of these areas and discretion as to the degree of severity remained principally in the hands of the states. A great deal of screaming went on in opposition to what was called the perils of big government, but most of that was coming from the Old Liberals within the Republican party, partly because they sincerely believed it but also because it could help them build bridges to the conservatives within the Democratic party who had begun to fear the direction of the expanded national government.

Politically, each of these items became a reason for the conservatives to mobilize and also a "wedge issue," as defined earlier. Some cut a wedge between northern and southern Democrats. Some cut a wedge between black and white. Some cut a wedge between old and young. Some cut a wedge not so much between rich and poor as rich-and-poor against the middle class.

Finally, the cumulative result of these initiatives cut a wedge between the neoconservatives and the rest of the Democratic party. Most neoconservatives had begun as Communists or otherwise pro-Soviet in the 1930s and then in the 1950s, turned into New Liberals on domestic policies and deeply hawkish and statist on matters concerning national security and Soviet foreign policy. Their spiritual development continued to strengthen, to the point in the 1970s when they articulated the belief that the West was doomed to failure, not because communism was the wave of history but because the self-indulgent liberalism of the West, especially of the Americans, was rendering us morally and characterologically weak. Neoconservative intellectuals were then embraced not only by the more extreme Right but also by the Republican party because they appeared to be procapitalist as well as

[27]Alfred H. Kelly et al., *The American Constitution, Its Origins and Development*, 2d ed. (New York: W. W. Norton, 1983), 635. Quoted in Byrnes, *Catholic Bishops in American Politics*, 46.

rightist. In fact, neoconservatives came to dominate the editorial pages of some of the largest newspapers in the United States, including the *Wall Street Journal*. By the time Ronald Reagan became president, most of the neoconservatives had become officially Republican and were a major force, probably the major intellectual force, in reconstituting the Republican party ideology in conservative as well as Old Liberal terms.

There was much about conservatism that was as incompatible with the Republicans as with the Democrats—except for one important thing. Old Liberals shared with conservatives at least an antipathy to the national government. Properly manipulated, that could make the Republican party the center of gravity for the emergent conservative movement.

But first there had to be a conservative movement. In the late 1960s and early 1970s, there was no conservative center of gravity to attract all the separate conservative elements to each other. Conservatives, encapsulated in their localities and separated from each other by their own parochialism, found their center of gravity in the judicial nationalization of the Bill of Rights and the legislative attempts to set national standards. Grievances against these actions, as they appear in table 5.1, gave conservatives a common national political experience—a sustained common national political experience that they had not had before. The small-town preacher, speaking with a heavy southern accent about a down-home approach to the Scripture, would discover, to his own immense surprise, a national audience. Many were called, few may have been chosen, but none would go away.

There had been signs, strong and distinct signs, of the emergent mobilization, if social science and journalism had not been looking through the misconceptions of the past. Some of the signs of resurgence were quite specific. Wald identifies the following local grass-roots campaigns that were particularly significant. One, in the mid-1970s, involved a protest over some of the English textbooks in a mining county of West Virginia. Led by the wife of a local fundamentalist minister, the campaign became a successful boycott of the schools by the parents of most of the students, supplemented by wildcat strikes in the coal mines and then by a teacher strike and the temporary closing of the schools. This "Battle of the Books" triggered similar challenges elsewhere.[28]

A second instance, in 1977, was a petition drive led by the well-known singer Anita Bryant and a number of religious leaders, through a new organization called Save Our Children. They took the initiative and won a referendum in Dade County, Florida (Miami), to reverse an ordinance adopted the previous year by the Dade County Commission to prohibit discrimination on the basis of sexual preference in housing, employment, and public accommodations. This campaign made Bryant famous as an activist and became the example for activists in other cities throughout the United States. The best-known local event was the "Stop ERA" campaign led by Phyllis Schlafly. State legislatures had been moving rather quickly to adopt the Equal Rights Amendment until the opposition formed behind Schlafly, just in time to stop the process a bare three states short of the required thirty-eight. Conservative churches had supplied most of the local anti-ratification activists.[29]

Another important local development that should have been appreciated far sooner was the "Christian academy" movement. Defenders of these independent Christian schools do not particularly deny that one of the motivating factors was their unwillingness to have their children attend school with racial minorities. But of equal and perhaps greater importance to these parents was their objection to what they called the liberal moral climate of the public schools and, in particular, the ban on prayer in schools, which was considered a ban on prayer per se.[30] This movement was further intensified by the effort beginning in 1977 by the Internal Revenue

[28]Wald, *Religion and Politics in the United States*, 187.
[29]Ibid., 187–88.
[30]See, for example, Bruce, *The Rise and Fall of the New Christian Right*, 40–41.

Service to revoke the tax-exempt status of schools it believed were racially discriminatory. Whatever the truth of the matter, the people in the movement sincerely believed that the IRS was attempting to impose racial quotas on those schools.[31]

Jerry Falwell of Lynchburg—Linchpin of the movement

Jerry Falwell founded the Thomas Road Baptist Church in 1956 in his birthplace, Lynchburg, Virginia, a town named for the man who gave lynching its name. Falwell's congregation was composed of thirty-five people, and his church was an abandoned factory building.[32] In 1964, he completed the construction of a thousand-seat auditorium. In 1967, he founded the Lynchburg Christian Academy, which soon thereafter became Liberty Baptist College and then Liberty University. Virtually from the start, Falwell built membership by using every available medium of communication, including radio and then television broadcasting. But for most of the first twelve years, his orientation, even through television, was to preach a sermon each week for local broadcast. And the orientation was not only local but nonpolitical. In an important 1965 sermon, Falwell argued,

> Nowhere are we commissioned to reform the externals. . . . Our ministry is not reformation but transformation. The gospel does not clean up the outside but rather regenerates the inside. . . .
> While we are told to "render unto Caesar the things that are Caesar's," in the true interpretation, we have very few ties on this earth. We pay our taxes, cast our votes as a responsibility of citizenship, obey the laws of the land, and other things demanded of us by the society in which we live. But . . . [b]elieving the Bible as I do, I would find it impossible to stop preaching the pure saving gospel of Jesus Christ, and begin doing

[31]See, for example, Moen, *Transformation of the Christian Right*, 16–18.
[32]Unless otherwise cited, the facts about Falwell's success are drawn from Frances FitzGerald, "A Reporter at Large: A Disciplined, Charging Army," *New Yorker*, 18 May 1981, pp. 53–141.

anything else—including fighting Communism, or participation in civil-rights reforms.[33]

Falwell would eventually change his mind. By the end of the 1970s, he explicitly and publicly repudiated this 1965 sermon as "false prophecy."[34] Whatever else had happened to him in that ten to fifteen years, two developments are absolutely certain. First, there had emerged a series of issues he would not be able to resist. Probably the most pressing were abortion, pornography, the Christian schools movement, and the issue of homosexuality.

The second development was pressing from within. The flock was growing, and like most developing organizations, and especially because of Falwell's tendency to stay ahead of himself and ahead of his financing, his organization had to grow or collapse. Basically, he found fairly early that "he could reach a far wider audience by talking about 'family' issues than by talking about theology."[35] Despite the pledge to stay strictly within the Bible, Falwell like most of the television evangelists had always veered into the political by preaching the "American way of life." Flag, freedom, anticommunism, and anti-anti-Americanism. As with so many passages in the Bible, those in the catechism of Falwell's "civic religion" required only the shortest of logical steps to get to contemporary politics.

As Falwell became increasingly current in his positions on political issues, he found more than merely a responsive audience in his own flock. Through social and political criticism, Falwell could transcend the limits of his southern accent, his bucolic and down-home rhetoric, and his extraordinarily right-wing positions on virtually everything. As he put it himself in a 1979 book, "If you would like to know where I am politically, I am to the Right of wherever you are. I thought Goldwater was too liberal!" Two years earlier he had

[33]FitzGerald, "A Reporter at Large," 63.
[34]Ibid.
[35]Ibid., 122.

called for a return to "the McCarthy era, where we register all Communists. . . . Not only should we register them but we should stamp it on their foreheads and send them back to Russia." On another occasion he said publicly that "the liberal churches are not only the enemy of God but the enemy of the nation."[36] If after the mid-1970s he continued to emphasize that he was involved only with moral and religious issues, it would have been because the distinction between moral and political helped him steer clear of the IRS and any possible change in the tax-exempt status of his organization.

After twelve years of preaching the Sunday sermon at his Lynchburg church and running down to the Lynchburg television station and later to the Roanoke television station sixty miles away, his growth of audience and income was sufficient to enable him to buy his own equipment, first in black and white, and to improve his programming. Then he upgraded to color and within two years was producing his own shows and buying time with local stations in the East and then in various parts of the country. By 1971, he was in competition, albeit smaller, with the more mainstream televangelists and, like them, was buying time on two hundred television stations around the country, meeting the millions of dollars of annual costs by over-the-air appeals and by direct mail. Within eight years, his "Old-Time Gospel Hour" had arrived, with 2.5 million loyal people on his mailing lists and an impressive reputation based on his ability to raise $115 million between 1977 and 1980. Although some skillful professional entrepreneurs were going to help him build up to the Moral Majority, Falwell was already ahead of them in experience and skill in compiling mailing lists through computer-analyzed searches. It was his mailing list, for example, that provided the database for Schlafly's anti-ERA campaign. Although Falwell had espoused separation of church from the outside world, this fundamentalist doctrine was given a rather expansive (liberal?) interpretation well before he broke away from it completely.

[36]Quotes from FitzGerald, "A Reporter at Large," 116.

Spiritually, organizationally, and technologically, Falwell was ready for the mobilization. And he was not alone. He serves here only as a case study, singled out not because he was the largest or most important but because he is richly illustrative and because he took the lead at the end—or I should say at the end of the beginning. Pat Robertson and his 700 Club was bigger, possibly more innovative, equally right wing or more, and equally modern in his command of the airwaves and the microwaves. Robertson was also southern, albeit more cosmopolitan. Moreover, Robertson had had a more impressive and dramatic conversion, the kind that seems to add credibility to people on the Right. The following is his own characterization.

> After all I'm a Yale law graduate, my father was a committee chairman of the U.S. Senate. . . . I harken back to a couple of presidents in my background and signers of the Declaration of Independence. So by the term "populist" I'm really not one of them. By heritage I'm more of the Eastern establishment . . . [but by] inclination . . . more aligned with the regular guy on the street.[37]

Yet Falwell best epitomizes the movement toward mobilization because it was Falwell who, in his own personal development and that of his flock, nationalized parochialism. The metaphor of metamorphosis does not fit. Neither Falwell nor his flock became something else, as the caterpillar becomes the moth. He and they remained the same, in values and outlook. What they had found, and what Falwell had tapped in his messages, was a set of shared national experiences and common irritants, which provided virtually a new national political culture for people with similar values but who spoke entirely different (albeit English) languages, had different tastes about the afterlife, and would ordinarily have found someone like Falwell a rather laughable sort—just as cosmopolitan (I should say

---

[37]Quote from an interview by Allen Hertzke, in Hertzke's *Echoes of Discontent*, 80.

Westernized) Jews find Hasidic Jews amusing or threatening or offensive (or all of the above) despite common values but because of their long hair and funny hats and mournful, unassimilated styles. As the stakes for Christian conservatives were nationalized, their focus and receptivity were nationalized accordingly, even though they basically remained parochial.

The rest is history, but no longer merely the history of Falwell and his flock of fundamentalists or Robertson and his Pentecostals and charismatics. By 1979, the movement optimistically called itself the Moral Majority, and it fell somewhere in between a congeries of small flocks and a national majority. The parochialisms, nationalized and mobilized in time for the 1980 presidential election, were far larger than the 2.5 million on Falwell's list plus the 16 million households tuned into Robertson's 700 Club broadcasts plus the other electronic evangelists and their followings. The first step had been from the Bible to contemporary political issues, through I Love America rallies and other initiation rites, to a few highly challenging specific issues. The next step was conversion of mailing lists into political constituencies. Although in many respects Falwell, Robertson et al. were ahead of the entrepreneurs, much of the credit goes to the entrepreneurs like Richard Viguerie for computerizing the Right. The next step required the entrepreneurs, because it required getting the Protestant flocks together with each other as well as together with the patrician Right on one side of them and the Catholic Right on the other.

A genuine challenge for entrepreneurs. During the Carter presidency, they began with the more secular right-wing organizations already in existence and got them together with the religious leaders to form three new organizations. The first, arising primarily out of western and southwestern states and probably the farthest to the Right, was Christian Voice, which addressed itself to particular electoral campaigns and candidates in regard to the issues of teaching evolution in the schools, pornography, immorality on television, and liquor and drug abuse.[38] The second was the Religious Roundtable, founded by Ed McAteer, a retired Memphis sales executive, and James Robison, an evangelist. Based primarily in the South and oriented primarily to the Southern Baptists, its expressed aim was to politicize evangelicals and to teach their pastors "the fine arts of political mobilization on behalf of various conservative causes."[39] It provided a platform for conservative speakers and gave conservative activists opportunities to become prominent as well as effective.

Finally, there was Moral Majority, the best known and the most comprehensive of the New Right groups. There seems to be some dispute over the origin of the name, with Falwell claiming to be its source but others claiming that it came from the entrepreneur Paul Weyrich's assertion made at their founding conference that evangelical Protestants, right-to-life Catholics, and orthodox Jews represented a "moral majority" that could tip the balance of national politics in favor of conservatism.[40] But there is no doubt that the two of them are the key figures in the formation of Moral Majority in 1979, at a meeting in Lynchburg, where Paul Weyrich and Howard Phillips had come to enlist Falwell's forces in some kind of conservative coalition. Weyrich, Phillips, and Viguerie were the Moral Majority's triumvirate of creative entrepreneurs.

And indeed it was and had to be a coalition. As Weyrich put it, "This alliance between religion and politics didn't just happen."[41] As Timothy Byrnes confirms, the alliance between religious leaders and political operatives that seemed to burst on the scene in the late 1970s was actually the result of a carefully implemented strategy.[42] The key to its success was more than a personal chemistry between some newly emerging religious leaders and some seasoned political entrepreneurs. It is true that Weyrich and Phillips, along with the

[38]Wald, *Religion and Politics in the United States*, 189–91.
[39]Ibid., 189.
[40]Byrnes, *Catholic Bishops in American Politics*, 89.
[41]Quoted in Byrnes, *Catholic Bishops in American Politics*, 89–90.
[42]Ibid., 90.

mass-mailing genius Richard Viguerie, had been working hard at such a conservative coalition throughout the 1970s, and had almost succeeded in forming a new third party with some of the patrician conservatives; but they did not find the essential missing ingredient until they, most probably Weyrich, came up with the "brilliant innovation" in 1979 to expand the "pro-life" agenda into a "pro-family" one.[43] This at last would give them the broader base, to incorporate the highly intense issue of abortion with a number of related and unrelated items on the agenda of social policies.

Abortion—Link to the Catholics

The founders of Moral Majority were fully aware that abortion was the key to their expansion, because it enabled the conservative Protestants, especially the Southerners like Falwell, to break "with the long fundamentalist tradition of anti-Catholicism." Falwell confessed that Catholic leaders had "stood alone and fought the abortion issue . . . [but] that Protestant ministers . . . have joined the fight." He spoke of Pope John Paul II, the successor to the notorious "popes of Rome," as the "best hope we Baptists ever had."[44]

Forming a coalition between Protestants and Catholics was a problem few today can appreciate. A long and bitter history of distrust between Catholics and other Christians was partly ideological and doctrinal, partly organizational, and partly ethnic, with all these factors intensified by Protestant fears that Catholics were more loyal to the Vatican than to America. This kind of distrust was extended and then further intensified by Irish opposition to the British and sympathy for the Germans during World War I and the involvement of Italy on the wrong side in World War II.

But there was a basis for an all-Christian coalition because Catholic conservatism was as localized as Protestant, and

[43]An observation by Connie Paige quoted in Byrnes, *Catholic Bishops in American Politics*, 88. For the longer account, see Connie Paige, *The Right to Lifers: Who Are They, How They Operate, Where They Get Their Money* (New York: Summit, 1983).
[44]Quotes from Byrnes, *Catholic Bishops in American Politics*, 90.

their concerns were about the same issues and focused on the same state and local governments. Disagreements between Catholics and Protestants could be intense, but they could see the same threats coming from the "social policies" outlined in table 5.1. As with other conservatives, Catholics and the Catholic hierarchy in America began to nationalize their political orientations in the 1960s.

Catholic reaction to these social issues came first from within the hierarchy. According to Byrnes, the national government had taken on "new authority and new responsibilities in a number of areas in which the Catholic hierarchy was ill-equipped to play a significant national role."[45] The National Catholic Welfare Conference, headquartered in Washington, had been active on such issues as contraception and aid to parochial schools, but it was a voluntary coalition not taken particularly seriously by America's Catholic bishops. Not all bishops attended the NCWC's meetings, and they rarely got together to make a collective announcement on behalf of the hierarchy and rarely permitted their priests to work there.[46]

All this changed after the Second Vatican Council (Vatican II, 1962–65) and a follow-up decree mandated establishment of national or regional conferences that under certain limited circumstances were to have "juridically binding force." Out of this came the National Conference of Catholic Bishops in November 1966 and their administrative arm located in Washington, the United States Catholic Conference (USCC). The NCCB went directly to work on the issues of contraception and abortion ("an unspeakable crime"), but even here, their focus was on coordinating the activities at state and local levels until *Roe v. Wade* in 1973 ("an unspeakable tragedy"). The NCCB took the lead nationally, and it was the bishops who gave antiabortion the "pro-life" spin and focused it on the relevant political campaigns, including the presidential campaign of 1976. The Catholic bishops and the Catholic

---

[45]Ibid., 47.
[46]Quoted in Byrnes, *Catholic Bishops in American Politics*, 48.

hierarchy were in national politics to stay, and no conservative entrepreneur could possibly overlook this opportunity.

THE MOBILIZED RIGHT

Pluralism for People Who Hate Pluralism

All the elements were in place for a nationally mobilized American conservatism. The nationalization of the many parochialisms meant that the "reconstituted Right" would be a coalition like the New Deal, composed of competing interests. But more problematic than the New Deal, the New Right was a coalition of, by, and for people who detest coalitions. It was a pluralist system of, by, and for people who hate pluralism. All the constituents of this coalition share a sense of certainty that the truth and the good can be known, but each can have a version of the truth and the good that may be considered the *only* truth and the *only* good. Each group in the coalition is a flock, and each flock shares a contempt for pluralism because in pluralism "*values* take the place of good and evil."[47] For patrician conservatives, even without an organized church, "there exists a transcendent moral order, to which we ought to try to conform the ways of society."[48] For them, there is a "body social, . . . a kind of spiritual corporation, comparable to the church."[49] Its moral authority "may take the form of the belief in 'natural law' or may assume some other expression . . ."; and, much to the contrary for liberals and pluralists, "theological postulates" can be derived from "this transcendent moral order."[50]

At a considerable distance from the patrician conservative position is that of the Catholic church; yet the two agree in their antagonism to pluralism. It had been a triumph in 1965 for the American delegation that the Second Vatican Council

---

[47]Allan Bloom, *The Closing of the American Mind* (New York: Simon and Schuster, 1987), 194. Emphasis in original.

[48]Russell Kirk, "Conservatism: A Succinct Description," writing for and in *National Review*, 3 September 1982, p. 1080.

[49]Ibid., 1081.

[50]Ibid.

had adopted a declaration of "the right to religious freedom" as one of its last acts before adjournment. As one liberal American delegate-observer put it, "A very ancient order of things, at least in principle—passed away. In principle, the era of Constantine—1600 years of it—passed away."[51] Seventeen years later, Richard McBrien, one of America's most renowned Catholic theologians and one who was thought to be much in sympathy with the 1965 declaration of religious freedom, felt moved nevertheless to make the following declaration of his own:

> There are many churches, but one Body of Christ. Within the community of churches, however, there is one Church that alone embodies and manifests all the institutional elements that are necessary for the whole body. In Catholic doctrine and theology, that one Church is the Catholic Church.[52]

A third view of pluralism, which cannot actually be characterized as in between or more moderate, is that of the populist Protestant Right. As A. James Reichley put it in his response to the Catholic claim to be the only true church, "Some of the fundamentalist faiths make somewhat similar claims, but not for their churches as institutions in history."[53] In other words, since there is no national or world church institution or hierarchy that can embody the true Protestant faith, the claim to exclusiveness has to be different. Nevertheless, there is an exclusiveness claim.

---

[51]Robert Cushman, as quoted in Reichley, *Religion in American Public Life,* 288. However, as Reichley puts it, the Church, in adopting that declaration, "had accepted the inevitability of social pluralism in a fallen world, but it had not accepted religious pluralism in the sense of acknowledging that all human institutions, including religious institutions, are finite and relative" (288).

[52]Quoted in Reichley, *Religion in American Life,* 288. Reichley, being a sincere pluralist, went to great lengths to be sympathetic to that position; and to put the most pluralist face possible on McBrien's figure, he accompanied McBrien's declaration with the observation that "Catholicism's enduring claim to be the one true church, while perhaps inevitably irritating to some non-Catholics, is not inconsistent with social pluralism. Indeed, if the Catholic Church were to give up its claim to *religious* primacy, America pluralism would be poorer . . . because the option of choosing an institution claiming unique spiritual authority . . . would no longer be available" (288; emphasis in original).

[53]Ibid.

The most extreme antipluralist statement of exclusiveness probably came from the Reverend Bailey Smith while serving as president of the Southern Baptist Convention: "God Almighty does not hear the prayer of a Jew."[54] The furious public response to Reverend Smith's assertion moved Falwell to make what might have been his most pluralist response, publicly assuring Rabbi Marc Tanenbaum of the American Jewish Committee that although he shared the faith that man comes to God only through Christ, that was merely a theological argument implying no anti-Semitism. "God is a respecter of all persons. He loves everyone alike. He hears the heart cry of any sincere person who calls on Him."[55] However, as the *New Yorker* reporter Frances FitzGerald observed, immediately following Falwell's assertion, "The price of ecumenical politics was apparently the renunciation of a fundamental tenet of faith." According to FitzGerald, Falwell was able to finesse Dr. Smith's orthodoxy only by "the maintenance of two separate audiences,"[56] because Falwell was regularly proclaiming to his own audience that "the liberal churches are not only the enemy of God but the enemy of the nation."[57]

Pat Robertson and his followers shared virtually all of these views but placed them in a larger context, adding distrust of big capitalism and eastern elites and placing it all within a conspiracy theory. Robertson saw a conspiracy to create a "new world order" involving the destruction of national sovereignty and "the elimination of traditional Judeo-Christian theism," under an elite rule that reaches back two centuries to a secret society called the Illuminati. The so-called international Communist conspiracy that was a favorite whipping boy of so many anti-Semitic agitators in Europe as well as in the United States was, to Robertson, "only a part of a broader movement that included the capitalist likes of Baron Rothschild, Cecil Rhodes, John D. Rockefeller, Andrew Carnegie,

---

[54]Quoted in FitzGerald, "A Reporter at Large," 133.
[55]Ibid.
[56]Ibid.
[57]Quoted in FitzGerald, "A Reporter at Large," 116.

and J. P. Morgan."[58] Just to emphasize the extent as well as the intensity of Robertson's antipluralist views, I should add that his conspiracy theory included the Council on Foreign Relations, the Trilateral Commission, New Age religion, and the Masonic movement; and one should add an etcetera.[59]

The neoconservatives offered a different kind of a problem for a coalition of the Right, because although inconsequential in numbers, they were powerful in intellectual influence, an influence that was a mixed blessing. From the standpoint of the conservative coalition, the plus side of the neoconservatives was that they shared a deep antipathy to New Liberalism, especially to the 1960s version with its social policies. Their criticisms of the antiwar movement, of student radicalism, of egalitarianism, and of the commitment of the New Liberals to policies of cultural diversity and affirmative action (later called political correctness) gave the rest of the conservative movement a great deal more intellectual respectability and a far wider public than would have been available through the *National Review* or through the various religious-sponsored publications. Neoconservatives and their journals had been secretly supported by the CIA, which gave them far greater access to American and European publics. But they hardly needed the CIA support after a while, because, since so many of them were extremely well educated and highly talented writers, their exposure and their views gained them honest access to the major "prestige papers," including the *Wall Street Journal*, the *New York Times*, and the *Washington Post*.

On the negative side (from the standpoint of the conservative coalition), most of the older, leading neoconservatives were former Communists. They had rejected Stalin, then the USSR, and then communism itself. But, unlike Whittaker Chambers, their conversion to Americanism did not include conversion to Christianity. Most of them were of Jewish

[58]Hertzke, *Echoes of Discontent*, 91.
[59]For Robertson's own views on the Illuminati and the "new world order" conspiracy, see Robertson, *The New World Order* (Dallas: Word Publishing, 1991), esp. chaps. 1 and 4. For an evaluation, see Hertzke, *Echoes of Discontent*, 91–95.

descent. Those who were not atheists were, for lack of a better term, religious functionalists or functional religionists. That is to say, although they themselves may not have believed in God, did not adhere to a church or observe the rituals of an established religion, or use God in their political analyses, they believed that it is essential that "the people" believe and that the people have a religion and be part of a religious institution of some sort. Virtually all neoconservatives have a "declinist" vision of history: with Chambers and more so with Aleksandr Solzhenitsyn, they believe that the West is going to hell in a handbasket not because communism is favored by history but because of liberal, capitalist self-indulgence, loss of character and self-reliance, rejection of authority, and skepticism and relativism toward Western morality, religion, and institutions. But despite their atheism, or deism, the neoconservatives were able to make their way into the inner core of the larger Republican/conservative coalition because their theories and policies were guided by such transcendent ideas as those of Solzhenitsyn.

> [We are threatened with destruction by] the spirit of Munich [that] dominates the 20th century. The frightened civilized world found nothing better than concessions and smiles to counterpose to the sudden renewed assault of bare-fanged barbarism. The spirit of Munich is an illness of the will of prosperous people. It is the daily state of those who have given themselves over . . . to material prosperity as the principal goal of life on earth.[60]

Religion, Race and Reagan

Mobilization provided not only a "reconstituted Right"[61] but a reconstituted Republican party that could definitely win and probably govern. But, for reasons given, it would be a

---

[60]Aleksandr Solzhenitsyn, *The Nobel Lecture on Literature*, translated from the Russian by Thomas P. Whitney (New York: Harper & Row, 1972), 27.

[61]Benjamin Ginsberg and Martin Shefter, "A Critical Realignment? The New Politics, the Reconstituted Right, and the Election of 1984," in Michael Nelson, ed., *The Elections of 1984* (Washington, D.C.: Congressional Quarterly Press, 1985), 1–26.

much more complex coalition than the New Deal coalition, and it would be far more difficult to maintain.

Every social movement is a contradiction. It must be built from the bottom up but also from the top down. People must become aware that they share grievances or goals, but people do not organize themselves. A movement requires an elite, an elite capable of exercising a very special kind of leadership. And if the binding of the various conservatisms into a movement was a particularly difficult challenge for a leadership, the task was all the more difficult if these conservatisms were to be tied to a still larger movement, a newly constituted Republican party with the novel and (to most conservatives) virtually alien mission of engaging in national electoral politics.

The very special leadership was indeed located in the person of Ronald Reagan, and the successful melding together of these various elements would in fact be the real Reagan Revolution. Reagan did not create the conservative movement, although he had made an important contribution to it in his prominent 1964 support of Goldwater and the momentary success of the conservative wing of the Republican party. Reagan's conversion prior to 1964 from New Deal Democrat to Goldwater Republican had made him all the more credible as a conservative. Conversion turns out to be as important in the politics as in the religion of the Right. It seems to be a kind of apotheosis. Moreover, the further into evil one might have descended, the more credible and respected one's testimonials after conversion. Nevertheless, Reagan was the catalyst, not the creator. He was not even the premier choice for president among right-wing leaders. But he had what none of the others had.

Reagan's gift was not charisma—a much misunderstood and abused word that actually means a gift of grace, partaking of the divine. Though there were many charismatics among the leaders of the religious Right, the quality of Reagan's leadership was far removed from that. He was a catalytic, not a charismatic, leader. A catalyst is a substance that can cause or change the rate of chemical reaction without itself being consumed in the process. In this he was like FDR and, in fact, like most great coalition builders. But his task was still more difficult because, as observed earlier, (1) he could not rely as much as FDR could on expanding government programs as patronage incentives; (2) his constituents required that he be more doctrinal and ideological during political campaigns; (3) the programs he did support had to be more doctrinal and also had to cost less, or nothing at all; and (4) he could not rely on Congress, even during the six years he had control of the Senate, because he had no two-house majority and also because appeals to districts could so quickly violate the party's own doctrinal position that "government is not the solution to our problem; government is the problem."

Complex as any national, presidential coalition would have to be, the Reagan/Republican coalition came together and was held together by three principal factors: race, religion, and negation. Apologies to those who recall "rum, romanism, and rebellion," but that particular alliteration was false and malicious, whereas the present one is, and is intended to be, descriptive and objective.

Race had been a defining factor in national politics for generations—first between the two parties and then principally within the Democratic party. Its relevance never really declined, but it was transformed during the 1960s, intermixed with religion. Within the Democratic party, religion had actually contributed to radicalization toward the Left, especially on issues of race, racial justice, and minority rights. And the contribution of race through religion to the liberal agenda helped send most conservative whites to the Republican party, at least for presidential purposes. This is why it is important to reiterate that the realignment of this era was largely an ideological one. Thus, for example, in 1980, white Protestants reported in exit polls that they voted 63 to 31 percent for Reagan, with born-again Protestants voting 63 to 33 percent. By 1984, white Protestants voted 73 to 26 percent for Reagan, and born-again Protestants voted a striking 80 to 20 percent for Reagan. There was of course a strong liberal wing on all social issues within each of the major religions and sects, but since a lot of the religious Left in the Democratic party was black and since so many of the white religious Left sympathized with the antiwar movement, the movement of the white faithful was further and further Right as well as Republican. I must repeat that Right and Republican were not always synonymous; but now they were moving closer together, in large part through the medium of self-selection within and among the Christian faiths. "Thus," as Hertzke so succinctly puts it, "were the seeds of Republican presidential hegemony planted in the soil of race and religion."[62]

Jimmy Carter was the first born-again Christian of prominence in national politics. His nomination "created an instant media fascination with his religion, and journalists made pilgrimages to Plains, Georgia, to discover what a 'born-again' Christian person was like."[63] When polls revealed that 34 percent of the total adult population shared Carter's born-again experience and when party leaders confronted that fact plus the fact that Carter was supported by both Jesse Jackson *and* Pat Robertson, there could be no denying that a genuinely new specter was hovering over America. Given that *all three* 1980 presidential candidates—Jimmy Carter, Ronald Reagan, and John Anderson—were professed born-again Christians, Reagan's speech with which this chapter began can be appreciated as an expression of a continuing strategic necessity.

THE STATE THEORY OF THE REPUBLICAN ERA

To elect is one thing. To govern is quite another, especially for this newly constituted coalition. It had to have some kind of operative principle that gave the appearance of a policy agenda but in fact had to transcend policy to avoid tearing the

[62]Allen Hertzke, "Harvest of Discontent: Religion and Populism in the 1988 Presidential Campaign," in James Guth and John Green, *The Bible and the Ballot Box: Religion and Politics in the 1988 Election* (Boulder: Westview Press, 1991), 5.
[63]Ibid.

fabric of the coalition. This is not to denigrate "the interests" that had to be held together in this newly energized Republican administration.[64] But interests have been far too overplayed in most academic and journalistic analyses. In this conservative era, ideology counts, for so much that an entirely new theory of the American state was emerging.

Elements of the Theory

A new state theory would take some doing for a party and a party leader with little taste for theory. But it happened, and this is precisely what put the Reagan Revolution on par with the Roosevelt Revolution. Table 5.2 is an outline of the most important elements of a Republican state theory, or, as an academic theorist might say, a pretheory. The dates chosen for this era are 1980 to 2000 because, at least in my opinion, the Republican theory is hegemonic even during the Clinton administration and is likely to remain hegemonic as long as the Democrats are as willing as they have been to carry on the discourse within its terms.

Elaboration of the elements in table 5.2 should begin with "Embrace," because these are the subdominant themes and can be given a lighter touch. Of these, the most important is the role of the presidency. Almost every treatment of American government embraces a strong and energetic president, to maintain public order, to use the office as a "bully pulpit," to protect and defend America not only from its external enemies but also from its internal enemies, such as an unstable economy, high living, and a tendency toward dysfunction. Intellectuals supporting New Liberalism and the Democratic party were great presidential power enthusiasts until the day

[64]For a thorough analysis of the elements of pure selfish interest that made up the "Reaganism" coalition, see Thomas Ferguson and Joel Rogers, *Right Turn: The Decline of the Democrats and the Future of American Politics* (New York: Hill and Wang, 1986). For a significant modification of the theory of interest groups in the politics of the 1980s and beyond, see Paul E. Peterson, "The Rise and Fall of Special Interest Politics," *Political Science Quarterly* 105, no. 4 (Winter 1990–91): 539–56.

their hegemony was broken; and even today they tend to find the Democratically controlled Congress something of an embarrassment, since it is largely a haven for protection of the agencies and programs that comprise their Second Republic. The presidency has become all the more attractive to the intellectuals of the Republican era, and this is genuine, not merely a product of the twelve-year Republican control, because most of the Republican intellectuals are conservatives for whom a strong executive is on principle essential. In fact, presidential scholarship itself has been virtually captured by conservatives.[65] Although Old Liberals as well as conservatives would prefer a Republican president, I think they have come to recognize that only a safe person, in their terms, can actually be elected—judging from the treatment given by the electorate to such unsafe candidates as Goldwater, McGovern, and Dukakis, as well as the electoral success of a safe Demo-

---

[65]The list of conservative scholars interested in and committed to the strong presidency is too extensive, and the issues too complex, for this book. But if in the future I were to undertake a review of the Right and the presidency, I would begin with Terry Eastland, *Energy in the Executive: The Case for the Strong Presidency* (New York: Free Press, 1992). Note Eastland's subtitle and a couple of introductory statements: "The purpose of this book is to recover and restate the enduring case for energy in the executive, which is to say: the strong presidency" (3). "The book is written for conservatives serious about politics and governing. But it cannot be for conservatives only, for the simple reason that the strong presidency is the American presidency" (4). And then I would turn to L. Gordon Crovitz and Jeremy A. Rabkin, eds., *The Fettered Presidency: Legal Constraints on the Executive Branch* (Washington, D.C.: American Enterprise Institute, 1989). In his foreword, Robert Bork states, "The rescue of the proper power to the presidency will have to be accomplished by strong and determined presidents who can make the case to the American people. . . . The president must make a public issue of congressional attempts to control his legitimate powers, perhaps by refusing to accept some restrictions even at the risk of political damage. It would be a prolonged and bloody fight, but our national well-being requires that it be made" (xiii–xiv). And from the Crovitz-Rabkin introduction, "This book addresses the proliferation of legal constraints on policymaking in the Executive Branch of the Federal government and highlights the risks and dangers this poses for public policy" (1). And, "The Executive has many inherent powers at his disposal to protect against the legal constraints that cripple effective policymaking. The lesson of the past eight years is that these powers must be used with greater vigor and resolve if the presidency is to fulfill its intended role" (12).

Table 5.2
Elements of the Republican Era State Theory, 1980–2000

Embrace	Negation
Of presidency independent of Congress	Of national government
Of administrative discretion	Of federal courts
Of state government	Of Congress
Of military force	Of party politics

crat like Clinton. All the presidency needs to satisfy the requirements of Old Liberals and conservatives is the line-item veto and term limits on Congress to become the good ruler in the name of responsible government.

The second element in table 5.2, embrace of administrative discretion free of court interference, is strongly related to the first. The conservative argument against the "imperial judiciary" has focused on the influence of the federal courts in "opening up the administrative process" by making it easier for citizen groups to sue federal agencies both to stop the agencies from doing unwanted things and, more important, to force the federal agencies to engage in more vigorous implementation of laws, especially in the field of environmental and consumer protection.[66] Some conservative authors have gone still further, accusing the court of engaging in a socialist plot virtually to turn the federal administrative process over to left-wing citizen groups trying to use the federal courts to advance goals that, after the 1960s, had been frustrated by their loss of the presidency.[67]

So much has already been said in these pages of the conservative embrace of state government that little more needs to be added here except to reemphasize potential for conflict with the Old Liberal component of the coalition.

[66]Sidney Milkis, "The Presidency, Policy Reform, and the Rise of Administrative Politics," in Richard A. Harris and Sidney Milkis, eds., *Remaking American Politics* (Boulder: Westview Press, 1989), 167.

[67]See especially, Jeremy Rabkin, *Judicial Compulsions* (New York: Basic Books, 1989).

Orthodox Old Liberals would prefer to negate state government as well as national government, while conservatives
view state government as the opportunity to impose virtue on
the population. What may help hold them together despite
this difference is the role of state government in the use of
uniformed force. Conservatives and Old Liberals stand together on the need for military force in the national government, and that becomes item number 4, which needs little
comment. Conservative support for maximum military force
in state government (through the police) against immoral
conduct, including crimes without victims, might be irksome
to Old Liberals, but they also recognize the need for military
force to maintain public order, defend private property, and
enforce the obligations of contracts. This is the irreducible
statist requirement of the free market that Old Liberals like to
pretend does not exist. Nevertheless, it is an important basis
for common cause between conservatives and Old Liberals.

In all other respects, the dominant theme of the Republican
coalition is negation, composed largely of the four items in
column 2 of table 5.2. Most important among these is negation
of national government. Republicans were so successful in
selling negation of national government that they implicated
the institutions as well as the policies, perhaps succeeding
beyond their own hopes. For well over a decade, Republican
party unity voting in Congress has been an ideologically
driven negation of national government growth, indeed national government action of *any* sort. Nowadays, almost every
candidate for Congress takes a strong stand against the
institution itself and devotes much time to expressing how his
or her tenure will be devoted to keeping the national government from doing anything. Members get heroic front-page
press if they retire for lack of being able to bring down the
deficit or to "get things done" in that context.

Negation of the federal courts, item number 2, is not inconsistent but is a rather curious stand, more complex than it
appears at first exposure. The basic argument goes well
beyond the previously observed criticism by conservatives of

judicial interference with administrative discretion toward the argument that the judiciary became imperial by infringing on the prerogatives of the legislature and therefore of the wishes of the people.

It sounds at first blush like pure democracy. The following is one example from Robert Bork, probably the most famous conservative critic of judicial infringement on the legislature. Having sought to bring "into the open the fundamental antipathy to democracy to be seen in much of the new scholarship," Bork went on to observe that

> the original Constitution was devoted primarily to the mechanisms of democratic choice. Constitutional scholarship today is dominated by the creation of arguments that will encourage judges to thwart democratic choice. . . . One of the freedoms, the major freedom, of our kind of society is the freedom to choose to have a public morality. . . . The makers of our Constitution thought so too, for they provided wide powers to representative assemblies and ruled only a few subjects off limits by the Constitution. . . . In a constitutional democracy the moral content of law must be given by the morality of the framer or the legislator, never by the morality of the judge.[68]

But what is the basis of Bork's complaint and the complaints of other conservatives on this point? Since the Supreme Court has not declared a significant act of Congress unconstitutional for five decades, where is the infringement? The infringement on the legislature of which Bork complains so passionately is the Supreme Court's application of the Bill of Rights to the power of *state* legislatures to act as they please against their own citizens in such matters as unpopular speech, school prayer, the races, and the status of females. Thus the negation they truly want is reversal of the decisions, and removal from the Court of the power to make decisions, incorporating the provisions of the Bill of Rights into the

---

[68]Robert H. Bork, "Tradition and Morality in Constitutional Law," Lecture on Public Policy, American Enterprise Institute, 1984; reprinted in Mark W. Cannon and David M. O'Brien, eds., *Views from the Bench* (Chatham, N.J.: Chatham House, 1985), 170–71.

Fourteenth Amendment to apply as restrictions on state government as well as on the national government. Back to *Barron v. Baltimore* and chapter 1.

Negation of Congress, item 3, ought to be clear already. Nothing has been more sincere and earnest on the part of members of the Republican coalition than the bashing of the national legislature. Americans traditionally criticize their government and rather enjoy an occasional congressional scandal. But I doubt there has been an era in this century that has engaged in more Congress bashing than the current one. Members of Congress have been rendered so fearful that they even vote against an increase in their own salary, and they tend to run against the very Congress for which they are candidates. Probably the best measure of the success of the campaign of negation against Congress was the unprecedented 1992 adoption by initiative and referendum of constitutional provisions for term limits in fourteen states, with at least six more states following suit in 1993. That means that twenty states out of the twenty where the attempt was made now put a constitutional limit of twelve years on the eligibility of a member to serve in Congress. Whatever the effect of term limits, the movement for their adoption was without a doubt a traumatic attack on Congress in particular and representative government in general.

Finally, as for the negation of party politics, there could be no stronger evidence than the continued increase of the preference among Americans for defining themselves as independent voters. Coupled with that is a dramatic increase in the proportion of *party-loyal* voters who reported that despite their continued party loyalty, they felt themselves to be neutral as to the significance of the difference between the two parties. Complementary to these developments is a significant decline in the percentage of those people who felt positive toward one party and negative toward the other party. The attack on party politics, coupled with the systematic avoidance of their party label by presidential and congressional candidates, has been counterproductive to the extent that

it definitely fed Ross Perot, whose campaign sought particularly "to capitalize on the perceived irrelevance of parties."[69]

The State Theory Applied to Policy

Although the basic elements of the Republican coalition's
theory of state are all concerned with institutions of government, the coalition leadership did use them as a source and
justification for a few specific policies. Table 5.3 is not an
exhaustive listing of twelve years of Republican policy efforts
but does not fall far short of one, because a coalition built so
heavily on negation would feel under far less obligation than
its predecessors to produce a lot of new policies. Moreover,
not all of the items in table 5.3 became law. To understand this
era and what held the Republican coalition together, it is more
important to identify and assess what they seriously asked for
rather than what they got. Table 5.3 therefore identifies the
most salient policy positions taken by the Reagan and Bush
administrations. Most of these are Reagan's, with Bush prom-
ising continuity and keeping the promise, almost to the end.

Each of the items in table 5.3 can and should be viewed as
an effort by the central leadership to come up with actions
that would give the public the impression of positiveness and
at the same time give certain segments of the Republican
coalition a sense that their main interests were being taken
into account. Granted, conservatives are far more concerned
with ideology and moral consistency. Granted also, *interest* is
a word closely associated with liberalism and is a sign of
sinful indulgence, implying that values are mere interests and
that all interests are equal. Nevertheless, interests are not
irrelevant to conservatives. As a matter of fact, the job of
serving interests is all the more difficult in a coalition consist-
ing heavily of conservatives. This is the proper context in
which to assess the policies.

[69]Martin Wattenberg, "The 1992 Election: Ross Perot and the Independent
Voter," prepublication copy of chap. 10 of Wattenberg's *The Decline of American
Political Parties, 1952–1992* (Cambridge: Harvard University Press, forthcoming).
Poll results reported in this paragraph are also from Wattenberg.

Table 5.3
Policies and Interests in the Republican Coalition

Policies	Interests Served	
	Old Liberal	Conservative
1981 tax cuts	x	
High interest, anti-inflation	x	
Tax rate indexation	x	
1986 tax reforms	x	
Capital gains tax cuts	x	
Economic deregulation	x	
Civil rights deregulation	x	x
Privatization	x	
Welfare: devolution ("the swap")		x
Welfare: "cleaning the rolls"		x
Welfare: stigmatization	x	x
Balanced budget amendment*	x	x
Line-item veto amendment*	x	x
Term limits amendment*		x
School prayer amendment*		x
End school busing and benign quotas		x
Defense buildup	x	x
War on drugs		x

*Sought but not adopted.

Table 5.3 would tend at first exposure to confirm the contention that the mainstream Old Liberals got significantly more satisfaction than conservatives from Republican era administrations. Initiatives of interest to Old Liberals were in fact sought by Republican leaders more frequently, supported more strongly, and adopted more readily than those of primary interest to conservatives. However, especially during the Reagan years, there seems to have been enough to keep most conservatives under the Republican tent. First, although the purely economic policies were more strongly salient to Old Liberals, conservatives were not unhappy to see at least some shrinkage of the national government. Second, the patrician Right in particular would share satisfaction in the upward redistribution of wealth forthcoming from "across-the-board" tax cuts plus elimination of several tax brackets and indexation of the remaining ones. And third, Reagan administration support for conservative constitutional amendments, even though not adopted, was highly gratifying because prime-time media coverage would contribute more to change in the climate of moral opinion than all the prayer meetings and Praise the Lord broadcasts.

Another point of great relevance to the interests of conservatives as well as Old Liberals was Reagan's commitment to policy initiatives that could be taken or maintained independently of Congress. Tax indexing, once adopted, works automatically, without further need of going through Congress. Cleaning the welfare rolls is largely administrative and takes a minimum of congressional clearance. Most significant, Reagan's approach to deregulation avoided Congress almost completely: he sought no terminations or even serious downward revision of the jurisdictions, powers, or methods of the major regulatory agencies. Those goals would have required legislation. Instead, like a good conservative, he left all the regulatory authority in place—ready to be called on if desired—and got his deregulation through significant reduction of the *output of agency rules and regulations.* The first thing he did was to weaken the regulatory agencies by cutting their budgets and staffs and by appointing people to the commissions who were not in sympathy with the regulatory mission of their agencies; in fact, some of these Reagan appointees were genuinely hostile.[70] Next, and most important, he employed a regulatory review process actually put in place by President Carter but little appreciated then. Through the Office of Information and Regulatory Affairs (OIRA) in the Office of Management and Budget, Reagan successfully subjected all

[70]See, for example, Kenneth J. Meier, *Regulation: Politics, Bureaucracy, and Economics* (New York: St. Martin's Press, 1985), chaps. 4, 6, and 8.

proposed administrative rules to review. (For those independent regulatory commissions where he did not have full
authority to require preclearance, President Reagan successfully
got hold of them through moral suasion.) There was indeed a
significant reduction of rules, a rough approximation of which
can be gained from the fact, as mentioned previously, that the
number of pages in the annual *Federal Register* was cut by
about half from its high of 65,000 between 1977 and 1984.[71]
Thus deregulation through "regulation management" was
attractive to virtually all constituents of the Republican coalition, first because they all tended to favor shrinkage of the
national government and second because they all contributed
to negation of Congress.[72]

Finally, and of especial significance to conservative interests, there was the stigmatization of welfare. For the Old
Liberals, the primary welfare policy goal was one of reducing
welfare expenditures, especially expenditures for discretionary, means-tested service delivery programs (as contrasted
with contributory, direct cash benefit entitlement programs).
Although the most radical of Old Liberals would have preferred
the complete dismantling of the entire welfare state, they
definitely could live with serious expenditure reduction, giv-
en political realities. For conservatives, expenditure reduction
was secondary: Stigmatization meant leaving virtually all
welfare state programs on the books but seizing them as an
opportunity to teach some moral lessons to dependent people. Citizens, privately and through their governments, should
be charitable to those less fortunate than themselves. But in
the consensus view of the Republican coalition, policy should
at the same time carefully distinguish between deserving and
undeserving poor, looking out only for the "truly needy." People,
however unfortunate their fate, should be made ashamed of

[71]For a good review of the entire process, see Harold Seidman and Robert
Gilmour, *Politics, Position and Power* (New York: Oxford University Press, 1986),
127–31.

[72]For more on the concept of "regulation management," see Lowi and
Ginsberg, *American Government*, 337–44 and 664–68.

accepting assistance, should always prefer work to welfare, and should be forced to work wherever and whenever possible. Dependency may not always be caused by moral weakness, but continued dependency will almost certainly contribute to weakness. The following passage is a good example. Referring to welfare as a "moral hazard" (bringing on the very evil it is aimed to eliminate), Gilder argues that extending benefits to families with unemployed fathers contributes to an increase in the rate of breakup of poor families

> because the benefit levels destroy the father's key role and authority. He can no longer feel manly in his own home. At first he may try to maintain his power by use of muscle and bluster. But to exert force against a woman is a confession of weakness. Soon after, he turns to the street for his male affirmations.[73]

THE TRAGEDY OF CONSERVATISM

Although the factor or impulse common to the Republican coalition's ideological and policy elements is negation, it can be given a more substantive political interpretation. The theory and policies of negation amount to rejection of representative government and democratic pluralism.

This formulation reveals the tragic flaw of the American Right. Just as each of the other public philosophies was shown to have its inherent contradictions—producing a tragedy by virtue of its lack of sufficient awareness of its own limits—so we now confront the inherent contradiction of the Right: It

---

[73]Gilder, *Wealth and Poverty*, 138–39. While there are data from experimental studies of welfare families that would tend to confirm Gilder's own impressionistic study of a relationship between increased welfare benefits and separations and divorces in poor families, there is nothing in these studies that would confirm his psychological theories as to what unemployed males go through; there is actually nothing in the data to suggest that the initiative for the breakup comes from the males, even among those who might be suffering from loss of self-esteem. That scenario is strictly from Gilder's own imagination. Until in-depth interviews of sufficient samples of males and females in such families have been conducted, there is an alternative theory that is just as likely to be confirmed, which is that the increased welfare benefits made it possible for poor married couples to get divorced because the extra money made it possible for them to imagine they could get along without their spouses.

has contempt for the pluralist political process that makes its own persistence possible. Since conservatism is a numerical minority seeking ideological hegemony, it must depend on the tolerance of opposing minorities, which, together, make a majority. Yet tolerance is the beginning of relativism and decline.

Allan Bloom, Advocate of the Closed Mind

Take the case of the late Allan Bloom, one of the leading conservative critics of this era.

> Cultural relativism succeeds in destroying the West's universal or intellectually imperialist claims, leaving it to be just another culture. So there is equality in the republic of cultures. Unfortunately the West is defined by its need for justification of its ways or values. . . . This is its cultural imperative. Deprived of that, it will collapse.[74]

To Bloom, truth can be discovered by use of reason, and truth will prove our culture superior to others. Relativity is political.

> History and the study of cultures do not teach or prove that values or cultures are relative. All to the contrary, that is a philosophical premise that we now bring to our study of them. The premise is unproven and dogmatically asserted for what are largely political reasons.[75]

In other words, the very "openness" of liberal America, including its universities, is nothing more than blind acceptance of all cultures as equal and refusal to see the truth Bloom's reason will reveal. The purpose of Bloom's book is to close the American mind around the genuine truth. But found where? In what? The Greeks? The Judeo-Christian tradition? The Bible? Old or New Testaments, or both? Translated or original language only? The English (or French or American) tradition? The local/country tradition? It is curious that the

[74]Bloom, *The Closing of the American Mind*, 39.
[75]Ibid.

leap of faith to embrace a particular text or tradition comes first, then reason follows. But that is not as advertised.

A key example of this point of view can be found in Bloom's treatment of his Yale colleague Robert Dahl. In one of the classic works of liberal democratic theory, Dahl turned to a confrontation of the problem of the "intensity" of commitment to a particular goal that groups might bring to the political process. That is definitely a basic problem for any political system, especially a democracy, because the radicalism resulting from intense commitments can destroy the discourse out of which political solutions can be developed. Bloom, however, takes Dahl's recognition of the problem as an indication of Dahl's willingness to replace reason with fanaticism.[76] What is doubly interesting about this attack on Dahl's effort to come to grips with a particular political problem is that Dahl's own tolerance of opposing ideologies made possible Bloom's appointment to the Yale political science faculty and, through that, Bloom's appointment and promotion to tenure at Cornell University. This is not to suggest that Bloom is to be condemned for a lack of gratitude. The point is quite a different one, that if Allan Bloom could have been cloned into a majority in the Yale Department of Political Science, Robert Dahl would have been denied an appointment.

Bloom's confidence that reason determines truth and that Western culture is the superior one was shared by a famous Yale alumnus, William Buckley. However, according to his arguments in *God and Man at Yale*, Buckley would have sought vigorously to deny Allan Bloom his appointment to the faculty, because Bloom did not accept the Christian faith as his own, was not "committed to the desirability of fostering both the belief in God and a recognition of the merits of our economic system" (Buckley, p. xiv), and was, besides all that, a practicing homosexual. Thanks to the exclusivity of conservatives like Buckley, a professor like Bloom had to depend on the open-mindedness and downright cultural relativism of liber-

[76]Ibid., 32.

als like Robert Dahl while at the same time having nothing but contempt for such views.

Pat Buchanan, Pan-Christian

Bloom is a limited case study for our purposes because he was concerned with absolute truth in contexts in which differences over absolutes were not matters of life and death. He was in the university. For the larger political universe, we have to turn to different cases, the richest of which is Pat Buchanan. Buchanan is the Gamal Abdel Nasser of panconservatism. Like Nasser, who preached broad third world unity but practiced a narrower Pan-Arabism, Buchanan preaches a broad panconservatism within a still broader Republican coalition but practices Pan-Christian conservatism.

We need not review here the details of Buchanan's revolt against Bush, his insurgent candidacy against Bush for the 1992 presidential nomination, and his ignominious defeat by Bush in thirty-three (of thirty-three) primaries. We can jump instead directly to his concession/unity speech before the Republican Convention on that famous opening night when the party was turned over to the conservatives.

> My friends, this election is about more than who gets what. It is about who we are. It is about what we believe and what we stand for as Americans. There is a religious war going on in this country for the soul of America. It is a cultural war as critical to the kind of nation we shall be as the Cold War itself, for this war is for the soul of America. And in that struggle for the soul of America, Clinton and Clinton [Bill and Hillary] are on the other side, George Bush is on our side.[77]

Buchanan's convention speech was pure panconservatism. He knew something that apparently few others did. Although the polls had revealed that conservatism is a minority ideology in America at large and that Christian conservatism is a

[77]Patrick Buchanan, "The Election Is About Who We Are—Taking Back Our Country," delivered at the Republican National Convention, Houston, Texas, 17 August 1992, reprinted in *Vital Speeches of the Day*, 15 September 1992, pp. 712–15.

still smaller one, more specialized polls disclosed that 47 percent of the Republican *delegates* were "born-again Christians" and that 79 percent of the delegates defined their ideologies as ranging from conservative to very conservative.[78]

> My friends, these people are our people. They don't read Adam Smith or Edmund Burke, but they . . . share our beliefs and convictions, our hopes and dreams. These are the conservatives of the heart [such as] the brave people of Koreatown who took the worst of those LA riots, but still live the family values we treasure, and who still believe deeply in the American dream.[79]

In his convention speech, Buchanan called only on the shades of Adam Smith and Edmund Burke. But following the election, with a renewed sense of having been confirmed by the embarrassing defeat of President Bush after only one term in office, Buchanan became the Pan-Christian rather than the panconservative, calling less on the English moralists and more on the prophets and the popes. Speaking to the national conference of the Christian Coalition in September 1993, "Pat Buchanan brought 2,000 Christian conservatives to their feet with a vow to rebuff Republican moderates and never 'raise a white flag to the culture war.'"[80] Although beginning on his 1992 convention speech theme, Buchanan turned quickly to a theme more narrowly appropriate for this homogeneous audience. This was an attack on "multiculturalism." He scoffed at those who accept all the world's cultures as equal: "Our culture is superior. . . . Our culture is superior because our religion is Christianity and that is the truth that makes men free. . . . We cannot raise a white flag in the cultural war because that war is who we are."[81]

The Christian Coalition, a product primarily of the leadership of Pat Robertson, was happy to have Pat Buchanan as a

[78]Gordon Black Poll, conducted for *USA Today* and NBC News, July 1992.

[79]Buchanan, convention speech, 17 August 1992.

[80]"Christian Group Keeping to Right," *New York Times*, 12 September 1993, p. 37.

[81]Ibid.

national leader and symbol of Christian conservatism, but its own official strategy was to seek votes and influence at the grass roots. Claiming to have learned their lesson with what they themselves call "a suicide mission" for Robertson's presidential bid in 1988, "their best policy is to struggle at street level, and leave national politics to look after itself."[82] And their grass-roots strategy was paying off, not only through their contributions to the defeat of several Democratic senators and members of Congress but also in their success in dozens upon dozens of cities in local and state legislative, school and library board elections, and Republican party committee elections. We have already seen that this localism fits a long tradition of conservative behavior. The difference now is that conservatives have tasted national mobilization, have had a bittersweet experience with it, appear to have no intention of rejecting it even as they return to local concerns, and hold tightly to the likes of Pat Buchanan for those occasions when a national presence is desired. And to repeat, Pat Buchanan is not alone in this role; he is simply the richest case study of it.

Buchanan's prose is the ambitious prose of a Christian Republic. It could be more grandiose; it could be the prose of a Christian Nation. But that is too risky, and it leaves them no escape route or moderating room in short-run dealings with non-Christians, especially the Jewish intelligentsia of the neoconservative persuasion. Intimations of the dynamite in the Christian Nation idea came home to Christian conservatives shortly after the 1992 elections when Mississippi Republican Governor Kirk Fordice asserted to a conference of Republican governors that it was a "simple fact of life" that the United States is a "Christian nation." Other governors were quick to rebuke Governor Fordice, and they joined with the Republican National Committee to insist on "Judeo-Christian," as used in the Republican party platform. Governor Fordice resisted at first, curtly responding that he would have said

[82]Quote from the *Economist*, "American Survey," 5 December 1992, p. 25.

"Judeo-Christian" if that is what he had meant to say; he meant "Christian nation" and that is what he said. Ultimately, Governor Fordice did back down, with apologies to those he might have offended. All of them were aware of the fact that Jewish support of President Bush had dropped from 35 percent in 1988 to 12 percent in 1992, and one of the important influences back of this decline was the emphasis the 1992 Republican Convention put on "Christian values."[83] In any event, "Christian Republic" is an adequate formulation, and it fits the temper of the times inasmuch as large parts of the Islamic world are hopeful of founding Islamic Republics.

Buchanan is almost certainly anti-Semitic, and most of the testimony comes from the fellow travelers in his own conservative movement. A. M. Rosenthal, *New York Times* columnist and prominent Jewish neoconservative, brutally made the charge in his regular op/ed column. The charge was confirmed by no less than William Buckley and expanded on by another neoconservative, the distinguished journalist Charles Krauthammer, who baldly asserted that "the real problem with Buchanan . . . is not that his instincts are anti-Semitic but that they are, in various and distinct ways, fascistic."[84] Buchanan has a lot of supportive company among most orthodox, observant Christians, who have a tendency toward anti-Semitism. Some are as naive and unapologetic about it as Governor Fordice and the Reverend Bailey Smith, former president of the Southern Baptist Convention, the one who asserted unqualifiedly that "God Almighty does not hear the prayer of a Jew." As observed earlier, the smiling, peacemaking Jerry Falwell stepped in to make amends, but Frances FitzGerald, the source of the story, went on to observe that during her extended visits and interviews with Falwell she did not hear a single racial slur among students and faculty at

[83]Reported in Adam Clymer, "Tiff Over Governor's 'Christian' Remark Underscores Fault Line in GOP," *New York Times*, 22 November 1992, p. 28.

[84]This quote and various references to attitudes of other conservatives toward Buchanan will be found in Charles Krauthammer, "Buchanan Explained," *Washington Post*, 9–15 March 1992, p. 28, national weekly edition.

Liberty Baptist College, but, she continued, "What I did hear was anti-Semitism."[85]

When Falwell and the other Christian conservatives made the decision to enter the portals of democratic politics, they had to embrace, or give the impression of embracing, "ecumenical politics." This meant that they would have to renounce or seriously weaken the "fundamental tenet of faith," that God is a Christian God. "Ecumenical politics" is just another name for the pluralism that conservatives have to accept even as they hold it in contempt. In politics, individuals may not be equal but every interest is. This is the ugly side of democracy and the sin of pluralism, with its profound implications for cultural relativism. On the way to the Christian Republic, toleration of democratic pluralism is necessary. But then there comes a point when the open-minded toleration of toleration can be concluded and the American mind can be properly closed.[86]

THE FATAL FLAW

This is not the first time a substantial minority has rejected democracy, political pluralism, and the equality of all interests, and these experiences support at least one generalization: Such rejection, whenever and wherever it occurs, arises out of a still deeper urge *to found a moral republic in which basic values are so homogenized that democracy can take place without risk of morally bad outcomes.* The moral republic can be a Christian Republic, an Islamic Republic, a Jewish Republic, or even a republic espousing a civic religion like communitarianism. They will all be morally homogenized republics.

[85]FitzGerald, "A Reporter at Large," 114.

[86]Organized legal and political pressure by Christian activists against tolerance as a public policy, especially in the secondary schools, was mounting all during the 1980s. For a brilliant and comprehensive assessment, including the difficulties and dilemmas in the liberal response, see Nomi Maya Stolzenberg, "He Drew a Circle That Shut Me Out: Assimilation, Indoctrination and the Paradox of a Liberal Education," *Harvard Law Review* 106 (January 1993): 581–667.

This is not to suggest that a New Christian Right is about to step up from hegemony within the Republican coalition to the founding outright of a Third Republic of the United States.[87] I speak of a "Third Republic" because it is better to be sober as to the possibilities and to *over*estimate the Right for a change; and I speak of a "Third Republic" in order to identify the logical extreme and fatal flaw of the American Right: its lack of faith in democracy. Every ideology is built on a contradiction. Here we have found theirs: *It can govern only if the state and its values are homogeneous.*

Can they discover their flaw in time to develop some self-restraint? That is, can this particular public philosophy prove superior to its competitors in its ability to engage in genuine *self*-government? Unlikely.

Here to conclude the chapter is an experience that may be close enough to simulate a conservative American Third Republic without having to actually suffer through it. Gaetano Mosca (1858–1941), one of the great historians and political theorists of his time, was also prominent in Italian politics as a minister and a senator between 1897 and the 1930s. Toward the end of his life, after enduring two decades of Italian fascism and witnessing the rise of Hitler, Mosca penned the following reflections for the final edition and for the English-language translation of his classic, *The Ruling Class.*

> Fifty years ago the author of this volume . . . sought to lay bare some of the untruths . . . of the representative system, and some of the defects of parliamentarism. Today advancing years have made him more cautious. . . . Specialization in the various political functions and cooperation and reciprocal control between bureaucratic and elective elements are two of the outstanding characteristics of the modern representative state. These traits make it possible to regard that state as the most complex and delicate type of political organization that has so far been seen in world history. From that point of view, and

---

[87]Since I had already labeled the system brought in by the Roosevelt coalition the Second Republic of the United States, I am obliged to designate this hypothesized change the Third Republic. See Lowi, *The End of Liberalism.*

from others as well, it may also be claimed that there is an almost perfect harmony between [that] political system and the level of civilization that has been attained in the century that saw it come into being and grow to maturity.[88]

Fascism in Italy and Germany arose out of the breakdown of liberal solutions to governance. The first thing to be attacked by the well-meaning European radicals of Left and Right was "parliamentarism." Liberal democracy offers a solution to the tyranny inherent in the morality of the far Right (and of the far Left in countries where it exists); liberal democracy removes morality from public discourse and thereby makes politics possible. Once absolute moral principle is introduced, homogeneity around principle becomes necessary, and in this context homogeneity and tyranny are virtually synonymous. That is the self-damnation of the American Right.

Unfortunately, liberalism (New or Old) shows no better promise of ability to preserve the democracy that bears its name. In other words, liberalism does not seem to understand liberal democracy any better than conservatism. When in power, it seems simply to produce a different kind of self-defeat. Is there an exit?

[88]Gaetano Mosca, *The Ruling Class* (New York: McGraw-Hill, 1939), 389 and 491.

CHAPTER 6

RESTORING THE LIBERAL REPUBLIC

Ideology and the Multidimensional Polity

> *There are enough illusions of*
> *inadvertence without making the*
> *creeds, the wants, and perceptions of*
> *others into illusions which we must*
> *first uproot before we can live*
> *together in peace. Even an optical*
> *illusion represents a genuine*
> *experience.*
>
> JACQUES BARZUN, 1941

THE MYTH OF THE UNIDIMENSIONAL POLITY

The French Model and the British Departure

IDEOLOGY AS WE KNOW IT today began with the French Revolution. Its first use, *ideologie,* is traced to Napoleon's attack in 1796 on writers who "misled the people by elevating them to a sovereignty which they were incapable of exercising."

It is the doctrine of the ideologues—[which] . . . seeks to find . . . primary causes and on this foundation would erect the legislation of peoples, instead of adapting the laws to a knowledge of the human heart and of the lessons of history—to which one must attribute all the misfortunes which have befallen our beautiful France.[1]

The Jacobins led by Robespierre occupied the benches in the National Assembly and the Convention above and to the left of the chair, thus earning them two designations, the Left

---

[1]Quoted in Raymond Williams, *Keywords: A Vocabulary of Culture and Society* (New York: Oxford University Press, 1976), 126.

and the Mountain.[2] Their main opposition was a breakaway faction called the Girondins, named after the province Gironde, where the leading members resided. The Jacobins and the Girondins were two of two dozen or more provincial clubs whose mobilization was a driving force in the Revolution.

Since neither the Left *montagnards* nor the Girondins on the other side could muster solid majority control of the Assembly or the Convention, they had to compete for the support not of a single club but of a diffuse collection of less committed deputies simply called Plain.[3] These included the sansculottes ("without knee breeches," i.e., the antiaristocracy), who were middle class but far from capitalists. The Church was an interest not to be considered synonymous with the aristocracy. Country people were not all peasants, and both were pressing Paris in their own ways through their deputies. Landed proprietors were very much present but had more in common with government officials than with any other faction. And the nobles, however personae non grata in Paris, were "local notables" and had a positive role in the political life of many communities. Dare one employ "pluralism" to characterize the political scene during the revolutionary 1790s?

The prevailing theory of the French Revolution in our own time is distinctly not a pluralistic theory, and for good reason. Called the classical theory, it is a class theory that, "despite its obvious Marxist overtones, most historians have accepted . . . in greater or lesser degree."[4] According to this theory of the Revolution, society was polarized by a capitalist class frustrated to a violent extent by the monopoly of power held in the hands of the aristocracy. Despite the many social and political cleavages, as indicated, the politics of France during the Revolution was unidimensional, with highly predictable pro-

---

[2]See, for example, D. M. G. Sutherland, *France 1789–1815: Revolution and Counterrevolution* (London: Fontana Press, 1985), 162–63; and Robert R. Palmer, *The Age of Democratic Revolution: A Political History of Europe and America, 1760–1800* (Princeton: Princeton University Press, 1964), 50ff.

[3]Sutherland, *France 1789–1815*, 163–65.

[4]Ibid., 11.

and anti-Revolutionists, that is to say, a radical Left and a radical Right. All of the observed plurality of interests were social cleavages, but the cleavages were cumulative. It is useful to picture once again a log being attacked by wedges. A politically pluralist society would appear as a log in which the wedges or cleavages were "crosscutting." A revolutionary situation can be defined as the converse, one in which the wedges are all cutting into the same crack.

It is hardly surprising, then, that French politics has appeared unidimensional—giving support to the practice of dividing a society or its polity into a single Left and Right, with a moderate and diffuse middle, all on the same plane. It made sense during the Revolution, and it made sense during the many regime changes in France during the nineteenth century. Marx's theory of a capitalist society careening through a simple dialectic toward a revolutionary synthesis appeared to have been validated by France in 1789 and again by France in 1848.

Elsewhere, especially in countries with an Anglo-Saxon tradition, a unidimensional political theory—Marxist or otherwise—is far more difficult to confirm. One immediately turns to the two-party system of Tory and Whig as shaping a single dimension of Right and Left; but that party system did not produce a nationally organized polarity that could in any conceivable way approximate a unidimensional polity. Even as late as 1867, with the formal appearance of the Liberal party, Samuel Beer is moved to ask, "May we say that at last the 'modern political party' has made its appearance?"[5] His answer was in the negative, followed by an insistence that Britain does not get two parties that nationally organize mass behavior and mass opinions until the twentieth-century emergence of the Labour party and the aping of their structure by the Conservative party. Before that, British politics was structured by "the vast proliferation of voluntary associations

---

[5]Samuel Beer, *Modern British Politics* (New York: W. W. Norton, 1982), 54–55.

formed for political purposes."[6] Moreover, by the time Britain gets modern political parties, it was not a two-party system but a three- and four- and even five-party system, depending on how one counts the Irish and Scottish Nationalists and when one ceases to count the Liberal party as a genuine party. How can there be unidimensional Left-to-Right belief system in such a country, where the older liberal tradition rests in and for parliament and where "Socialist Democracy and Tory Democracy have a great deal in common [including the fact that] both . . . reject parliamentarism"[7] while disagreeing with each other in other fundamental ways? Unidimensional politics is simply not Anglo-Saxon. This is why the famous Gilbert observation in *Iolanthe* was immediately understandable and quite funny to almost any English ear:

> I often think it's comical
>   How nature always does contrive
> That every boy and every gal,
>   that's born into the world alive,
> Is either a little Liberal,
>   Or else a Conservative!

America—Where Theory Masks Reality

The unidimensional polity never made sense in America either. Beer's generalization that "the political culture of a country is rarely monolithic" would encounter no exceptionalism here.[8] Yet being nonsensical did not prevent its adoption by political theorists and political behaviorists. A major influence on American thinking on the matter during the past half century comes from a French intellectual, Maurice Duverger, who, in his classic book, observed,

The two-party system seems to correspond to the nature of things, that is to say that political choice usually takes the form of a choice between two alternatives. A duality of parties does

[6]Ibid., 43–44.
[7]Ibid., 70–71.
[8]Ibid., 71.

not always exist, but almost always there is a duality of tendencies. . . . *The term "centre" is applied to the geometrical spot at
which the moderates of opposed tendencies meet. . . . The Centre is
nothing more than the artificial grouping of the Right wing of the Left
and the Left wing of the Right.*[9]

Even the inimitable V. O. Key was enthralled by the dualism
theory, which is nothing more than a unidimensional polity
arranged on a continuum. Although Key could find no combination of factors to explain the American two-party system,
he nevertheless accepted "dualism" as the "pattern of political faith," going further to express his own political faith
that

a pattern of attitudes exists that favors, or at least permits, a
political dualism. . . . Powerful mechanisms of education and
indoctrination, along with the accidents of history, maintain
broad agreements, if not universal conformity, upon political
essentials. At times it can be said, with a color of truth, that we
are all liberal; at another time, it may be equally true that we are
all conservatives. Given this tendency for most people to clus-
ter fairly closely together in their attitudes, a dual division
becomes possible on the issue of just how conservative or just
how liberal we are at the moment. Extremists exist, to be sure,
who stand far removed *from the central mode of opinion*, but they
never seem to be numerous enough or intransigent enough to
form the basis for durable minor parties.[10]

Dualism means two halves of one dimension, roughly equal,
held together by consensus on "the rules of the game" and
agreement on what to disagree about, anything to the contrary not only notwithstanding but pathological.

The unidimensional polity was given its most formal and
influential statement not by a political scientist but by an
economist, Anthony Downs, in 1957. Downs drew his inspiration from a rational model of real estate choice, or "spatial

[9]Maurice Duverger, *Political Parties,* trans. Barbara and Robert North (New
York: John Wiley, 1954), 215. Emphasis added.
[10]Key, *Politics, Parties, and Pressure Groups,* 210. Emphasis added.

competition," published in 1929.[11] This model could explain why it is that we find a Wendy's and a Burger King and a Pizza Hut very near the spot where a McDonald's has located. Harold Hotelling and associates applied the model to politics, based on the assumption that people are evenly spaced along a straight-line scale and that competing parties would move toward each other on the assumption that extremists at the far end of the scale would prefer the party on that side, because they had no other place to go. The Downs model was a clearer and more sophisticated application of the real estate model to politics.

Our version of Hotelling's spatial market consists of a linear scale running from zero to one hundred in the usual Left-to-Right fashion. To make this politically meaningful, we assume that political preferences can be ordered from left to right in a manner agreed upon by all voters. They need not agree on which point they personally prefer, only on the ordering of parties from one extreme to the other.

In addition, we assume that every voter's preferences are single-peaked and slope downward *monotonically* on either side of the peak (unless his peak lies at one extreme on the scale). For example, if a voter likes position 35 best, we can immediately deduce that he prefers 30 to 25 and 40 to 45. . . . The slope downward from the apex need not be identical on both sides, but we do presume no sharp asymmetry exists.[12]

Figure 6.1 is drawn directly from Downs (118). Assuming there are, say, 100,000 voters "whose preferences cause them to be normally distributed with a mean of 50," Parties A and B

[11]Anthony Downs, *An Economic Theory of Democracy* (New York: Harper & Row, 1957). The model of real estate choice was that of Harold Hotelling, "Stability in Competition," *Economic Journal* 39 (1929): 41–57. The Hotelling argument is drawn from Downs, p. 116.

As a matter of personal interest it should be added that Downs had two careers. One was as an economist with a Ph.D., in the normal academic faculties and think tanks; the other was as a member and ultimately as chairman of the Board of the Real Estate Research Corporation of Chicago, founded by his father, James Downs, who was an important figure in Chicago real estate and Chicago Democratic politics.

[12]Downs, *An Economic Theory of Democracy*, 115–16. Emphasis added.

placed initially at points 25 and 75 will converge rapidly toward the center. Wendy next door to McDonald. The parties would not, however, converge toward the center if voter preferences were distributed bimodally. But in a world with full information about parties and preferences, the voters would still be scalar and would choose the party candidate nearest them because "it is always rational *ex definitione* to select a greater good before a lesser, or a lesser evil before a greater." (118–19). Before 1957, but especially afterwards, all but the most sophisticated surveys of attitudes, analyses of congressional roll call votes, and interpretations of political speeches and academic discourse were reduced to the simple spatial model: On the Left, more government; on the Right, less government. On the Left, less free market; on the Right, more. On the Left, more civil liberties; on the Right, contraction of civil liberties. And there was no reflection whatsoever on the inconsistency between and among these criteria. Adjectives were introduced to provide some nuance, but liberal and conservative remained, regardless of the amount of fudging it took; to the Left and Right of each other on a single line across the page, with people distributed in such a way as to create spaces above the line—usually tending toward a normal distribution of space—and with the Democratic party to the Left of the mean and the Republican party to the Right.

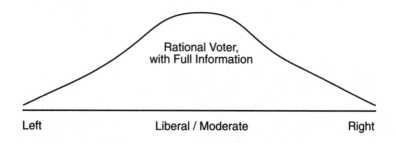

Fig. 6.1. The Unidimensional Polity

The unidimensional model, with all its rational trappings, has had a deeply mischievous effect on American politics because it has corrupted and degraded political discourse. Reducing rich concepts and complex arguments to thin dichotomies and self-serving definitions has done more to foul political language and adulterate civic education than could have been achieved by deliberate conspiracy of all the print media and the broadcast media. We enjoy blaming so many things on "the media"; but the language has already been cheapened before it ever reaches the scriptwriters and the talking heads.

One example will have to suffice, but it is a rich one: Michael Kinsley, whose moment of fame may, we hope, have passed by the time this book is published. A genuine celebrity among political pundits in the 1990s, Kinsley refers to himself on his highly rated CNN "Crossfire" as "on the Left" and to his friend Pat Buchanan as "on the Right." If Kinsley is on the Left, Karl Marx is a monkey's uncle. Kinsley has been a longtime editor and senior editor of the *New Republic,* a neoconservative magazine with a good record on civil liberties and a memory trace of support for New Deal domestic policies. He has also been an American editor of the *Economist,* a brilliant English journal with a distinctive libertarian or free market slant, and a factor at the *Washington Monthly,* a self-styled "neoliberal" journal whose founders were pushing toward a "New Democratic" party of privatization and deficit reduction even before Bill Clinton joined that position. What Kinsley has done is to contribute to the stigmatization of liberalism by cooperating good-naturedly in the spirit of healthy debate with people who understand exactly what they are doing and are cynically exploiting Kinsley's naïveté. People like Buchanan, genuinely "on the Right," operate in an entirely different dimension, not merely a few steps to the Right of Mr. Kinsley's Left. And they know it. They are through the looking glass, where people like Kinsley appear either as comic figures or just plain fools.

BREAKING OUT OF THE PROCRUSTEAN BED
OF UNIDIMENSIONAL THOUGHT

The Reagan Revolution, of which Buchanan is a product as well as a founder, confronted American politics with the multidimensionality it had never recognized. Here is how and where Reagan, the boy from Eureka, Europeanized American politics. The Downsian spatial analysis has masked the significance of this revolution. Yet with the same spatial analysis, slightly altered, it is possible to pictorialize the multidimensional space and, through that space, inch toward a truer picture of ourselves in front of the looking glass rather than through it.

The First Break—Liberalism as a Dimension All Its Own

Figure 6.1 represents the economist's effort to incorporate the entire universe of discourse, showing a Left and a Right as one set of extremes defining a single middle, with a liberalism slightly to the Left of center and a conservatism slightly to the Right. Figure 6.2 is the first step toward breaking out of the single dimension, showing liberalism as a dimension all its own, on a continuum *without the Right and Left present at all.* Right and left on figure 6.2 are simply conventional designations for either side of the page. Each side does designate radical extremes because radical indicates the commitment to "go the limit," that is, to insist on doctrinal purity. But this is not Left and Right in a substantive sense; it is literally "radical liberalism." Radical liberalism or extreme liberalism may sound like an oxymoron, but that is only because people are not accustomed to treating liberalism as an ideological dimension or belief system all its own.

The shape of figure 6.2 is presented as a moderately bimodal distribution to indicate that in the real world one side consists of basically Old Liberal, Republican party preferences and the other side primarily of New Liberal, Democratic party preferences. Obviously the dip in the distribution was much deeper during certain periods of intensified partisan-

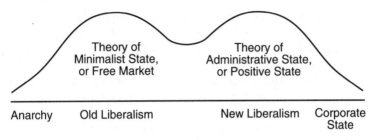

| Anarchy | Old Liberalism | | New Liberalism | Corporate State |

**Fig. 6.2. Liberalism as a Dimension All Its Own,
with Radical Liberalism at Both Ends**

ship; and during the 1980s and 1990s the dip may be more
gentle than shown here because of the general willingness of
the Democratic party leadership to accept Republican party
positions about big deficits and big government. But everybody on figure 6.2 is a liberal. The logical extreme of liberalism on one end is not "the Right" or conservatism but a place
occupied by extreme or radical liberals for whom almost no
instrumental argument about potential injury would be sufficient to justify a policy of government intervention. They are
anarchists on principle, and that is a genuine radical position—but a radical *liberal* position. The other logical extreme—
and I emphasize logical—is not Left but another extreme of
radical liberalism whose instrumental view sees all conduct
as potentially injurious and therefore envisions an enormous
state apparatus committed to the reduction, if not the elimination, of all risk. In chapter 2, I referred to this end of the
continuum as totalitarian or totalistic, in the sense that this
kind of radicalized liberalism assumes responsibility for all
injury, even if no programs are (yet) established for certain
types of conduct and certain types of risk. Here is where
many critics of New Liberalism begin to make the charge that
liberalism is socialism. That is plainly incorrect. There *is* a
Left and a Right in the world; however, they are not in the
world of liberalism but in a world all their own.

Suppose we now reimpose Left and Right on the continuum with liberalism. On figure 6.2, Old Liberalism, being on the left side of the page, becomes the Left. That makes some sense, because socialism also embraces anarchy; after the socialist revolution, the state withers away. Let us then switch sides, as on figure 6.3, making New Liberalism the Left, as Reagan and most Republicans have been trying to do for years. That makes sense, too, considering that New Liberals rely more on government. Nevertheless, that makes no more sense than putting it back on the Right (as most Europeans see it), because New Liberalism, like all liberalism, is pro-capitalist, and most of the policies supported by New Liberalism have either been supportive of capitalism itself or an effort to use government to make up for the imperfections of capitalism. Most everyone outside the United States recognizes this. In fact, "capitalism" is a term rarely used in liberal discourse anywhere. The word was appropriated and developed by Marx and then given special connotations in the socialist critique of the capitalist system. Thus, to a genuine socialist, the American welfare state is right-wing.

By now, the main point of all this logical analysis should be apparent, that liberalism is a dimension of belief and state theory all its own, and so are Left/socialism and Right/conservatism. Anomalies of logic and of substance in public discourse are created when each is treated as an extreme or

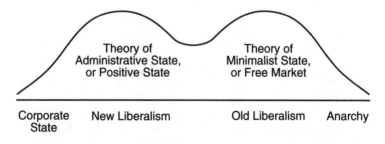

Fig. 6.3. **The Liberal Continuum with the Extreme Reversed**

direct opposite of the other. Previous chapters are reinforced by this logical or spatial analysis: there are at least three separate communities of values or beliefs, each with its own center, each with its own radical extremes, each with its own logic, and each with its own limits that, when disregarded, give each its own form of tragedy. But back for the moment to the real world of political ideology.

Right (and Left) in Review

Figure 6.4 is drawn as a bimodal distribution so as to indicate not only that there is a range of positions on the Right, but that it, like the Left and liberalism, is its own dimension with its own dual nature. Unlike the others, however, the differentiation within the conservative community is more along class lines, as indicated here (and in earlier chapters) by the labels "Patrician" and "Populist." Although both types of conservative belief are at bottom antidemocratic, antipluralist, and anticapitalist in their stress on elite knowledge and on transcendent moral order, there are considerable differences between them in sacred sources and strategy, and these differences can separate them and can have significant political consequences. The Noble Lie of the patrician elite is not so much a matter of hypocrisy as a belief that although the truth is available only to a small elite capable of reason, what is

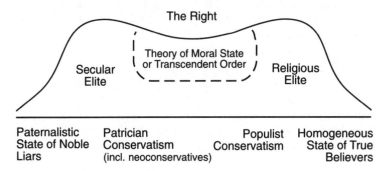

Fig. 6.4. The Conservative Community of Belief

important is not that the elite believe but that citizens—the masses—believe. Many patrician conservatives draw on religion, but their primary sources are quite secular, particularly classical antiquity.

The following example involves a sacred source, but the attitude is patrician conservatism through and through. It is Dostoyevsky's story of the return of Jesus for his brief Second Coming at the time of the Spanish Inquisition. The speaker is the Grand Inquisitor.

> Why have you come to interfere with us now? . . . Do not answer. . . . I know too well what you would say. And you have no right to add anything to what you already said once. . . . Tomorrow I shall condemn you and burn you at the stake as the most evil of heretics, and the very people who today kissed your feet, tomorrow, at a nod from me, will rush to heap the coals up around your stake. . . . But we shall say that we are obedient to you and rule in your name. We shall deceive them again, for this time we shall not allow you to come to us. This deceit will constitute our suffering, for we shall have to lie.[13]

While both sides on figure 6.4 share confidence that the true and the good can be known, the populists tend to be the true believers. They have found the truth in a sacred source. But it is likely that they would have welcomed the Second Coming regardless of His threat to established order.

The labels Right and Left make no sense, of course, as distinctions among people who are all on the Right. But it should also be clear by now that the Right makes no sense as the limiting radical extreme of liberalism. Liberal and Right are two quite different things—separate dimensions. Each has its own extreme, and therefore each plays itself out in a different kind of tragedy.

The Left will once again be relegated to brief treatment because of the relatively small role it has played in American

---

[13]Fyodor Dostoyevsky, *The Brothers Karamazov* (San Francisco: North Point Press, 1990), 250, 253, and 255.

history and in this book.[14] Figure 6.5 is offered as still another case of the incompatibility of belief systems and the absurdity of a rational choice analysis that treats them all as a fluid but orderly, indeed scalar, continuum. But this is much more than merely an irritating issue among intellectuals. The universal continuum incorporating all beliefs is precisely what made possible and successful the effort of the Right to stigmatize liberalism as having become leftist, then socialist, then, according to Ronald Reagan, so far Left as to have left America.

Figure 6.5 also demonstrates the unique character of the logical limits of each belief system. As with figures 6.2 and 6.4, the Left does not change by decaying and declining and moving along the line toward the neighboring belief system. It self-destructs by becoming too much of itself, generally without recognizing the danger until too late. We have so recently seen this in the USSR, where after years of having become a totalitarian system as a logical extension of social-ism, the Old or Marxian Left exists no longer. Had it gone to the extreme left of the Left or the extreme right of the Left in its self-destruction? Time was when the most revolutionary extremists were defined (as shown in figure 6.5) as on the far left of the Left. But lately, the remaining Communists in the Mikhail Gorbachev coup of 1991 and the Boris Yeltsin counter-coup of 1993 were referred to as the conservatives, that is, the extreme right wing of the Left. Right and Left have come to mean nothing in this context. Once again, through the look-ing glass.

[14]George Will has observed that the Right did not "put the morality in politics" but that it began by a liberalism turned Left, developing into "a doctrine of liberation." This, he argues, provoked fundamentalist and evangelical Chris-tians to reshape American moral life without due regard for the convictions of millions of other citizens. George Will, "Who Put Morality in Politics?" in Richard John Neuhaus and Michael Cromartie, eds., *Piety and Politics: Evangeli-cals and Fundamentalists Confront the World* (Boston: University Press of America, 1987), 259. But as Will's own views elsewhere indicate, especially in his book, *Statecraft as Soulcraft,* cited earlier, the Right—populist and patrician—has hardly needed provocation. And while many liberals were radicalized by the Left in the 1950s and 1960s, the actual policies adopted by liberals when in power in the 1960s were genuinely liberal, not Left at all.

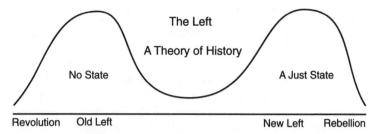

Fig. 6.5. Where the Norm Is Not Normal: Polarization Between the Orthodox Left and the Revisionist Left

Finally, one extreme on figure 6.5 has been labeled "Revolution"—a radicalism based on a theory and strategy of reconstituting the society and the regime. The other extreme is labeled "Rebellion"—an extreme using radical means to redeem the existing regime by forcing it to live up to its own ideals or the alleged ideals of the people at large. At either end of the continuum, the Left (all of figure 6.5) is its own tragedy—quite foreign to any experience of liberal or rightist theories or regimes.

EUROPEANIZATION: THE END OF COALITIONAL POLITICS?

A more direct and practical conclusion to be drawn from this account is that ideologies do not readily enter into electoral, party, or legislative coalitions, regardless of interests that the individuals or groups may share. In fact, although it is so commonplace as to be overlooked, *ideological differences can prevent coalitions that would appear to be quite rational on the basis of shared interest alone.* Different ideologies may coexist, as in the old American federal scheme in which each ideological tradition could be hegemonic in its own geographic realm. But in the same arena, they will be confrontational, generally to the detriment of each other and of representative democracy. This is another statement of the Europeanization of American politics, a contribution of the Reagan Revolution's turning ideology on its feet, from coexistence in the two separate spheres of federalism to direct, eye-to-eye confrontation by national mobilization of the Right.

The End of the Republican Era—and the Republic?

The most significant contributor to the Europeanization of American politics was the 1980s mixing of Old Liberalism with conservatism inside the Republican party. Since these are logically incompatible systems of belief, their coalition— Mr. Reagan's masterwork—lasted well beyond what anyone could have expected, but only by maintaining two principles in common: (1) negation of the national government, both its policies and its institutions; and (2) concordance between capitalism and Christianity, treating them as mutual blessings rather than contradictions. But how can such a coalition hold? Or, how can it hold without doing damage to democratic institutions? To moralize capitalism is to make it immensely oppressive, for then, criticism of capitalism is equal to treason. It is already tough enough to regulate capitalism when it violates its own market principle or pushes wages below Ricardo's "iron law of subsistence." But once capitalism sheds its instrumental character and becomes infused with heavenly grace, what then? The Right (and also the Left, when it exists) moralizes all of political life, transforming variation into deviance, deviance into shame, and disagreement into culture war.

Once again Allan Bloom provides the philosophical grounding for the cultural absolutism that promises an end to the republican era—in both senses of the word:

> If democracy means open-endedness, and respect for other cultures prevents doctrinaire . . . condemnation of the Soviet reality, then some day their ways may become ours. . . . (33) One of the techniques of opening young people up is . . . to force students to recognize that there are other ways of thinking and that Western ways are not better. . . . But [actually all cultures] think their way is the best way, and all others are inferior. . . . A very great narrowness is not incompatible with

the health of an individual or a people, whereas with great openness it is hard to avoid decomposition. (37) The fact that there have been different opinions about good and bad in different times and places in no way proves that none is true or superior to others. To say that it does so prove is as absurd as to say that the diversity of points of view expressed in a college bull session proves there is no truth. (39)[15]

Bloom is working on the assumption that there is one Western culture, that all who are in it hold the same truths, and that, as a condition of their own cultural survival, all other cultures must be treated as inferior—all conflicting cultures being bull.

If out of the mouth of a sage we can get such an absolute view of culture, imagine the result when true believers apply it to politics. For example, Pat Buchanan:

Profoundly uncomfortable with "moral" issues, the congressional Republican abhors a political brawl. By breeding, he is a political diplomat, not a warrior. . . . And, unfortunately, you cannot make an attack dog out of a cocker spaniel.

What he fails to understand, however, is that, as Norman Podhoretz writes, there is a "war going on in this country." It is a civil war, one that is at root a religious war; it is a war over our conflicting beliefs about good and evil, morality and immorality, justice and injustice, and, yes, even patriotism and treason.[16]

Obviously the Right never fully joined the Republican coalition—not by a long shot. Attacks on Old Liberal George Bush were far more savage from his own right wing than from the Democrats. George Will denounced Vice President Bush as a lapdog. Pat Robertson ran against candidate Bush for president in 1988. Pat Buchanan crusaded against President Bush in 1992.

In the wake of his failed 1988 presidential campaign and the withdrawal of Falwell and the disappearance of Jimmy Swag-

---

[15]Bloom, *The Closing of the American Mind;* page references in parentheses next to each specimen.
[16]Patrick J. Buchanan, "Commentary," *Washington Post,* 16 November 1987, p. 23, national weekly edition.

gart and Jim Bakker, Pat Robertson decided to rebuild Christianity's political clout with a new organization, the Christian Coalition. Within two years of its founding in the summer of 1989, the Christian Coalition had grown from the mailing lists of the 700 Club viewers to a solid organization of 350,000 members, 750 local chapters, a full-time staff in fifteen of the states, representation in Washington, a highly professional executive director, and an annual budget of $10 million. They have attracted relatively little national media attention, but this is more deliberate than it is a reflection on their size or their influence. Christian Coalition is a genuine grass-roots organization no longer concerned with the media operation of the earlier Pat Robertson or of Ross Perot. Perot's United We Stand America is strictly top-down, despite Perot's protestations. Christian Coalition is much more truly a bottom-up organization.

Christian Coalition is quite genuinely the "army who cares," as put by Robertson himself. It is committed to absolute and exclusively Christian values in politics, but unlike so many previous Christian Right organizations, this tiger wears a smile. It has quietly and cooperatively gotten control of six or seven state Republican delegations, it can confidently claim nearly 20 percent of the 165-member national Republican Platform Committee, and it can also legitimately claim significant influence on the electoral outcome of a goodly number of congressional and senatorial races—a number that is hard to count but is nevertheless impressive to the entire Republican party.

But influencing the Republican party does not define the primary objectives of the Christian Coalition. Their objectives go beyond that and particularly beyond the economic issues around which the mainstream of the Republican party flows. With the smile on the face of the tiger, the Christian Coalition is campaigning for and winning school board seats in such disparate but liberal states as California and New York. It is joining with other groups to push and to win initiatives on abortion and homosexuality laws as well as term limit provisions. The tiger smiles as it consumes local Republican organizations and school districts by following fairly strictly a strategy developed nationally but best expressed in a "county action plan" distributed by the Pennsylvania Christian Coalition.

> After getting the [local Christian Coalition] organization going you will have plenty of time to get involved in issues. But for now stay clear of issues and focus on organization. . . . If we have 75–150 people in each county we could become the most powerful political influence in the state.[17]

Before the decade of the 1990s is over, there will be a civil war inside the Republican party, or the right wing will break out of the party altogether. The price of the Old Liberal/ conservative coalition has proven to be more than the party can bear, not to speak of the country. By cutting taxes without terminating any programs, it gave us the intractable deficit that robs American national government of its options. But the costs went far beyond the particulars of Republican public policy, such as it was. First, because the right wing was intellectually the most powerful member of the coalition, the Republican era moralized national politics, "realigning man's law with the laws of nature and God."[18] As one of the leaders of the Christian Coalition put it, "Any Christian that tells you that on some of these issues it's all a matter of perspective just doesn't read the Bible."[19] The smiling accommodationist tactics of Ralph Reed are not liked by everyone in the Christian Right. For example, Martin Mawyer, president of the Chris-

---

[17]Quoted in *Harper's Magazine*, January 1993, p. 27. Sources for the account in the previous paragraph are from Robert Sullivan, "An Army of the Faithful," *New York Times Magazine*, 25 April 1993, pp. 33ff.; Joe Conason, "Pat Robertson's Coalition: The Religious Right's Quiet Revival," *Nation*, 27 April 1992, pp. 1ff.; Ralph Reed, Jr., "The Religious Right Reaches Out," *New York Times*, 22 August 1993, sec. 4, p. 15; and Guy Rogers, Christian Coalition National Field Director, "The Importance of Local Politics," *Christian American*, published nine times per year by the Christian Coalition, September 1993, p. 31.

[18]Robert Sullivan, "An Army of the Faithful," *New York Times Magazine*, 25 April 1993, p. 44.

[19]Quote in Sullivan, "An Army of the Faithful," 44.

tian Action Network, published a long and pointed criticism of Reed's "new strategy to Christianize the Republican Party by Republicanizing the Christian Right," in the *Washington Post*. But it is quite clear there and elsewhere that their differences are merely differences of tactics.[20] The end of the Christian Right is the moralization of national politics. And already their influence reaches the Democratic party as well as the Republican party. Not only are President Clinton and Vice President Gore meticulously observant Southern Baptists but they also regularly add a significant moral and religious dimension to almost any public policy argument they make. It has become politically perilous for liberals to make purely instrumental arguments—perilous, in fact, to call themselves liberal.

The influence of the conservatized Republican party is that it has given Americans a determined opposition to representative government and an antagonism to the discourse of cultural relativism that politics in a heterogeneous—yes, pluralistic—society must have. A pluralistic society is composed of many cultures, each built on absolute values. The *OED* actually defines *culture* as an absolute. Its first definition is "worship; reverential homage"; and it cross-references *culture* to *cult* and the French *culte*—"reverential homage rendered to a divine being or beings." Do they mix? Can cultures melt together into that distinctive American alloy?

The American ideal of the melting pot actually came from a popular play of 1908 by that name, written by an English Jew, Israel Zangwill,[21] at precisely a time when "melting and fusing" into the new American alloy seemed particularly remote. In a *political* sense, there was a great deal of truth in the melting pot: citizenship, common political values, shared love of flag and country, equality before the law. But *culturally*, the more accurate image was the tossed salad or salad bowl.

[20]Martin Mawyer, "A Rift in the Ranks of the Christian Right," *Washington Post*, 4–10 October 1993, p. 24, national weekly edition.
[21]Carl N. Degler, *Out of Our Past: The Forces That Shaped Modern America* (New York: Harper Colophon Books, 1959; rev. ed., 1970), 295–96.

In fact, every time local political bosses made an effort to integrate a cultural or ethnic group by nominating one of its members to elective office—thus creating "the balanced ticket"—or by appointing one of its members to an important administrative or judicial post, they were at the very same time reinforcing the separate identification and pride of that group. Cultures—each one with its own absolute values and sense of superiority—coexisted in the society. "Cultural war" broke out only when one culture or religious sect sought to subsume others by a "realignment of man's law with [their] God's law."

The other potential civil war—within the conservative community itself—could arise out of the social class differences between the patrician conservatives and the populist conservatives. If it does, it will be driven by the conflict between the genuine religiosity of the populists versus the lack of religiosity of the patricians and the genuine morality of the populists versus the more consequential morality of the patricians, that is, "I believe" versus "I believe that society ought to believe."[22]

As a Jewish liberal cultural relativist, I look with not a little sympathy on the plight of a Jewish, atheist, homosexual

[22]After completing this chapter, I read a valuable piece by the conservative Charlotte Allen, who complained bitterly about the hypocrisy of the elite of her own conservative movement, who were leading highly self-indulgent lives, violating the family values they ardently espouse in their writing. For example, "right-wing elites have long used religion to mobilize their followings. But today the disconnect between right-wing leaders and followers on moral—meaning religious—values may cost the Irreligious Right not just moral points, but its hold on the Republican Party." Allen made a special case of the hypocrisy of George Will and Newt Gingrich, but she drew on the contradictions of Allan Bloom for her summation. Observing that Bloom became a conservative icon because of his exaltation of traditional family life but privately viewed family-bolstering laws as "a kind of unnatural force," she went on to conclude as follows: "That Bloom took care to advocate something more conventional when preaching to the Right-wing masses was perhaps a product of his sense of himself as 'a naturally superior person,' one who has no need for the virtues he wishes others would practice. Bloom is hardly alone." Charlotte Allen, "Throwing Stones from a Very Fragile House," *Washington Post*, 26–31 October 1993, p. 24, national weekly edition.

cultural absolutist like Allan Bloom in a community of Christian Right political activists, whose minds are closed around absolute values, as Bloom prescribed, but whose absolutes are not the ones Bloom reached by use of his own gifts of reason. At the same time, I must look with more than a little suspicion at Bloom's view of the polity. He drew it largely from his great mentor, Leo Strauss; but Strauss was honest enough to confess that the well-being of the polity requires deliberate obfuscation and mystification even though that goes against the grain of the philosopher.

> The living respect for old laws, "the prejudice of antiquity" which is indispensable for the health of society, can only with difficulty survive the public questioning of the accounts regarding their origin. . . . Society has a continuous need for at least an equivalent to the mysterious and awe-inspiring action of the legislator.[23]

And, although this is mere speculation on my part, Strauss's own explicitness about the need of antidemocratic thoughts to be couched in obscure and esoteric language could be the reason Bloom hides his obligation to his teacher. There is only one reference to Strauss—and this a very casual one—in Bloom's four hundred-page book.[24]

Given this tendency among patrician conservatives to hide their antidemocratic fears in elitism mystified by notions of morality drawn from reason and nature, the American Right has relied on its populists to do its dirty work because of the

[23]Leo Strauss, *Natural Right and History* (Chicago: University of Chicago Press, 1953), 287. This quote and a very good discussion of the view of Strauss and other classicists that belief needs to be widespread but truth needs to be reserved to a minority will be found in Shadia Drury, *The Political Ideas of Leo Strauss* (New York: St. Martin's Press, 1988), 156, and esp. chaps. 7 and 8.

[24]Another of Strauss's students, a contemporary of Bloom's, saw in this neglect not dishonesty but "impiety . . . which is rather odd considering that Bloom's book stands for a return to an older way of education. . . . Leo Strauss, Allan Bloom's principal teacher, is ignored, even though there are in his book dozens, if not hundreds, of echoes of that teacher's work." George Anastaplo, "In Re Allan Bloom: A Respectful Dissent," in Robert L. Stone, ed., *Essays on the Closing of the American Mind* (Chicago: Chicago Review Press, 1989), 268.

willingness of true believers to tell the truth about their beliefs. There is a strong streak of democracy, albeit Christian democracy, among populists—for example, Pat Robertson on the Right and Jesse Jackson on the Left—that cannot for long tolerate either the elitism or the hypocrisy of their brothers and sisters in the patrician camp. Yet, even if they should divorce, their legacy is shared. That is the end of the Republican era; let us hope that it is not also the end of the republican era.

The threat to the republican era was not limited to conservatism. Another came from Old Liberalism, which also failed America because of its exclusiveness, its simpleminded and uncritical adherence to the faith that human beings are perfectible and that a system based exclusively on individual rational self-interest, *Homo economicus*, is self-perfecting. No Republican administration ever lived entirely by this faith—not even the Church can claim it lives uncompromisingly by its faith—but the Old Liberal faith was so hegemonic that it was all the Hoover leadership could offer as political sustenance when confronting a depression not of its own making; and, of course, Old Liberalism in the 1980s was winning only by making political use of its more intellectually powerful right wing, whose price was the moralization of capitalism as well as politics.

Threat to a Democratic Era

This inability to participate in a coalition helps explain why the Left, the genuine Left, was not a serious player in the Democratic party's coalition in the New Deal. The immensity of that coalition and of its electoral majority reduced what there was of the Left to relatively microscopic scale, but in any case, it failed to radicalize any aspect of New Deal policy even though it may have contributed in some small way to the items that went on the New Deal agenda. The New Deal actually destroyed what there was of the Left, most of whose adherents either sank into the labor movement—a distinctly procapitalist, liberal, "business unionism"—or disappeared into neoconservatism, as we have already seen. The only important role of the Left in that entire epoch was in foreign policy; and this came at the end of the domestic New Deal, and only then because the USSR had become an ally against the Axis.

The New Left played a more influential role in the Democratic coalition of the 1960s. In fact, its influence contributed to the collapse of the New Deal coalition itself, after which the New Left itself dwindled to the point of disappearance. The Left has been far, far less important than the Right; but, like the Right, each time it has appeared in national politics, the Left has had a corrosive influence on democratic politics.

Despite Republican ravings about the insidious influence of the Left and despite the willingness of people like Michael Kinsley to accept that designation for sound bite purposes, there is almost no evidence of an influence from a genuine Left in American politics today. It no longer even has a vigorous Left in Europe to draw on for inspiration and support. But there is today a genuine threat to a new Democratic era, from a recent source, or I should probably say, the adaptation and application of an older source, communitarianism. Communitarianism was not confronted up to now because it does not fit as a genuine, separate tradition of ideology but instead attempts to be the texture of any and all of the others.[25] Communitarianism can best be defined by Robert Bellah, who tied it to his own concept of "civil religion." Following Bellah, it can be defined as a republicanism in the tradition of "the republics of classical and modern times . . . dependent on that inner spirit of republican character and mores that make for republican citizenship," to be distinguished from "a liberal constitutional regime governed

[25]This section owes a great deal to two colleagues: Professor Thomas Dumm of Amherst College in his wise critique of the book manuscript, and Professor Stephen Newman of York University in his superb unpublished review essay, "The New Communitarian Critique of Liberalism."

through artificial contrivance and the balancing of conflicting interests."[26]

Professor Amitai Etzioni has attempted to start a communitarian movement on just such a grounding, resting on a "single core thesis" that Americans "can act without fear . . . to shore up our values, responsibilities, institutions, and communities [without charging] into a dark tunnel of moralism and authoritarianism that leads to a church-dominated state or a right-wing world."[27] Although Etzioni has not succeeded in organizing a movement, communitarian views have reached the White House and are indeed influencing the Clinton agenda. Vice President Gore appears with Etzioni in a photograph on the dust jacket of Etzioni's book, and his most influential communitarian colleague, William Galston, is an important intellectual in the Clinton White House and has been close to Clinton through the Democratic Leadership Council since its founding in the mid-1980s.

At one level, communitarianism today is just a form of good old-fashioned sentimentality about traditional values. Nobody likes crime, and almost everybody agrees with the proposition that rights and responsibilities ought to be linked. Who could possibly disapprove of Bellah's discovery that the family meal will result in a stronger family and has an "indispensable educational function"—that is, if you have a family.[28] One might even be able to muster up a majority in some communities for Galston's invention of a "braking" mechanism that legally imposes a nine-month waiting period

[26]Robert Bellah, *The Broken Covenant: American Civil Religion in Time of Trial*, 2d ed. (Chicago: University of Chicago Press, 1992), 170–71.

[27]Amitai Etzioni, *The Spirit of Community: Rights, Responsibilities, and the Communitarian Agenda* (New York: Crown Publishers, 1993), 2.

[28]Bellah's discovery and its endorsement by the U.S. Department of Health and Human Services is reported in Etzioni, *Spirit of Community*, 80. In fact, the Department of Health and Human Services has become so communitarian that they have declared officially that "father's presence is crucial for [family dinner] to be a family hour. Workplace expectations of fathers will need to adapt accordingly."

before a divorce may be granted.[29] But sometimes the influence has gone beyond sentimentality to serious policy—serious if only because it is very difficult for legislators to vote against these commonplace sentiments when they become policy proposals.

But there is a deeper level. Every president—Clinton among the best—engages in communitarianism in almost every presidential address. That is why Theodore Roosevelt called the presidency a bully pulpit. But this has gone much further with President Clinton, and the communitarian influence on him can be seen clearly to be a rightward public policy influence, reassurances of Etzioni to the contrary notwithstanding. President Clinton has proposed a "three strikes and you're out" provision for criminal offenders, and he would bring state law enforcement into this by building federal prisons to nationalize the housing and treatment of these life-timers. Clinton has also extended the process of stigmatization of the welfare state that began with the conservatives in the Reagan administration. Implying strongly that everybody on welfare prefers it to working, Clinton proposed a two-year limit on eligibility for women on AFDC, and he coupled that with the requirement that they take a job after the end of their twenty-four-month welfare maximum. Since there are far too few low-income jobs even for those already looking for work and since the income from those jobs would not be sufficient for subsistence plus child care, this stress on "workfare" is clearly and patently an effort to stigmatize. Add to that a national war on deadbeat fathers. That is a case of right-wing communitarianism. In other words, President Clinton is proposing to use a form of national police power to shore up our deteriorating communities with the nationalization of all extreme cases of law enforcement and all extreme cases of economic dependency.

In the narrowest political sense, these words and actions can be interpreted as President Clinton's effort to extend and

[29]Cited in Etzioni, *Spirit of Community,* 81.

expand a minority Democratic coalition that won in 1992 only because of a split in the Republican coalition. But it is an expansion of his coalition in directions that are taking the Democratic party back toward its pre–New Deal days, albeit without racism. Communitarianism is a linkage to Old Conservatism, and it can succeed only by accepting the antagonism of communitarian conservatism to the Godlessness—or let us call it what it truly is, the open-mindedness—of liberalism.

Liberalism is concerned with communi*ties*. Conservatives are concerned with communi*ty*. Liberalism is replete with communities. Liberalism literally resides in its recognition of the existence of cultural, territorial, economic, religious, and all other groupings. Liberalism even accepts the exclusiveness of each community—its close-mindedness—as long as all communities remain civil religions in the *civil* society and not in the polity.

Bellah concludes his argument that republicanism and liberalism "are profoundly antithetical" with the proposition that "exclusive concern for self-interest is the very definition of the corruption of republican virtue."[30] Bellah and the current communitarians freight far more meaning into republicanism than can be supported in the writing of that founding republican, James Madison. In *Federalist 10*, Madison defines a republic as "a government in which the scheme of representation takes place . . . [as well as] the delegation of the government . . . to a smaller number of citizens elected by the rest." Madison goes on in *Federalist 39* to define a republic as "a government which derives all its powers directly or indirectly from the great body of the people." No substantive notions of virtue are anywhere to be found in the definition, and no substantive notions of virtue are given as a prerequisite to a republic. Any virtues to be found anywhere related to Madison's concept was in the consequences that

[30]Bellah, *Broken Covenant*, 172. In this point he is joined most eloquently by one of the leading thinkers in communitarianism, Michael J. Sandel; see Sandel's *Liberalism and the Limits of Justice*, esp. 148–54.

would flow from the republican principle. In other words, Madison took an instrumental (liberal) view of the concept. Even as regards "exclusive concern for self-interest," Bellah is correct only for the most radical, extreme form of anarchist liberalism.[31] But liberalism need not be held to its most radical expression. We can take Bellah's observation as a lens to help focus more clearly the particular remedy that liberalism needs to make it the one public philosophy that can bring the "American civil religion" out of its "time of trial."[32]

EXIT: THE UNLIKELY BEGINNING OF LIBERALISM

What we have here is an inventory of ideologies competing as theories of the state. In actuality they are off-the-shelf disasters for any people foolish enough to attempt to govern themselves by uncritically selecting any one such theory. Most Americans, being pragmatic, would tend to agree and proudly embrace the alternative "none of the above." But this is not a genuine alternative; rather, it is a collision course with a dilemma presented best by Lord Keynes in an aphorism that cannot be repeated too often:

> Practical men, who believe themselves to be quite exempt from any intellectual influences, are usually the slaves of some defunct economist. Madmen in authority, who hear voices in the air, are distilling their frenzy from some academic scribbler of a few years back.

The Instrumental over the Moral

New Liberalism wins, because it can provide the only theory of the state capable of enduring all the alternatives. But it wins only by default. We have already seen how dangerously tragic New Liberalism can be. It is aging and decadent, useless without regeneration. Its core values require generous application of prudence and practical reason (words loved by

---

[31]For a very informative and well-balanced review of the various approaches to the problem of balancing individualism against community, see Newman, *Liberation at Wit's End*.

[32]The quotes are taken from the subtitle of Bellah's book, *The Broken Covenant*.

conservatives). This is close to a philosophic temperament but one accessible to practicing politicians: to be aware—almost to the point of immobility—of the contradictions inherent in one's own situation.

Such prudent self-consciousness, however difficult for liberalism, is nevertheless only a first step. More are needed to move out of the cave into which liberalism was driven by its fear of the moral superiority of the Right (and of the Left, whenever it was present). Another step, equally necessary, is a thorough rededication to the instrumentalism that liberalism has always brought to government. Liberalism must engrave in large letters over the portals of the political system "Abandon God, all ye who enter here." And it will work, if the letters are large enough, because eventually most people on the moral extremes must come to recognize the fatal flaw inherent in their situation, that there is more than one God and that each is the jealous God who said, "Thou shalt have no other Gods before me." Historians and philosophers have never fully appreciated the tremendous contribution liberalism has made to the theory of democracy by its attempt to cleanse the political process of morality.

Taken all alone, being instrumental is also inadequate, as liberal disasters of the past will demonstrate. But liberalism can also be substantive without abandoning the instrumental commitment. Family values, community values, traditional values, religious and philosophic sources of values—all have a place in liberalism, *as long as the practical consequences of disregarding or violating these values can be convincingly demonstrated to be sufficiently injurious to warrant intervention.* Most people who embrace moral sentiments and complain about the lack of liberal regard for the same would like to skip the demonstration of injury and jump right ahead to letting the articulation of the value be its own justification. What the Right (and the Left and, we might add, the communitarians) want is moral hegemony. The moral and the instrumental can coexist in politics—only as long as the instrumental has the last word.

There is still one more step at least before liberalism is fully out of the cave, liberated from the shackles of its fear of the moral superiority of the extreme ideologies and ready once again to govern, not merely to preside over a temporary party majority. This last step requires an embrace of the principle of *self*-government, *applied by liberalism to itself.* A constitution is a set of limitations that rulers impose on themselves in return for the people's consent to be governed. Each constitutional principle is a limitation on power that cannot be altered except by an extraordinary process specified in advance. Some constitutional principles, such as federalism, have been, more often than not, observed. The Bill of Rights is a bundle of constitutional principles adopted in 1791 that we began to take seriously in the 1960s. But there is one principle that has been conspicuous in its absence, and its absence was, as I argued as early as 1969, responsible for the collapse of New Liberalism and the decline in the legitimacy of the post-1937 positive liberal state. This is the principle of the rule of law.[33]

In 1935, the Supreme Court used two arguments to invalidate the National Industrial Recovery Act, thereby endangering the entire New Deal.

> On both the grounds we have discussed, the attempted delegation of legislative power and the attempted regulation of intrastate transactions which affect interstate commerce only indirectly, we hold the code provisions here in question to be invalid.[34]

The Court promptly reversed itself two years later on the second of those two questions, regarding the regulation of

---

[33]In my 1969 book, *The End of Liberalism,* I chose to use the term "juridical" as the synonym for rule of law and "juridical democracy" to refer to an ideal system in which democracy limited itself by its commitment to the rule of law. Although the argument here is an extension of the previous one, I have dropped the juridical reference and have retained rule of law because it is the most likely to be directly understood and because too many people got "juridical" mixed up with "judicial."

[34]From the majority opinion by Chief Justice Charles Evans Hughes, in *Schechter Poultry Corporation v. United States.* The second case was *Panama Refining Company v. Ryan.*

intrastate transactions, and thereby virtually put an end to the doctrine of interstate commerce as a limitation on the power of the national government.[35] *But to this day it has never reversed itself on the first question, the delegation of legislative power.*

Two dismissive things have been said about the 1935 cases that declared broad delegation of legislative power unconstitutional. First, it is argued, *Panama* and *Schechter* were unusual cases; no cases prior to 1935 had ever declared unconstitutional a delegation of power, and the Court up to that point had allowed wide discretion in "filling in the details of legislation." The second point is that since *Panama* and *Schechter* have been systematically disregarded since that time, they have been effectively reversed even though the Court has never explicitly reversed them.

All this is true, and I have already argued at some length in chapter 2 that the liberal state paid a heavy price for its disregard of the principle. My purpose here is not to argue further about the bad political consequences of having disregarded the rule of law but to argue in favor of the good consequences of its embrace.

Building a Constituency for the Rule of Law

It would be useful to begin with a definition of the principle of the rule of law. In the first place, it is taken to mean that no person is above the law and that all persons, regardless of rank or position, are subject to the same set of laws and to the jurisdiction of the same tribunals. But beyond that, it means that law is to be contrasted with authority or discretion; in other words, rule of law requires that no person

> is punishable or can be lawfully made to suffer in body or goods except for a distinct breach of law established in the ordinary legal manner before the ordinary Courts of the land. In this sense the rule of law is contrasted with every system of government based on the exercise by persons in

[35]*NLRB v. Jones and Laughlin Steel Corporation.*

authority of wide, arbitrary, or discretionary powers of constraint.[36]

Compare this with John Locke:

And so whosoever has the legislative or supreme power of any commonwealth, is bound to govern by established standing laws, promulgated and known to the people, and not by extemporary decrees.[37]

The supporting quotations could continue, but the opposing lineup of apologists for broadly delegated power against the rule of law is more contemporary and more influential. In fact, there is today virtually no constituency or market for the rule of law. Antagonism to the rule of law includes practically the entire community of law professors, I suppose because the purpose of law is to support lawyers. In the twenty-five years since the publication of *The End of Liberalism* and the foolhardy recommendation made there that we revive the *Schechter* rule, the echoes of horselaughs from the law school classrooms and legal periodicals can still be heard. The lawyers are joined by most conservatives, who prefer authority to rules.[38] They are also joined by the New Liberals (referred to in my earlier work as "interest-group liberals"), who have always been impatient to get on with the goals defined by group claims. Also against the rule of law are the "new politics" groups, whether liberal or genuinely on the Left, who are even more concerned with goals and with getting a favorable administrative environment. To them, the rule of law is a cover for vested interests.

Yet if liberalism is to return as a public philosophy capable of governing the large positive state and at the same time preserving at least a memory trace of representative government

---

[36]From the distinguished jurist A. V. Dicey, *Introduction to the Study of the Law of the Constitution* (Indianapolis: Liberty Classics, 1982; first published 1885), 110.

[37]John Locke, *Second Treatise of Government*, ed. C. B. MacPherson (Indianapolis: Hackett Publishing Company, 1980), 68.

[38]This distinction between authority and rules is one that I owe to one of the few modern defenders of rule of law, F. A. Hayek, *Law, Legislation and Liberty*, vol. 1, *Rules and Order* (Chicago: University of Chicago Press, 1973), 120.

against the triumph of bureaucracy, it has no alternative but to embrace the rule of law. Rule of law is the only absolute that liberalism can afford, and the only one it needs. If there is to be a criterion or justification for a particular policy or government action other than "the process itself," it has to be the rule of law. If there is to be any foundation for liberal regimes to say No (other than the power or influence of the group participants), it has to be the rule of law. If there is any civic virtue liberalism can teach, it has to be this. Without it, liberalism enters the stage once again as tragedy. If it attempts to replace the rule of law with any substantive moral content, it becomes farce.

Most antagonists to the rule of law apologize for congressional incompetence with the argument that Congress is already doing as much as it possibly can, given the complexity of our society. But no data or arguments are ever provided to support this apology; and I can provide two strong arguments the other way.

First, to state legislators of the 1840s, society must have seemed immeasurably more complex than ours seems to us today. They were living in the midst of the industrial revolution; there was not yet even any established economic theory of capitalism; there was no clear grasp of fractional reserve banking or insurance; and many traditional notions of law and obligation were coming unstuck. Meanwhile, those legislators had less education, they had virtually no staff help at all, and they had no budget to buy expertise and research. There was greater party domination and, presumably, more corruption. Yet statutes produced by state legislatures in the nineteenth century had much more legal integrity than the average statute coming out of Congress today. How did they do it? By not trying to ordain a desired outcome for the "whole system" but dealing through rules applied to one piece of the problem at a time, as sensory experience with real consequences directed them.[39]

---

[39]A longer argument on this point will be found in Lowi, "Toward a Legislature of the First Kind," in Robinson and Wellborn, *Knowledge, Power, and the Congress*, 9–36.

There is still the second response to this apology that modern society is too complex for representative government to govern by law. In actual fact, *proposals* for legislation today are usually very clear and provide a sound basis for articulating a good rule that would satisfy even a strict criterion of the rule of law. When organized interest groups come before Congress, they tend to know exactly what they want, and they have the lawyers and the staff to articulate their wants as rules that would be clearly understood not only to members of Congress but to citizens on whom these proposals, if adopted as law, would be imposed. It is true that rules developed by groups would tend to be too narrow and self-serving, but it is precisely the job of Congress to take those proposals and to work out compromises with the various contrary and conflicting proposals until a majority is ready to vote final passage. The burning question here is not why the modern Congress is unable to formulate legislation with clear rules but *why Congress takes proposals that embody clear rules and turns them into the vague and meaningless delegations of power that apologists call inevitable and unavoidable.*

What the defenders of delegation do not say is that serious commitment to the rule of law would produce a significantly smaller government. If legislators seriously lived by the principle "tell them what you're going do to them before you do it to them," few proposals would become law. When people actually know what is at stake, intelligent discourse expands, but so does opposition. Smaller government would be a direct consequence of the rule of law principle, but that is a far better reason for smaller government than mere ideologically based negation of representative government itself.

Thus the healthiest possible development for the Congress of the future is movement away from leadership based on analytic, budgetary, or procedural skills toward leadership based on skill in legislative drafting. But the judiciary must also be included, if Congress is to be saved from itself. My proposal twenty-five years ago to revive the *Schechter* rule was most heavily criticized for inviting the nonelective judiciary to displace the elected legislature altogether by exercising the power to invalidate legislation that embodies no guidelines. But everyone knows that the judiciary already intervenes constantly against the legislature. Through "statutory interpretation" federal courts are writing and rewriting legislation all the time. This is an application of the self-imposed rule that the judiciary should always try to give a statute an interpretation that can maintain its constitutionality—no matter how much legal sophistry they have to employ. But why? The separation of powers was supposed to *invite* confrontation between the branches; and it would seem to me that frequent conflict at the level of constitutionality would make for superb civic education. Moreover, courts do not have to be arrogant in their confrontation by an explicit holding that "this provision is unconstitutional." The Supreme Court developed an excellent alternative to such arrogance in one of the earliest civil rights cases, *Shelley v. Kraemer.* In that case, the Court held that although the Fourteenth Amendment "erects no shield" against private contracts that provide for racial discrimination, the state courts would be violating the Fourteenth Amendment if they attempted to enforce those contracts. In that same spirit, the Supreme Court could confront Congress by holding, in effect, that "Congress can pass a completely vague and stupid Public Law, or an empty Section 1066 or a totally opaque Title V, but the Courts cannot enforce it."[40]

Laying to Rest Two Principled Objections to the Rule of Law

Most objections to the rule of law are, as shown, illogical, frivolous, or self-serving. But two, being objections in principle, are threatening to the entire liberal project: (1) putting a rule of law cap on liberalism amounts to putting a cap on democracy, which will never stand; and (2) rule of law, being

---

[40]*Shelley v. Kraemer,* 334 U.S. 1 (1948). This discussion and the previous paragraphs regarding objections to the rule of law were taken liberally from Lowi, "Two Roads to Serfdom: Liberalism, Conservatism, and Administrative Power," *American University Law Review* 36, no. 2 (1987): 295–322; and Lowi, "Toward a Legislature of the First Kind."

an amoral constitutional principle, cannot effectively oppose morally objectionable bad laws if those laws can meet the rule of law criterion.

The first, though serious, can be dealt with rather briefly. Rule of law definitely puts a cap on democracy. But every constitutional provision does that. The whole point of a constitution is to make some rules for the proper conduct of government and then to permit alteration only by extraordinary, supra-majoritarian means. Democracy is not the sole and exclusive value in our system. American government is a "mixed regime." Thus what we have here is not a question of whether but *what kind* of caps are placed on democracy. Rule of law is one, the one least observed. Moreover, this cap is reasonable. It is reasonable to deny government the authority to act when it refuses to say in advance how it wants to act.

The second objection is the more difficult to deal with. How can the amoral rule of law generate a No to a proposal that meets the criterion of legal integrity but is nevertheless objectionable on substantive moral grounds? How can it deal, for example, with a racial segregation law or a criminal abortion law?

A patently racial discrimination law is a fairly simple case. A law in Virginia declares as a crime any interracial sexual contact, such as marriage or intercourse between a white person and a person of color. The rule of conduct is clear and the punishment is equally clearly specified, say, imprisonment for two to seven years. Or take Alabama's school segregation law, providing separate facilities for each race and the application of the laws of trespass with use of severe injunctive power to prevent parents of one race from putting their children in schools provided for the other race.

There is no question that such laws meet the standard of legal integrity, providing a clear definition of the conduct in question, a solid and standardized method of implementation, and a clear and appropriate sanction for violation. Yet once racial segregation became objectionable in the nation at large, it was those very states of the Old Confederacy whose practices were first to be attacked and whose people were required to make the biggest changes in their laws and conduct. The very explicitness of the southern laws had brought them under attack more quickly and thoroughly than the vague and extralegal methods of segregation outside the South. The amoral rule of law applied to public discourse enabled citizens individually and through their representatives to bring their private moral judgments to bear on public choices. At the same time, the amoral rule of law principle tied these private moral judgments to consideration of the actual consequences of preferred outcomes. (See once again the argument of the unanimous Court in *Brown v. Board*.)

The second case is a mock-up of the type of criminal abortion statute that would have to be adopted by a post-*Roe* legislature with a pro-life majority. (See below.) Imagine under such circumstances a pregnant woman at her country club who is overheard at lunch saying to her tennis companions, "I need this fourth child like a hole in the head." Imagine then that she goes out for two vigorous sets, disregarding her physician's advice, and ends up with a miscarriage. This has to be reported to the Panel of Inquest, whose leading question is, Is this woman guilty of negligence, criminal negligence, manslaughter, or premeditated murder?

THE HUMAN LIFE PROTECTION ACT
Whereas life begins at conception, when a human spermatozoan fuses with a human ovum,

The state of Alaga declares that abortion, being an abomination, constitutes an act of murder, except when the pregnancy endangers the life of the mother or when the pregnancy is the result of sexual assault or incest.

Any pregnant woman who, with intent to terminate a pregnancy, submits to invasive or noninvasive medical procedures aimed at effecting an abortion, or who ingests abortifacients for the same, shall be guilty of capital homicide.

Any person who assists a pregnant woman to terminate an abortion by providing medical or pharmacological services, or in any way directly assists, aids, or procures abortion services on behalf of that woman, shall be guilty of capital homicide.

Any pregnant woman who acts with willful and wanton disregard for the consequences to human life and thereby effects a miscarriage, shall be guilty of manslaughter.

Any individual who has knowledge of a woman's pregnancy and is aware of her efforts to terminate that pregnancy or is aware of her blatant disregard of factors that might increase the risk of spontaneous abortion, and fails to report the same, shall be guilty of obstruction of justice. Any individual failing to report an abortion shall be an accessory to murder.

Pursuant to the proper implementation of this law, all pregnancies shall be registered with the Office of Maternity (OM) in the county of residence, within 30 days of a medical test or 90 days of onset pregnancy, as determined by a certified physician. Failure to register a pregnancy will be subject to not more than a $1,000 fine and two years in prison.

Normal birth shall be reported to the OM, formal certification thus terminating OM jurisdiction.

In the event a pregnancy does not go to term, an inquest shall be held to determine the cause of the interrupted pregnancy. Documentation of interrupted pregnancy shall be received by a Panel of Inquest, which shall have the status of a grand jury, with authority to hand down indictments, where appropriate.

Someone asked President Bush during his 1992 campaign what kind of punishment he would provide in his antiabortion law. He confessed he had not thought about it. Pro-lifers have not had to think about it. What the pro-lifers seek in a criminal abortion statute is a delegation of state authority, concrete enough to establish the crime but vague enough to provide legally sanctioned moral hegemony over women. What we can see in the hypothetical law presented above is a law with full legal integrity whose consequences, leading to a police state for women, can be clearly seen and evaluated.

Contrast the mock statute to two real examples. The Texas law voided by *Roe v. Wade* did not actually define abortion as a criminal act but provided criminal punishment for those persons who "shall designedly administer to a pregnant woman or knowingly procure to be administered with her consent any drug or medicine [or other means to] procure an abortion." If the pregnant woman did the whole thing by herself, would she be scot-free? Since the punishment was imprisonment for a mere two to five years, was the fetus not a human life after all? If the mother died in the process, assistance in the abortion was defined as murder, but assistance was only a minor crime if the abortion was successful. Again, does this mean that the fetus is not human life after all?

The second example, a ballot initiative in Wyoming in 1994, provided that any abortion or contraceptive measure that interferes with the "life of an unborn child" carries criminal penalties for both mother and related medical personnel. But although life is defined as beginning with conception, the crime of abortion is not defined as murder. And would the use of an intrauterine device (IUD) amount to an abortion? Would recommendation of an IUD by a physician amount to complicity to commit murder? The proposed law is silent on how the abortion action would be found out and reported. Capabilities and complicities are left open-ended. The proposed law is completely silent on methods of implementation, including scrutiny of pregnant women.[41]

It is extremely difficult for elected legislators to vote against a morality law. How can anyone be against home, family, motherhood? But a bill such as the mock-up, properly drafted to meet the rule of law standard, would give doubtful legislators a variety of arguments; it would provide many opportunities to direct the debate toward consequences; and the proponents of the law would have to recognize its implications and be prepared to take responsibility for them. The mock abortion statute paints a not outlandish picture of a police state for women. It points also to a still larger universe of morality laws, especially "crimes without victims" involving voluntary activity among consenting adults. Any morality

[41]The Texas abortion law is reproduced in full, along with an excellent commentary, in Barbara Hinkson Craig and David M. O'Brien, *Abortion and American Politics* (Chatham, N.J.: Chatham House, 1993), 11 and chap. 1. My thanks to Professor Alice Hearst for the Wyoming example and for her help in constructing the mock-up. However, responsibility for the final version of the mock-up is entirely my own.

law with genuine legal integrity, providing not only a clear rule but clear provisions for implementation, would immediately expose itself as requiring full access to private moral spheres. Those who favor such laws must be prepared for a police state for the immoral. The rule of law criterion would inhibit such laws from being adopted, except where there is virtual unanimity as to their necessity. In such a case, politics is over for the immoral minority and they must look for opportunities to emigrate. But there will not be many such laws, as long as they are written with a clear rule and a clear intent to be implemented.

The same considerations apply to all laws. The more solid the legal integrity of a proposed law, the clearer are its consequences and implications, and the harder it is to get a majority to adopt it. But it is also true that, once adopted, such a law will much more likely produce the results sought by its supporters. The great mystery to me is why New Liberals have not recognized that a smaller government based on clear and solid rules is not only constitutionally superior but much more effective in reaching their own goals. The only people who should be comfortable with vague legislation are those on the radical Left and Right, for whom government means putting the right persons with the right values in power and letting them make morally good decisions.

But even if the liberals were suddenly converted, the task of getting rid of the hundreds of soft, badly drafted statutes would be extremely difficult for the following fairly obvious reasons: (1) the apparatus of the Democratic party is dominated by public employees with a stake in the present system; (2) professional careerists in the bureaucracy as well as professors in law and public affairs schools believe that government by expertise is superior to a government of laws; and (3) vaguely drafted legislation provides discretion that enables agencies and their congressional and interest-group supporters to convert agency resources into patronage.

Voltaire, a frequent victim of arbitrary and capricious, that is, discretionary, uses of the state, once asserted that "if you want good laws, burn those you have and make new ones."[42] It is reported, although I cannot find the source, that Frank Lloyd Wright was once asked what he would do about "the problem of New York," to which he responded, "I'd start all over again on the second floor." This is the revolution we need. Starting all over again, but in the basement where the foundations are. The Third Republic we need would be an enlightened liberal republic, not enlightened by greater knowledge than lawmakers have today but enlightened as to the virtues and the limits of liberalism.

THE BISHOP ORDERS HIS TOMB

Even as I compose these final passages, I already know that everything said here will be disregarded. I conclude feeling a kinship with Robert Browning's dying Bishop. After giving line after beautiful line of instructions to his sons for construction of his tomb, it begins to dawn on the Bishop that his sons ("Nephews—sons mine . . . ") have gathered round him, bored and indifferent, just waiting for him to die.[43]

What is there about an ideology that blinds its believers to the limits of its applicability? Whatever it is, it makes tragedy the universal drama, in which politics imitates art. What woes could be avoided if only men and women of action could maintain a sense of history and a sense of humor about the beliefs that guide them. How much better off we would be if political elites could call up, as a catechism, the immortal words of Ogden Nash:

> Do you think Der Fürher could keep on being Der Führer
> If he saw what everybody else sees every time he looks in the mührer?[44]

---

[42]Voltaire, *Dictionnaire Philisophique*, quoted in F. A. Hayek, *Law, Legislation, and Liberty*, 25.

[43]Robert Browning, "The Bishop Orders His Tomb at Saint Praxed's Church," 1845.

[44]Ogden Nash, "Don't Grin, or You'll Have to Bear It," *The Ogden Nash Pocket Book* (New York: Pocket Books, 1944), 1.

Conservatism can never govern America because its view of authority is contrary to democracy: that there are persons who can know the truth and should, with the truth, govern. But, of course, if they appreciated this flaw inherent in government by moral absolutes, they would no longer be conservatives but would have passed back through the looking glass into another dimension—not merely a few steps along a continuum but into another realm altogether, not merely as liberalized moralists but as moralized liberals. They would be in good company, because all liberals are moral; they simply accept the burden of leaving their morality at home when they enter into the public domain. Is this too much to expect of the Right (or the Left), to abandon their homeland and to accept liberal hegemony for the sake of the republic?

The ultimate end of the republican era is therefore in the hands of liberalism, and what a dismal prospect that is. If war is too important to be entrusted to generals, at least we have reassurance that there is someone else to turn to. The republic is too important to be entrusted to liberalism. But what else is there?

That identifies the task not only of good citizenship but of good political science: Either we enlighten liberalism to the true task of governing, or we will again be betrayed by it.

INDEX

Abolitionists, 80; evangelicals as, 119, 164
Abortion, 255; Bush vs., 255; Catholics and (*see* Catholic church, vs. abortion; Catholics, right-to-life); conservative focus on, 129; criminalization of, 159, 255–56; evangelicals vs., 183, 188, 235; Medicaid and, 26; mock legislation re, 254–56 & n. *See also* Catholic church, vs. abortion; Catholics, right-to-life
Academies, Christian, 181
Acton, John (Lord John Emerich Edward Dalberg-Acton), 26 & n, 44
Adams, Henry, 118
Adams, John Quincy, 4
Adoption, child: as political issue, 171
Adulterated substances, Congress vs., 46–47
Adultery, Reagan vs., 159
Affirmative action: neoconservatives vs., 193; during New Deal, 40–41
African-Americans: disenfranchisement of, 35; evangelical, 163n.6. See also *Brown v. Board of Education of Topeka;* Ku Klux Klan; Lynching; Prejudice, racial; Race; Segregation, racial; Slavery
Agencies, federal, 50, 74–76; growing powers of, 48–49; New Deal and, 40; and patronage, 257; Reagan focus on, 66n.21, 206–207. *See also* Bureaucrats; Regulation

Agricultural Adjustment Administration (AAA), 134
Agriculture, U.S.: Democrats and, 84; 80th Congress and, 134; evangelicals and, 164; food stamps as boon to, 52; New Deal and, 36, 132; political independence of, 84; price supports for, 134; Republicans and, 83–84, 89
Agriculture, U.S. Department of, 83
Aid for Dependent Children (AFDC), 52, 68, 243
Airlines, regulation of U.S., 50
Air Quality Act, 72
Alabama, state of: school segregation in, 253
Alcohol, Christian Voice focus on, 186. *See also* Prohibition
Allen, Charlotte, 238n
Amendment(s), constitutional: conservative-proposed, 206; First, 31n.33, 154, 160, 161 (*see also* Church, state and); Fifth, 29, 30n (*see also* Double jeopardy; Due process; Property, private); Tenth, 28, 29; Fourteenth, 15, 30–31n, 133n.45, 154, 178, 203, 252 (*see also* Civil rights; Due process); Nineteenth, 166 (*see also* Women's suffrage); Twenty-second, 95. *See also* Bill of Rights; Equal Rights Amendment
American Civil Liberties Union (ACLU), 42